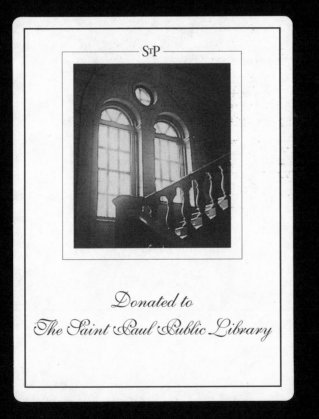

Shark Attacks

Their Causes and Avoidance

Thomas B. Allen

THE LYONS PRESS

2 4 6 8 10 9 7 5 3 1

Printed in the United States of America

Library of Congress Cataloging-in-Publication Data

Allen, Thomas B.
  Shark attacks: their causes and avoidance / Thomas B. Allen.
  p. cm.
  Includes bibliographical references (p. 285) and index.
  ISBN 1-58574-174-4 (hc)
  1. Shark attacks. I. Title.

QL638.93.A39 2001
597.3'1566—dc21
                                                    00-67782

We need to remember that we are invaders of a natural system that has large animals living in it that occasionally can cause us harm. Sharks share the waters with humans, or more rightfully put, humans share the water with sharks. It's a wilderness experience every time we enter the sea.

     —George H. Burgess
     Director of the International Shark Attack File

CONTENTS

PRELUDE

The New Shark

The blue water suddenly turned a vivid crimson, stained by the blood of a struggling [victim]. The huge shark, much of its body out of the water in clear view, swam vigorously back and forth. It appeared to be enjoying its meal.

Shark attacks are not remarkable. Attacks like this one happen countless times a day in the seas of the world. The blue water here is about seventy-five feet off the California coast. The shark is a great white (*Carcharodon carcharias*).[1] The victim is a northern elephant seal.

When we think about shark attacks, we do not think about seals. We think about ourselves. A swimmer at a beach on a summer's day. A diver plunging into the blue-green paradise of a Pacific reef. A windsurfer gliding down a

1

Hawaiian wave. A weekend sailor who sees a triangular fin heading toward a boat that suddenly looks so frail.

Shark attack. Ever since Peter Benchley's 1974 novel, *Jaws*—and the movie that followed a year later—the words have conjured up terror and adjectives: murderous, monstrous, ferocious, vicious. The movie, which had the working title "Shark Attack," is only in its ninth minute when Police Chief Martin Brody (Roy Scheider) types up a report that says, "*Possible cause of death—SHARK ATTACK.*" Later, when the mayor learns that a shark is stalking his town's beach, he says to the chief, "Martin, it's all psychological. You yell barracuda, and everyone says, 'Huh? What?' You yell shark, we've got a panic on our hands. . . ."

Shark attack. The words still close beaches. But today there is more behind the words than a scary movie. The witness to that bloody attack on the elephant seal was Dr. Peter Klimley, an associate research behaviorist at the Bodega Marine Laboratory, University of California at Davis. Klimley knows sharks up-close. He has made one-hundred-foot dives to tag hammerhead sharks with a dart gun. He has worn a costume to make him look like prey so that he can see the reaction of lemon sharks, long a favorite of researchers. One of the lemons showed a reaction: It tried to bite him.

Klimley's studies of great white sharks inspired his effort to save them. To Klimley and his fellow scientists, *shark attack* involves the relationship between the apex predator and its prey. Looked at from another angle, *shark attack* also means what human beings have been doing to sharks. Each year, fishermen kill as many as 100 million sharks.[2] This annual massacre, which threatens some species with extinction, has brought on the era of the New Shark.

One of the leading champions of the New Shark is Peter Benchley himself. Twenty-five years after the release of the

2

movie *Jaws*, Benchley took up a mission to "de-demonize" the great white shark. In the *National Geographic* magazine and in interviews, he cited an increase in knowledge as driving a new appreciation of sharks. "I haven't said that I regret having written *Jaws*," he insisted during questioning on the magazine's Web site. "I've said that with the knowledge that we have today, *Jaws* would be impossible. Any story about an animal that I would write today would have to portray the animal as the victim, not the villain."

The transformation of the shark from foe to victim began with crusades by environmentalists. And no crusade looked more quixotic than the one launched by Burr Heneman and Marci Glazer, California environmentalists who lobbied for a law to protect the great white shark in a state where great whites regularly attack people. First, after some convincing, they got Assemblyman Dan Hauser, an avid diver, to introduce Assembly Bill (AB) 522. "The joke passed around was that, with politics so brutal, protection for white sharks became the easiest conservation issue," they later wrote.[3]

The origins of the save-the-great-white crusade date to the 1980s when three white shark researchers—Heneman, Klimley, and David Ainley—got together at the Point Reyes Bird Observatory, headquarters for behavioral studies of great whites. The observatory, a non-profit conservation organization, originally focused on the rich bird life in its islands, the Farallons, a national wildlife refuge twenty-six miles west of the Golden Gate Bridge. Shark researchers were drawn to the Farallons to get accessible, long-term opportunities to see sharks prey on sea lions, elephant seals, and harbor seals. Klimley's vivid description of a great white attack on an elephant seal came from Farallon shark watching.

The legislative campaign began in 1992 with attempts to educate legislators in the need for protection of the great white. One of the teachers was a shark researcher, Peter Pyle, whose eloquent description of the great white became a paean for the New Shark:

The white shark may be the last of the Earth's primary predators capable of evoking irrational fear and response in humans. Although land-bound predators such as lions, tigers, and wolves once held this authority, they have all been subdued, nearly eradicated, or restricted to wildlife preserves where we point at them from the safety of our automobiles. But *Homo sapiens* remains out of its element in the ocean, and it is from this perspective that the white shark still lurks in the primal quarters of the human mind. By revealing the white shark's natural story, we hope to supplant fear and vindictiveness with respect and understanding for this beleaguered citizen of the sea.

Unexpected endorsement of the great white shark bill came from a diver who had been attacked by one of those citizens of the sea. "I am writing to express my support for AB 522 to protect white sharks in California," Eric Larsen said in a letter to Hauser. "As you may know, I was mauled by a shark thought to be a Great White on July 1, 1991. . . . My experience with the shark convinced me that sharks are an important part of the natural order of things. Any creature which is as well-adapted to its environment as the shark deserves a lot of respect."

The shark had clamped its jaws around Larsen's left leg and pulled him down on that July day. Larsen, a thirty-two-year-old surfer, tried to pry his leg from the jaws. The shark let go of his leg and bit down on his arms. Larsen managed to extract one arm, ripping it to the bone as he dragged it through the shark's razor-sharp teeth. He pounded his bloody fist on the shark, and as suddenly as it appeared, the shark vanished. Larsen managed to paddle to shore, losing half the blood in his body. It took four hundred stitches to sew up his wounds.

Along with a shark victim, support of AB 522 came from the Pacific Coast Federation of Fishermen's Associations and representatives of surfer, diver, and sea kayaker organizations, every one of which had in its membership victims of shark attacks. Mike McHenry, a commercial fisherman who had been a victim of shark conservationists, also gave his support. McHenry had been pilloried as an enemy of sharkdom after he had caught four large great whites at the Farallons in a single day in 1982. Now he was hailing the New Shark.

No one seemed to bear a grudge against the great white. As the *San Diego Union Tribune* put it, "Suppose you're a 4,000-pound ocean predator with a mouthful of dagger-like teeth and a nasty habit of occasionally snacking on humans. Where do you look for friends? Where else but California, *amigo.*" Commercial fishermen and other foes of fish-eating seals and sea lions saw sharks performing a service they could not dare do. "White sharks," said the California Urchin Divers Association, "may be one of the few lethal controls on marine mammals that are acceptable to the general public."

AB 522 won approval of Hauser's Joint Committee on Fisheries and Aquaculture. Then he skillfully steered it through three other committees and onto the floor of the Assembly, where it passed without a vote against it during a bitterly partisan session. The bill had a similar fate in the Senate. Legislators were not swayed by a *San Francisco Chronicle* headline of June 10, 1993: GREAT WHITE SHARK DEVOURS NEWLYWED DIVING OFF AUSTRALIA. Or the

Chronicle's August 13 headline: SHARK SWALLOWS MAN, THEN SPITS HIM OUT. The August attack was off Mendocino, in Hauser's own district. A shark opened its jaws and took a diver by the head but gave him up. He was able to swim to shore. The possible loss of a Californian voter to a man-eater did not diminish Hauser's support of the great white.

The bill reached the desk of Republican Governor Pete Wilson, who had to decide whether to hand an environmental victory to Hauser, a Democrat. Wilson already had vetoed a stack of bills when one of Hauser's staffers put up a drawing of a shark fin in a window that could be seen from Wilson's office in the Capitol. "Please sign AB 522," said the drawing. On October 11, the last day on which Wilson could act on bills, a poster appeared in the gubernatorial window opposite Hauser's. The poster showed a large shark in pink sunglasses leaping out of the water. On the poster was a message in the governor's handwriting: "Dan— Cordially, Pete Wilson." America's first white shark protection bill had become law.

South Africa, long a notorious locale for shark attacks, had passed the world's first white shark protection law in 1991 after researchers determined that human predation, including anti-shark net barriers, were wiping out great whites and other species. Along the twenty-four-mile stretch of netted beaches on the KwaZulu-Natal coast, an average of 1,354 sharks, including thirty-nine great whites, were being snared each year. The gill nets had begun going up in 1952, and year after year net guardians killed all potentially dangerous sharks caught in the nets. That practice stopped in 1988 in what would be the first step toward protecting great whites, which were also being killed by spear fishermen, big-game anglers, and commercial fishing boats. Customers for great white jaws and teeth also preyed on white sharks. (Great white jaws in prime condition can sell for as much as $50,000 on the South African black market.)

The unprecedented 1991 law forbade the killing of great whites within 200 nautical miles of the South African coast. Anyone who harmed a great white could be fined the equivalent of $22,000. The law also prohibited the selling or buying of the jaws, meat, or teeth of a great white in South Africa.

In Australia, trophy hunters and commercial fishermen killed so many great whites that conservationists pressed for protective legislation. The states of New South Wales, Tasmania, Queensland, Western Australia, and South Australia passed white shark protection laws, including the prohibition of chumming within two nautical miles of the coast, restrictions on white shark sports fishing, and regulations on the selling of thrills to divers by sending them down in cages and luring sharks with food offerings. New South Wales also gave similar protection to the gray nurse shark (*Odontaspis arenarius*), which has been implicated in many attacks.

Most people supported the laws, but there was opposition from what could be described as Australia's white-shark industry. Vic Hislop, an Australian professional shark hunter—and shark hater—said, "For a government to protect something that can tear your children apart in seconds is brainless." Despite such opposition, Australia's federal government completed the campaign for protection of the white shark. In December 1997 Australia announced the prohibition of hunting, molestation, or harassment of great whites.

As the save-the-great-white campaign swept on, Florida passed a white shark protection law similar to California's. Then, early in 1997 Florida's action was overshadowed by a federal response: The National Marine Fisheries Service

(NMFS) outlawed the taking of great white sharks, other than tag-and-release sport fishing, in waters of the East Coast and the Gulf of Mexico.

The New Shark is a victim of humans, a shark that must be given the kind of protection that we have bestowed on cuddly pandas, magnificent whales, and photogenic dolphins. Something deep in us initially resists the New Shark. We do not intuitively feel compassion toward a beast that can rip us apart. It takes education to change our emotion from fear to pity.

The education comes primarily from environmentalists, who point out that large sharks like the great white and the tiger (*Galeocerdo cuvier*) render the same service in the sea that large carnivores do in ecosystems on land. On land and in the sea, the predators seek out weak, sickly, or injured prey, allowing only the strong and healthy to survive and reproduce. "It's Darwin's survival of the fittest at work," says Craig Sowden of the Sydney Aquarium in Australia. "If you remove sharks, you are interfering with the natural order that makes fish and other sea creatures stronger by selective culling."

In the Atlantic Ocean, fishermen long interfered with the natural order by acting as predators on the spiny dogfish (*Squalus acanthias*). Off Massachusetts, fishermen once took as many as 27 million spiny dogfish in a single season. Nineteenth-century Long Island fishermen measured their catch in wagonloads. Fishermen considered them pests, for they preyed on more valuable market fish, and millions were discarded rather than harvested. Then, beginning in the late 1980s, dogfish became targets of fishermen who saw them as market fish, and they began to disappear. Marine biologists of the National Marine Fisheries Service noted in 1998 that the number of mature females had dropped by an estimated 50 percent since 1989. The NMFS put this once plentiful shark on the list of overfished stocks. The NMFS also cut the legal quotas on commercial harvests of several other species of coastal sharks in U.S. waters.

Most of the decline could be traced to a side effect from China's embracing of capitalism. By endorsing private wealth and elitist life styles, China's rulers inevitably authorized the return of shark-fin soup, once a forbidden bourgeois luxury. To meet the sudden huge demand for shark fins, fishermen from Hong Kong to Hawaii sought large oceanic sharks, whose fins were preferred by Chinese gourmets. When the large sharks became scarce, fishermen turned to the lowly dogfish. And the finding of fins for shark-fin-soup consumers became a major source of income for fishermen throughout the world. All that the shark-fin market wanted were the fins—and would pay $100 or more a pound for them. So fishermen hacked off fins and dumped the sharks back into the ocean to die. The practice was called "finning."

Marine biologists hoped that isolation would preserve some populations in remote areas. One such place was the Chagos Archipelago, a string of islands in the middle of the Indian Ocean. Scientists in the 1970s reported that the Chagos seas swarmed with several species, including the tawny nurse shark (*Nebrius ferrugineus*), silvertip shark (*Carcharhinus albimarginatus*), gray reef shark (*Carcharhinus amblyrhynchos*), blacktip reef shark (*Carcharhinus melanopterus*), and whitetip reef shark (*Triaenodon obesus*). But a scientific expedition in 1996 reported finding "minimal numbers" of sharks. Fishermen in quest of fins had found even the Chagos.

Fin suppliers were drawn to North American waters because they contained some of the world's last great shark populations. Of the 390 recognized species of sharks in the world, seventy-two are found in the U.S. Atlantic, Gulf of Mexico, Puerto Rico, and the U.S. Virgin Islands. These populations were never of great interest to American fisher-men because North Americans had never developed a taste for shark. But when sharks began vanishing from tradi-tional Asian fisheries, fishermen put sudden new pressures on North American populations. Among the hardest hit species are the sandtiger (*Eugomphodus taurus*), the sand-bar (*Carcharhinus plumbeus*), tiger shark, and dusky (*Carcharhinus obscurus*). Some populations have been re-duced as much as 80 percent. Scientists studying Atlantic shark populations expressed some hope, however. "What we're seeing is an increase in the number of small sharks," according to Jack Musick of the Virginia Institute of Marine Science, regarding sandbar sharks in the Chesapeake Bight. But the sandbars must be thirteen years old before they can reproduce. So it will be some time before scientists can con-firm a comeback.

In December 2000, President Clinton signed the Shark Finning Prohibition Act, banning finning in the U.S. Exclusive Economic Zone, which extends 200 miles from shore. The action was aimed primarily at Hawaii, where finning had increased 2,000 percent between 1991 and 1998. The proposed legislation would prohibit Hawaiian fisher-men from possessing or landing shark carcasses without fins. And Thai Airways International, Thailand's national flag carrier, took shark fin soup off its menu. Another pro-shark move came from an American animal-rights organization that was against bullfighting and other animal exploitation. The organization called itself SHARK (Showing Animals Respect and Kindness). *Shark* was no longer a nasty word.

The U.S. awakening to the worldwide shark slaughter may have come just in time. But if extinctions seem at least temporarily postponed in U.S. waters, recovery of popula-tions is far over the horizon. Sharks are not prolific. Males and females in some species may live as long as twenty years before they mature. And they produce few young after gestation periods of a year or more. Some species may breed only every other year. Commercial fishermen know this, but their own short-term interests often transcend the long-term needs of the environment. Fisheries need regulators. But governmental stewardship over the fish of the sea is rare. Of the 125 countries whose fishermen hunt sharks, only four—the United States, Canada, Australia, and New Zealand—manage shark fisheries.

Finning is not the only peril for sharks. Their skins are tanned for high-quality, high-price leather. The oil of their livers is used in cosmetics, lubricants, vitamins, and pharmaceutical products. And in recent years, sharks have been sought for their unique skeletons. (Unlike typical bony fish, sharks and their close relatives, such as rays and skates, have skeletons made of cartilage.) The craze for cartilage began after it was touted as a magic anti-cancer drug. In Costa Rica, for example, a company that markets crushed shark cartilage to American and European pharmaceutical firms is shipping 22,500 pounds of cartilage a month. Before the dubious anti-cancer claims were widely publicized, the company had been producing 3,000 pounds a month, mostly as an ingredient in fishmeal. The slaughter goes on despite a study conducted by the independent Cancer Treatment Research Foundation on terminally ill cancer patients. The investigators concluded that shark cartilage did nothing to slow their disease or to improve their quality of life.[4]

In the Mediterranean, where Aristotle and Pliny wrote the West's first accurate descriptions of sharks, studies show that sharks are dwindling rapidly. Ian Fergusson, a biologist who has maintained a computer database on Mediterranean sharks since 1989, says that sharks and rays there "are now on the verge of collapse." Malta took heed and in 1999 listed the great white shark as a protected species, becoming the first

Mediterranean nation to enact such a law. Malta also gave protection to the basking shark (*Cetorhinus maximus*) and the devil ray (*Mobula mobular*).

As an apex predator, the shark maintains the equilibrium of the ecosystem. When its populations plunge, populations of its prey soar. In Australia, for example, researchers discovered that lobsters were becoming scarce in areas where sharks had preyed upon lobster-eating octopuses. Along the U.S. Atlantic and Gulf coasts, if sharks vanish, stingrays will flourish in the shallows that are now the domain of waders and swimmers.

While dinosaurs came and went, sharks prevailed. They have existed, little changed, for 350 million years because their anatomy and their behavior made them sovereigns of the sea. Nothing in their evolution prepared them for voracious fishermen or polluters of the coastal areas where shark nurseries had existed for millennia.

The New Shark, protected and imperiled, is still the old shark, feared as a killer, a lethal shadow in a sea that we humans claim as our own—while knowing that somewhere out there may be an animal that can maim or kill us. We have mostly rid ourselves of other dangerous beasts. We hike wilderness trails unconcerned about the other carnivores around us, or about ticks that carry Lyme's disease or about malarial mosquitoes. But in the sea there is always the shark, the fearsome shark.

We can be told that more than 75 percent of shark species are harmless. We can be told again and again that bees, wasps, and snakes kill far more people than sharks do, that risk of death from lightning is thirty times greater than death from shark attack, that actuarial statistics—of drowning, seaside cardiac arrest, and automotive travel to and from the beach—stalk us far more lethally than sharks do. Yet only the shark kindles within us a primordial fear.

Not until the twentieth century did the reality of shark attack become widespread. *Jaws* the book and movie get most of the blame. More important than the big movie screen, however, is the television screen. A shark attack off a Durban beach once would have been reported only in South African newspapers and radio stations. Now television, spread by CNN and other news purveyors, carries word of that attack throughout the world—even if the only image is a deserted beach and a blue-and-white sign with a shark warning in English and Afrikaans.

Added to the phenomenon of instant visual news is the fact that more and more people are venturing into the sea. Once the amateurs who went down to the sea were merely swimmers. Now the weekend adventurer and the thrill-seeking vacationer are plunging into the sharks' own realm as divers, surfers, spearfishers, and underwater tourists. Those are the human beings who are seeing sharks, being seen by sharks, and occasionally being attacked by sharks. In Fiji, where some believe that dead chiefs inhabit certain sharks, they say that you always swim at your peril, for the shark decides who lives and who dies.

In this book you will read about many shark attacks. But the sharks that attack on these pages will not be called murderous, demonic, diabolical, or vicious, as the old shark was labeled. This book will tell how attacks happened and how some of them could have been prevented, thanks to the knowledge and the respect that has come in the wake of the New Shark.

CHAPTER 1

By the Sea, By the Sea . . .

A killer shark suddenly appears off a popular beach and snatches a swimmer before the horrified eyes of other bathers. In panic, officials demand that beaches be shut down. Resort owners insist there is no shark—and it strikes again. Beaches are closed as the shark hunt begins . . .

This is not *Jaws* the book or *Jaws* the movie, its sequels, or its TV reruns. This is reality in New Jersey in 1916.

> MAN EATING SHARK IN MATAWAN CREEK
> CAUSES DEATH OF MAN AND BOY
> —headline in *The Matawan* (New Jersey) *Journal*
> July 13, 1916

BEACH HAVEN, NEW JERSEY, SATURDAY, JULY 1, 1916: Charles Van Sant, a twenty-three-year-old man from Philadelphia, is taking his first swim of the day. Up in the

Van Sant's shorefront suite, his father and two sisters are still unpacking. He could not wait to plunge into the surf after the long train ride from Philadelphia to Long Beach Island, a narrow strip of land dotted with resorts like Beach Haven. The sea is cool and sparkling. This is the year everyone is singing, "By the sea, by the sea, by the beautiful sea . . ."

Other bathers said afterward that they had seen the shark before Van Sant did. They said they had screamed, but he did not seem to have heard them.

He was still close to shore when the water churned and red foam billowed around him. Alexander Ott, a former U.S. Olympic team swimmer, dived into the sea and swam toward the red blotch on the water. Ott saw the shark turn toward him, then disappear as Ott reached Van Sant and pulled him to shore. Van Sant's legs had been horribly ravaged. He died that night from shock and loss of blood.

Word of Van Sant's death quickly spread through Beach Haven, but there was no panic. Many who heard about the tragedy doubted that Van Sant had been killed by a shark. *The New York Times* reported the attack in a two-paragraph story on page eighteen.

No one could remember a shark ever having killed a swimmer before. That was something that happened in the South Seas, not in New Jersey. But some people remembered that three years before, on August 26, 1913, a fisherman had caught a shark off Spring Lake, New Jersey, forty-five miles up the coast from Beach Haven. When the shark was cut open, a woman's foot wearing a tan shoe and a knitted stocking was found in its stomach. Sure, that had been in the papers, said the skeptics. Sailors will tell you that sharks might eat bodies but they don't eat live swimmers.

SPRING LAKE, NEW JERSEY, THURSDAY, JULY 6, 1916: At the elegant and tranquil resort of Spring Lake, where the socially

16

prominent spent their summers, they did not talk of sharks. There were about 500 people on the beach, and a few recognized Charles Bruder, a twenty-eight-year-old bellboy at the Essex and Sussex Hotel, as he began his afternoon off with a swim in the surf. They would say of him afterward that Charles, ever so polite and helpful, was *part* of Spring Lake for them. On their generous tips he supported himself and his only known relative, his mother, who lived in Switzerland.

Bruder's powerful strokes quickly took him beyond the lifelines that marked off the bathing beach. George White and Chris Anderson, the lifeguards on duty, did not call him back. Everybody knew that Charles Bruder was a strong swimmer. Then a woman screamed and shouted at the lifeguards: "He has upset! The man in the red canoe is upset!"

Even as she screamed, White and Anderson were racing toward their boat. They knew that it was not the reflection of an overturned canoe that they saw, for even now the red blot was spreading, and in the midst of the red blot Bruder's face appeared for a moment. He flung up a bloodied arm. When the boat reached him, White leaned from the bow and held out an oar to Bruder. Somehow, he grasped it. His face was white and his eyes were shut. "Shark—shark got me—bit my legs off!" he gasped. Then he fainted. White hauled him over the gunwale.

Mrs. George W. Childs, one of the principal envoys of Philadelphia society at Spring Lake, was standing on the private balcony outside her suite at the Essex and Sussex when she heard the screams from the beach. She turned to her maid and asked for her spyglass.

Below on the shore, she saw White and Anderson beaching their boat. She saw them hesitate to put Bruder on the sand. From the crowd a woman darted forward and laid out her linen coat, turning her eyes away as she did so. Several women fainted. Mrs. Childs, who was seventy-four years old and famously indomitable, did not faint. She went to the phone in her room, called the manager, and told him what she had seen. She also asked that her car be brought around. Minutes later she was speeding to Deal Beach, some five miles north. Her niece took a plunge in the surf there every afternoon, and Mrs. Childs wanted to get to Deal Beach before the shark did.

By the time a doctor reached Bruder, he was dead. The doctor began tending to the women who had fainted. At the Essex and Sussex, the telephone operator was ringing up every central switchboard from Point Pleasant to Atlantic Highlands. Within twelve minutes, swimmers were streaming ashore along twenty miles of New Jersey beaches.

But was it a shark? Was it true that man-eaters were prowling the shore of New Jersey? Everyone—the hotel managers, the resort operators, the beach goers—wanted to be told that it could not happen. The answer came from Colonel William Gray Schauffler, an eminent physician and surgeon general of the New Jersey National Guard. He had examined Bruder about fifteen minutes after he had been taken from the sea.

"There is not the slightest doubt," Schauffler reported, "that a man-eating shark inflicted the injuries." The colonel went on to clinically describe the injuries: "Bruder's right leg was frightfully torn and the bone bitten off half-way between the knee and ankle. The left foot was missing, as well as the lower end of the tibia and fibula. The leg bone was denuded of flesh from a point halfway below the knee. There was a deep gash above the left knee, which penetrated to the bone. On the right side of the abdomen, low down, a piece of flesh as big as a man's fist was missing."

That night, while hotel residents, at Mrs. Child's suggestion, took up a collection for Bruder's mother, motorboats equipped with searchlights slipped out to sea in a futile hunt for the shark. Colonel Schauffler called a meeting of resort owners and town officials to discuss ways to make the beaches safe from sharks. Rifle-toting boatmen were hired to patrol the beaches. Fishermen prowled the shore, trolling for the shark with great hooks, sturdy lines, and chunks of prime mutton—said to be the best shark bait—donated by Spring Lake meat markets. "I am certain that the bathing beaches will be made safe within two or three days," Councilman D. H. Hill announced. No shark was caught, shot, or even seen.

This attack made page one of the *New York Times*, which reported the beginning of a shark-attack panic. Each resort town along the New Jersey coast reacted in its own way. Atlantic City was more upset by a ban on bathing suits that exposed "the nether extremities" than by sharks, although some daring souls made an adventure out of the shark scare by contemptuously swimming beyond the end of the piers. At Asbury Park, with a flourish of publicity, a motorboat shark patrol was begun and workmen started to enclose the bathing area with "shark-proof" wire netting.

The Atlantic seemed alive with sharks and tales of sharks. At Spring Lake, a lifeguard told of battling a twelve-foot shark with an oar only fifty feet offshore. At Bayonne, New Jersey, boys swimming off a yacht club float said they saw a shark. A policeman, hearing their cries, emptied his revolver at what he said was a black fin. In shallow water off Eldred's Bar near Rockaway Point in Brooklyn, eight men digging for sand worms saw a shark driving a school of weakfish toward shore. They said they killed it with eel-tongs, oars, spears, and spades—a shark that was doing what sharks do every year when the weakfish appear. But this year was different. All along the coast, shark hunters were firing their rifles at anything that looked big and moved in the sea.

Some resorts reported that bathing had fallen off more than 75 percent. But the anti-shark defenses were being built, and, as the *New York Times* reported from Asbury Park on July 10, "Tiger sharks will hold but little terror for bathers in the waters hereabouts within a few days. Today the final work was being rushed on the net protectors about the Asbury Park beaches, and in Ocean Grove the contractors who received the job of erecting steel nets began work. At Fourth Avenue, where the grounds had been enclosed by the steel nets, a record-breaking crowd of bathers enjoyed the surf."

But shark sightings continued: Four off Asbury Park. One cruising 200 yards off Bridgehampton, Long Island. That report came from Esterbrook Carter, nephew of Charles E. Hughes, the Republican candidate for president. Carter, along with all other Republicans, was relieved to learn that Hughes had spent the day indoors.

Officials of the U.S. Bureau of Fisheries in Washington theorized that a *single* shark was probably responsible for both fatal attacks. Because of a scarcity of food off the New Jersey shore, they said, the renegade shark may have been driven far inshore, and maddened by hunger, attacked Van Sant. Then, having acquired a taste for human flesh, it continued swimming near shore until its appetite was satiated by Bruder. "The case is extremely unusual," said the U.S. Commissioner of Fisheries, Hugh M. Smith. "I don't look for it to happen again. The fact that only two out of millions of bathers have been attacked in many years is evidence of the rarity of such instances."

MATAWAN, NEW JERSEY, WEDNESDAY, JULY 12, 1916: In this inland town, eleven miles west of the Atlantic Ocean, the only link to the sea is Matawan Creek, which flows into Raritan Bay, a body of water that blends into the Lower Bay, gateway to the great port of New York. But late this morning, Captain Thomas Cottrell, a retired sailor and part-time local fisherman, saw a shark in Matawan Creek. Eleven days had passed since Charles Van Sant had died at Beach Haven, seventy miles as a shark would swim, from Matawan. Six days had passed since Charles Bruder had died at Spring Lake, twenty-five miles as a shark would swim, from Matawan.

The most popular swimming hole in Matawan Creek was at the old Propeller Wyckoff Dock, named after the tug-sized steamer *Wyckoff* that used to come up the creek with the tide to pick up farmers' produce and carry it to the New York market on the next tide. All that was left of the dock was a dozen or so pilings that jutted close to one another along the edge of a broken-down pier.

One day in early July, fourteen-year-old Rennie (for Rensselaer) Cartan dived into the creek. As his head and shoulders entered the murky water, he felt something like a strip of very coarse sandpaper grate along his stomach. He clambered up a piling to the dock. His stomach was streaked with blood. "Don't dive in anymore!" he had shouted to the other boys. "There's a shark or something in there!"

The swimming hole was about a mile and a half up the creek from the spot where Captain Cottrell saw the shark. He shouted to two workmen. They had seen something, too, but they weren't sure what. They ran to a telephone and called John Mulsonn, a barber who was also Matawan's chief of police. Captain Cottrell ran the half mile to Matawan center. He tried to stop groups of boys who were heading for the creek. Running down Matawan's short lower Main Street, he shouted his warning to merchants and their customers.

One of the shops was Stanley Fisher's new dry-cleaning establishment. Stanley, one of Matawan's best-liked young men, also took orders for men's suits. A few days before, a man had bought a suit and, instead of paying cash, had bought Fisher a $10,000 life insurance policy. Fisher, a blond-haired, 210-pound giant of a man, was taking a ribbing from his friends. He was, after all, only twenty-four years old.

A little after 2 P.M. on this scorching, muggy day, twelve-year-old Lester Stilwell left his box-making job at Anderson's Saw Mill and headed for Wyckoff Dock with his pals—Johnson Cartan, Frank Clowes, Albert O'Hara, and Charles Van Brunt. Most of them jumped into the creek naked. Eleven-year-old Albert O'Hara was near the dock, about to climb out of the water, when Lester yelled, "Watch me float, fellas!" Albert turned to look.

Lester was so thin he usually had trouble floating. At that instant, something hard slammed Albert's right leg. He looked down and saw what looked liked the tail of a huge fish. Charles Van Brunt, thirteen years old, also saw the fish—the biggest, blackest fish he had ever seen, and it was streaking for Lester Stilwell. Lester screamed. Charles saw the fish strike, its body suddenly twisting as it hit Lester, and Charles saw that the fish was not all black, for as it rolled it exposed a stark white belly and gleaming teeth. In an instant, the fish nearly closed its jaws about Lester's slim body and dragged him beneath the reddening waters of Matawan Creek.

Lester's pals and other boys who had been swimming nearby got out of the water as fast as they could. Some ran up the steep dirt road from the creek and raced to the center of town. Boys who had seen the shark were yelling, "Shark! Shark! A shark got Lester!" Along the shore by the dock, those who knew only that Lester Stilwell had gone under were calling his name: "Lester! Lester!" Out of this tumult somehow came the report that Lester, "a boy who took fits," had been seized by an attack and was drowning. People began running to the creek. Among them was Stanley Fisher, who had ducked into the back of his dry-cleaning shop only long enough to put on a bathing suit.

Fisher took command at Matawan Creek, where some two hundred townspeople, including Lester Stilwell's mother and father, lined the dock and nearer bank. Fisher soon had men in boats, poling for Lester's body. Fisher ordered a couple of young men to get into a rowboat and string chicken wire, weighed down with stones, along the bottom down-creek from the dock, where the channel was about twenty feet wide.

Fisher knew there was a deep spot, off the farther bank, directly opposite the dock. There, he believed, the shark was lurking with Lester's body. Fisher planned to flush out the shark, driving it into shallower water down-creek, where the chicken-wire barrier would trap it. Fisher, with two powerful overhand strokes, swam to the deep spot and dove down.

Arthur S. Van Buskirk, a local deputy of the Monmouth County Detectives' Office, was sitting on the forward deck of a small boat when he saw a thrashing in the water at the farther shore. Even as he looked, the water calmed and a rapidly widening red stain spread on the surface. Van Buskirk yelled at the other man in the boat to start the engine. While it sputtered to life, Van Buskirk sculled forward. Then Stanley Fisher suddenly appeared in the midst of the red stain.

Fisher was drawn up, half crouching in waist-deep water. He seemed to be tottering on one leg. The boat pulled up directly behind Fisher. Van Buskirk could see that Fisher was holding bloody remnants of his right leg in both hands. Just as Fisher was about to pitch forward, Van Buskirk reached out and pulled him into his arms. He could get Fisher only halfway out of the water. The boat backed out of the shoal water and, as it turned to head to-

Searchers probe the muddy bottom of Matawan Creek for the body of Lester Stilwell.

ward the dock, the crowd could see that the flesh was gone on Fisher's right leg, from groin to kneecap. Little Alfreda Matz, one of the many children on the dock, tried to look. But her father threw the tail of his suit coat across her eyes and hugged her face to his side. She thought, *A crocodile bit Mr. Fisher.*

At the dock, men placed the still-conscious Fisher on a stretcher improvised from planks and bore him to the Matawan railroad, about a quarter of a mile away. At the station, they placed him on a baggage cart and waited for the next train. A doctor had been found. There was little he could do. Nearly three hours went by until the 5:06 train from Long Branch was flagged down. Fisher held onto consciousness. Not until 7:45 that night, as he was wheeled into the operating room at Monmouth Memorial Hospital, did he die. Before he died, he said that on the bottom of the creek he had reached the body of Lester Stilwell and wrested it from the jaws of the shark.

According to one newspaper report, the physician who conducted the autopsy on Fisher's body supposedly found that his flesh had been "impregnated with a poisonous liquid, which seemed to have a deadening effect on the nerves and muscles." Some modern researchers believe that such a substance may indeed exist, but it has not been discovered.

While Fisher lay on the baggage cart, several men went to Asher P. Woolley's store and got dynamite to blow up the shark. The creek was cleared of boats. Moments before the charge was to be set off, a motorboat hove into view from down-creek. Jacob R. Lefferts, a Matawan lawyer, was at the wheel. Lying on the bottom of the boat was a boy, his right leg swathed in bloodied bandages. "A shark got him," Lefferts shouted, as he pulled in to shore. The boy was trans-ferred to a car that sped him to St. Peter's Hospital in New Brunswick.

The boy, fourteen-year-old Joseph Dunn, had been swimming with his older brother, Michael, and several other boys off the dock of the New Jersey Clay Company brickyards about a half-mile down Matawan Creek, near Keyport. Someone had run to the brickyards and told the boys about the shark in the creek. They were all in the water when the warning came, and they swam swiftly to the dock. Joseph Dunn, the youngest, was the last one out of the wa-ter. As he started up the ladder, something that felt like a big pair of scissors, he said, grabbed his right leg. "I felt my leg going down the shark's throat," he said later. "I believe it would have swallowed me."

Townsfolk of Matawan gather on the banks of the creek to exact retribution from the shark. Dynamite, shotguns, handguns, harpoons, and pitchforks were all employed to hunt down the killer. BROWN BROTHERS

Joseph screamed. Michael Dunn and two other boys already on the ladder began a tug of war with the shark, which hung on for a moment or two. Then, suddenly, Joseph Dunn, the shark's third victim in less than an hour, was free of the great jaws.

In St. Peter's Hospital, hope was high that Joseph Dunn's life would be saved, but saving his torn leg—slashed with tooth marks, a major tendon severed, muscles badly mangled—seemed hopeless. Dr. R. J. Faulkingham, on general surgical service at the hospital, was given the case.

All that night and into the morning, Matawan Creek was the scene of an orgy of vengeance. Blast after blast of dynamite sent geysers of water and fish skyward. Hundreds of men lined both banks, armed with scythes, pitchforks, and old harpoons taken from living-room walls. By lantern light and by the first glimmer of dawn, men fired shotguns and pistols into the creek. At low tide, men waded into the water with knives—and even hammers.

The creek was soon laced with tangles of chicken wire and fishing nets. Newspaper reporters and photographers swarmed into Matawan, and one newspaper organized a

A charge of dynamite sends a huge geyser of water into the air on Matawan Creek.   BROWN BROTHERS

shark hunt by chartering a boat loaded to the gunwales with men carrying rifles. Extra-large charges of dynamite were set off for the benefit of newsreel cameras. Stores in Matawan and Keyport ran out of explosives and ammunition.

"We've got a shark!" a man shouted here . . . then there. Reports came in with the tide: One shark, two sharks, three sharks, four sharks were trapped in Matawan Creek. In reality, no shark was found.

The boys who had been the last to see Lester Stilwell alive later bore him to his grave. At the First Methodist Church, Stanley Fisher's voice was missing from the choir that mourned him. But his memory would live on in the church. With the money from the new insurance policy, Fisher's parents purchased a stained glass window—a landscape of Bethlehem.

At St. Peter's Hospital, Dr. Faulkingham skillfully sutured Joseph Dunn's severed tendon and ripped muscles. The boy would walk again, on two strong legs.

Six days after the attack, a shark was finally caught in Matawan Creek by none other than Captain Cottrell, one of the first people to see a shark there on July 12. He was coming up the creek in his motorboat *Skud* with his son-in-law, Richard Lee, when, about 400 yards from the bay, not far from the bridge where he had first seen a shark, he again saw a dorsal fin. He and Lee let out several yards of gill net and caught the shark. It weighed 230 pounds and was almost exactly seven feet long. Cottrell put the shark on exhibition in his fish shed and charged people a dime each to view the "Terror of Matawan Creek."

The actual killer of Matawan Creek may have been caught two days after the attack by one of the many shark hunters prowling the local waters. The shark tangled itself in a drift net that the hunter was dragging behind his boat in Raritan Bay, off South Amboy, New Jersey, less than four miles northwest of the mouth of Matawan Creek. Within the shark were fifteen pounds of flesh and bones; one, eleven inches long, was identified as the shinbone of a boy. Another fragment appeared to be part of a human rib. There was no doubt that the shark had certainly eaten, and probably attacked, at least one human being. The shark was a great white shark, never before reported along beaches as far north as New Jersey. The shark was placed on exhibit in a New York newspaper office. Later, "The Jaws of the New Jersey Man-Eater" wound up in the window of a Broadway fish shop.

The capture of the apparent killer did not stop the shark scare, which was sweeping the Eastern seaboard from Rhode Island to Florida. Several hundred sharks were reported off Fire Island, Long Island, and posses were formed to track them down. A neighbor of Teddy Roosevelt's said he saw a shark off the beach in Oyster Bay, Long Island, and called upon him to do something about it. A long-distance swimmer announced that he would brave the terrors of the lower bay of New York Harbor in a round trip from the Battery to Sandy Hook—in a wire basket. In the *New York Times*, America's leading woman swimmer, Annette Kellerman, advised bathers to dive under an onrushing shark. "As he is coming at you upside down," she explained, "you have a chance to get away, if the distance to shore or safety is not too far." A chorus girl rushed into print with the claim that she had frightened off a shark with an impromptu ballet of splashes and kicks. People signed up for "special swimming courses" that were supposed to teach bathers how to outwit sharks. Arguments broke out over whether the shark attacks weren't rather the doings of giant turtles.

Theories abounded, too. One was that heavy cannonading in the North Sea had driven sharks across the Atlantic to more tranquil seas. Another theory held that sharks were

feeding on swimmers because they had been deprived of their usual diet of refuse from passenger liners, whose sailings were being curtailed by German U-boats. The European war also spawned the idea that sharks had been feasting so well on war dead floating down rivers into the sea that they had undergone a change of dietary habits. One *New York Times* letter writer estimated that sharks had gobbled up more than 12,500 war casualties.

After losses estimated at $1 million in canceled reservations, the mayors of ten New Jersey resort towns met at Beach Haven, where the first shark attack had occurred, and pleaded for an end to the panic. They asked newspapers to refrain from publishing stories that "cause the public to believe the New Jersey seacoast is infested with sharks, whereas there are no more than in any other summer."

The mayors' plea went unheard. Shark stories continued. "Sharks are the undisputed masters of the Atlantic coast," one New York newspaper exclaimed. "The federal government yesterday abandoned its proposed campaign of extermination along the New Jersey beaches. The enemy was too numerous for the Coast Guard to tackle, it was said."

There was some truth in the story of the government's so-called surrender. The federal government had indeed declared war on sharks. A Coast Guard cutter had been dispatched to New Jersey to fight them. A congressman, predictably from New Jersey, had asked for a $5,000 appropriation to launch a federal crusade against the shark.

Ultimately the strategy of the shark war was discussed at the highest possible level. At a time when presidential worries included Pancho Villa's raids, a national election campaign, and possible U.S. participation in the Great War, President Wilson's Cabinet placed the subject of sharks on its agenda. After this Cabinet meeting, Secretary of the Treasury William G. McAdoo announced that the Coast Guard had been ordered to do what it could, which eventually turned out to be nothing. Secretary of Commerce William C. Redfield stated that his Bureau of Fisheries had not yet discovered why the sharks had appeared. Later, the Bureau of Fisheries officially warned bathers to stay in shallow water, because there was no known way to get rid of sharks.

Examination of the victims established beyond a doubt that large sharks had attacked them. Measurements of the wounds indicated fish with large jaws. But experts did not agree on the species. Modern analysis of the findings raises the possibility that a bull shark (*Carcharhinus leucas*) attacked the Matawan victims. Bull sharks (see Chapter 10) ascend rivers, which great whites rarely do. Almost certainly one or more great whites killed the bathers at Beach Haven and Spring Lake.

In his book *Jaws*, Peter Benchley recaptures the shark panic of 1916, moving it through time to the 1970s and geographically to a mythical New England resort. *Jaws* and the movie that followed rekindled the panic of 1916, a panic that had been intensified by general ignorance about sharks in general and shark attacks in particular.

Ignorance and fear have been eclipsed by knowledge and the rise of the New Shark. When a shark attacked two swimmers in the Gulf of Mexico, off Gulf Shores, Alabama, in June 2000, the beach was closed for only one day. There were no shark hunts, no massacres. The reaction seemed to be the kind that comes after a lion or a tiger attacks someone at a zoo: People don't blame the animal, and they keep going back to the zoo.

CHAPTER 2

Real Jaws

When a man fell from our ship into the sea during a strong wind, so that we could not wait for him or come to his rescue in any other fashion, we threw out to him on a rope a wooden block, especially prepared for that purpose, and this he finally managed to grasp and thought he could save himself thereby. But when our crew drew this block with the man toward the ship and had him within half the carrying distance of a musket shot, there appeared from below the surface of the sea a large monster called Tiburon; it rushed on the man and tore him to pieces before our very eyes. That surely was a grievous death.

That nameless sailor opens the modern records of documented shark attacks. He fell overboard one day in 1580 on a voyage from Portugal to India. The officer who wrote the account had witnessed the attack. (*Tiburon,* the Spanish word for shark, appears in many places where sharks prowl, including off the Tiburon Peninsula of Haiti, Cape Tiboron in Columbia, and Tiburon Island in the Gulf of California.) Another, less detailed account of a shark attack comes in 1643 from Sebastiao Manrique, an Augustine friar, who wrote of seeing sharks attack pilgrims wading into the sea at Hugli, in Bengal.

Descriptions of shark attacks continued down the decades. But when the New Jersey attacks occurred, scientists who had studied sharks were as shocked as anyone else. The common scientific belief was that sharks did not kill people. In April 1916, three months before the New Jersey attacks, two leading experts on sharks had displayed the kind of hubris that haunts the history of science. They had solemnly proclaimed that sharks almost certainly do not attack people. The assurance had come from Dr. John Treadwell Nichols, curator of the Department of Fishes in the American Museum of Natural History, and Dr. Robert Cushman Murphy of the Brooklyn Museum. "Probably few swimmers have actually met in him their fate," they wrote, "but doubtless many a poor drowned sailor has there found his final resting place."[1]

In a postscript, a third expert, Dr. Frederick A. Lucas, director of the American Museum of Natural History, added his voice of authority: "Cases of shark bite do now and then occur, but there is a great difference between being attacked by a shark and being bitten by one, and the cases of shark bite are usually found to have been due to someone incautiously approaching a shark impounded or tangled in a net, or gasping on the shore. And, under such circumstances, almost any creature will bite." Even after the attack on Charles Bruder, Lucas had dismissed Dr. Schauffler's description of the injuries. A shark's jaws, Lucas said, were simply not powerful enough to snap off a man's leg "like a carrot." He suggested that the next time the reader "carves a leg of lamb, let him speculate on the power required to sever this at one stroke—and the bones of a sheep are much lighter than those of a man."

The three experts needed only to have looked up "Watson and the Shark," the famous painting by John Singleton Copley. The painting portrays an attack on a future Lord Mayor of London, Brook Watson, who in 1749, at the age of fourteen, lost his right leg below the knee to a shark. An orphan who was a member of a ship's crew, he was attacked while swimming in Havana Harbor. Years later, when he became a baronet, Watson created a coat of arms that showed a shark and "a human leg erect and erased below the knee"—as "an allusion to an awful event in his life" and as "a memorial of his gratitude to Heaven." As a further memorial, in 1778 he asked Copley to reconstruct the attack in a magnificent painting.

Or the experts could read Pliny the Elder, who wrote in *Natural History* around 77 A.D. about the "vast numbers of sharks" infesting the sea around sponges "to the great peril of those who dive for them." Leonidas of Tarentum, writing in the third century B.C., told of a specific sponge diver, Tharsys, who was attacked by a shark that tore away part of his lower body. Tharsys' companions took his remains to shore, and thus, the poet cynically noted, Tharsys was buried "both on land and in the sea." In 1566, the naturalist Guillaume Rondelet, a pharmacist who became a biologist and produced a pioneering ichthyologic study of the Mediterranean, wrote of sharks' appetites for tuna and for human beings, suggesting that a shark, not a whale, swallowed the prophet Jonah.

If it is asking too much for scientists to visit an art gallery or a library, they at least could have examined medical records of shark attacks, scarce as those records may have been in 1916. In the *Indian Medical Gazette* of April 1, 1881, for example, a British surgeon routinely reported that "more than 20 persons have been severely bitten by sharks this year. Almost all were fatal." Another report came in 1899 from Dr. William Bryce Orme, the medical officer at Port Said, at the Mediterranean end of the Suez Canal. After treating three boys who were attacked there on a single day, he wrote, "Many people have expressed the opinion it must have been one shark which bit all three boys, and I think this very likely."

Such reports are scattered through reports of British colonial officials who set down what they saw while doing the business of empire. Where Britannia ruled the shores, there are records of shark attacks. But because the victims were what Kipling called the "lesser breeds" of empire, few records of such attacks exist. Other reports are scattered through medical records in other countries. An Italian medical report, published in 1909, for example, describes the remains of an adult male, an adult female, and a young girl found in a fifteen-foot female white shark captured off eastern Sicily. The victims were probably swept into the Straits of Messina following a tidal wave triggered by a massive earthquake. The physicians who examined the bodies could not decide whether the victims drowned before being eaten.

The Times of London, that good gray authority, had reported on December 24, 1910, in a dispatch from Australia, that sharks there had devoured a ship's crew. "Theodore Anderson," the dispatch said, "was engaged in a pearling schooner on the Australian coast, when, during a storm, the vessel drove ashore between Broome and Fremantle. All the men with the exception of Anderson and the captain put off in the ship's boats, which capsized one by one, the men being eaten by sharks. The captain tried to reach the shore, but was seized before the eyes of Anderson, who eventually swam ashore."

Eventually, researchers would search out those records, along with others ignored through the years, so that sober, comprehensive analyses could be made about attacks. But it would take more than the New Jersey attacks to produce such analyses.

Nichols and Murphy did concede that "the New Jersey accidents" had indeed brought "the whole shark question before us in a new phase." But "deaths from shark bite within a short radius of New York City would seem to be one of those unaccountable happenings that take place from time to time to the confounding of savants and the justification of the wildest tradition." They theorized that the deaths could be explained by a "shark year," a phenomenon comparable to "the sporadic abundance during certain years of army worms, or jellyfishes, or even western grasshoppers, or northern lemmings—movements that all have their source in overproduction and other little-understood natural agencies."

The belief that shark attacks were mythical or, at most, an inexplicable phenomenon had been persistent long before "the New Jersey accidents," and that belief endured long afterward. After the first reports of the attacks, newspapers frequently cited the challenge of Hermann Oelrichs, a socially prominent New York banker who summered at Newport, Rhode Island. Oelrichs had offered a $500 prize to anyone who could prove to him that any bather actually had been attacked by a shark anywhere north of Cape Hatteras. By 1916, the prize had gone unclaimed for thirty years.

Oelrichs represented the dominant belief about sharks at that time. Scientists scoffed at shark tales, whose sources were dismissed as sailors cadging drinks in waterfront bars. And even in that seagoing fraternity there was dissent. In 1881 an anonymous author published a fairly popular book entitled *Are Sharks Man-Eaters?* based on "a lifelong service to the sea." After talking to "hundreds of seamen, whalemen, pearl divers, South Sea Islanders, kroomen[sic], wreckers, those whose lives are mostly spent upon the water," he concluded that "he has never seen or heard of a well authenticated instance of a shark's seizing and carrying off a living man or a living land animal of any kind whatever." He even conducted an experiment by throwing dogs overboard to sharks—"large dogs and small dogs of all colors," including a puppy dropped "in the midst of five hungry sharks . . . and in no single instance was a dog touched."

Sharks, he wrote, were merely scavengers and never took live prey. He did admit that "men and women, horses, oxen, dogs, and other animals" are "caught in the water and dragged beneath the surface to be devoured." But the "monster of the deep," he maintained, was invariably an alligator or a crocodile, never a shark.

Lore about sharks around 1916 was largely anecdotal, an adjective that scientists abhor. Even though most of the anecdotes came from seafarers, the span of claims—from the it-was-a-crocodile to sharks-are-man-eaters—showed the unreliability of eyewitnesses. And belief in the innocence of sharks extended to eyewitness scientists, such as William Beebe, an American biologist and popular natural-history writer of the 1920s and 1930s. Beebe, who became famous as a deep-sea explorer, wrote in *The Arcturus Adventure* (1926) that sharks were "harmless scavengers . . . indolent, awkward, chinless cowards." Beebe, like most scientists, ignored such reports as a shark attack described in the *U.S. Naval Medical Bulletin* in 1922.

A contemporary of Beebe, Captain William E. Young, saw sharks as dangerous. But he was merely a seafarer. Young wrote and lectured in the 1920s and 1930s about his adventure as a hunter of sharks (for their hides, a source of tough leather).[2] He told of catching hundreds of sharks and treating large ones as dangerous. "I had seen too many of the ugly killers at their work not to have a deep respect for their armament," he wrote. While shark fishing near Big Pine Key, Florida, Young found a piece of blue serge cloth and a human arm in the stomach of a brown shark (*Carcharhinus plumbeus*). Authorities learned that a man wearing a blue serge coat had gone down in an aircraft the day before. Young later wrote that he did not know whether the brown shark, believed to be harmless, ate the man while he was alive. But in lectures and in newspaper interviews, Young repeatedly reported on shark attacks, particularly in Australia.

An Australian surgeon, Victor M. Coppleson, who had been chronicling shark attacks in his country since 1916, published his findings in the *Medical Journal of Australia* in 1933. He reported on thirty-seven attacks between 1916 and 1933. During his pioneering, lifelong research, Coppleson developed the theory of the "rogue shark," comparing a shark with a taste for human flesh to man-eating lions and tigers that reputedly sought out only human prey after eating one or two.

Coppleson dramatically demonstrated his theory in 1940. After reading in a newspaper that sharks in Georges River near Sydney were attacking dogs, Coppleson suspected a rogue shark. He became convinced when a shark at North Brighton Beach, not far from Georges River, killed a thirteen-year-old boy. The fatal attack occurred on January 23, 1940. That day Coppleson wrote a letter to the *Sydney Morning Herald*, warning that a man-eating shark was in the area and might strike again. Eleven days after his letter was published, a shark killed a man 400 yards from the scene of the first attack.

Another series of attacks revived the rogue shark theory in 1966. On August 21, in the waters of the Duke of York Islands, off Rabaul, a shark carried off a seven-year-old girl and fatally mauled a thirteen-year-old girl. Natives said there had been no attack in villagers' memory. On October 29, an eight-year-old girl was bitten in half while bathing off the southwest coast of New Ireland, about seventy miles from the August attack. The next day, sixteen miles away, a thirteen-year-old girl was fatally attacked; shortly after, a shark snatched a small child from her father's arms, leaving him untouched. Then, on March 1, 1967, a shark attacked but did not kill a fourteen-year-old boy near Rabaul.

Coppleson's rogue-shark theory became a popular explanation for researchers who looked back at such multiple attacks as those that bloodied the waters off New Jersey in 1916. There was also an old account of three attacks, two fatal, within nine days in the waters around Havana. In South Africa, a researcher[3] speculated about "rogue-type" behavior when he found eight clusters of attacks, including two fatal attacks in three days in 1962 and five attacks in twenty-three days in 1957–1958. But shark behavioral studies in recent years have cast doubt on the rogue theory.

During the 1940s, ichthyologists began to look more closely at the still unresolved scientific issue of shark attacks. In their masterful *Fishes of the Western Northern Atlantic*,[4] H. B. Bigelow and W. C. Schroeder of the Museum of Comparative Zoology conceded that "many shark fatalities are on record, well attested by hospital reports or otherwise." They then listed the places where shark attacks had been reliably reported: South Africa, the Red Sea, India, Ceylon, the East Indies, the Philippines, the Pacific coasts of Mexico and Panama, the coast of Ecuador, the Gulf of Mexico, the West Indies, the Guianas, the eastern coast of the United States, tropical West Africa, the eastern Mediterranean, and Port Said. They believed that shark attacks were unlikely in any temperate waters. Among the shark-safe zones that they declared were the coasts on either side of the North Atlantic, where "the danger to a swimmer

40

of attack by a shark, although existent, is so exceedingly remote as to be wholly negligible."

America's entrance into war in 1941 intensified shark research because of concern about U.S. servicemen serving in what newspapers inevitably referred to as the "shark-infested" Pacific Ocean. Attacks were seen primarily as a morale problem—especially for worrying mothers back home. While the researchers took up the problem, the U.S. Navy shrugged off the threat, stating in a publication called *Shark Sense* that "the shark offers no unusual hazards to a swimming or drifting man." Researchers focused on ways to ward off sharks, beginning the long quest for a shark repellent.

By the time Bigelow and Schroeder made their list of attack locations, other ichthyologists were also at work, ushering in a new era of shark research. In 1958 the American Institute of Biological Sciences sponsored a shark conference in New Orleans, drawing scientists from thirty-four nations. From a working group formed at that conference came the Shark Research Panel. Its chairman was Perry W. Gilbert, a renowned Cornell scientist; members included Leonard P. Schultz, the leading ichthyologist at the Smithsonian Institution; Stewart Springer, and later Albert L. Tester and H. David Baldridge, who, as a U.S. naval officer, had been involved in the Navy's search for a shark repellent. The panel began the Shark Attack File, the first worldwide compilation of documented attacks. Schultz and Marilyn H. Malin prepared the list, which was published in 1963.[5]

Now, finally, there could be no doubt that sharks attacked people. The Shark Attack File listed more than 1,000 attacks. The list bristled with dates and places: There are four attacks on the Hooghly River at Ghat, India, in May and June 1870; all survived. The body of a man named Barfoot is found in a shark in Warson Bay, Sydney, Australia, in March 1887. A Somali boatman is killed off Aden, Saudi Arabia, on July 15, 1898. A ship's pilot dies in 1911 off Pensacola, Florida. A U.S. Marine dies in an attack in Haitian waters in 1921. Two men die in attacks at Coogee, near Sydney, within a month in 1922. Between 1923 and 1932, nine pearl divers are attacked in Australian waters; all survive. Three people are attacked in separate incidents off Charleston, South Carolina, in the summer of 1933; all survive. Miami Beach suffers a shark casualty in April 1933. Alan D. McArthur survives an attack at Winkelpruit, South Africa, on Easter Sunday, 1934. An unidentified boy is killed at Winkelspruit two days later; two more die off Winkelspruit within two days in February 1962 (one of the "rogue" clusters). Two die in separate attacks in Havana Harbor in 1931. A sailor on the tuna vessel *Seiju-Maru* is lost to a shark in Port Kilindeni, Mambasa, on July 18, 1958. A man survives an attack in Long Island Sound, off Bridgeport, Connecticut, in 1960.

The list was divided into categories—"provoked," "unprovoked," "attacks on boats," "attacks following air and sea disasters," and "doubtful." By studying old medical journals, ships' logs, hospital and physicians' records, and newspaper files, the compilers of the list were able to sift through incidents, separating actual attacks on living people from cases in which sharks were scavengers, not attackers. The "doubtful" category covered those ambiguous incidents that had made scientists skeptical about shark attacks. Included are gruesome cases based on the stomach contents of caught sharks: "head of Mr. Johnson (drowned)" in Sydney Harbor in 1839; arms, legs, and other body parts in Australian sharks; a human leg in a Bermuda shark in 1960.

Another report, by Baldridge of the original Shark Research Panel, was published in 1973.[6] Using a computerized study that sought common factors in the attacks, the report examined 1,165 reported attacks. More than two-thirds of the reports were from attacks that occurred after 1940—except for World War II, a period for which records are spotty.

From the decades of reports and research has come the International Shark Attack File (ISAF), a compilation of all known shark attacks. The file is administered by the Florida Museum of Natural History and the American Elasmobranch Society, whose members professionally study sharks and their close relatives, skates and rays. The ISAF has information on more than 3,000 reported attacks, dating to the sixteenth century but consisting primarily of twentieth-century attacks. Much of that information comes from cooperating scientists who serve as regional observers throughout the world. These observers forward investigations of attacks in their areas to ISAF headquarters, where the data is analyzed and computerized. Hard-copy documentation includes original notes, press clippings, photographs, audio/video tapes, and medical/autopsy reports. "The File," says an official statement, "is utilized by biological researchers and research physicians; access to the data is granted only after careful screening on a case-by-case basis. Direct access by the press and general public is strictly forbidden since much sensitive information is considered privileged."

Drawing from the ISAF's authoritative information on shark attacks, scientists have been analyzing shark behavior and learning more in the last few years than had been ever known before. Douglas Long of the University of California, for example, has been studying the feeding habits and predatory behavior of great white sharks on marine mammals around the Farallon Islands off the central California coast. One of his techniques: He and his research team watch for injured marine mammals, which are magnets for great whites. When a shark begins feeding on the prey, the researchers hop into a small boat and head for the shark. They come close enough to stick a small hand-held water-proof video recorder under the water to film the shark. They got to know the sharks so well that they could identify them by scars and other skin marks.

Such research has produced two new wellsprings of knowledge—shark behavior in general and shark behavior that results in attacks.

First, a look at the shark.

Sharks live in all oceans except for seas south of the Antarctic Circle. The Greenland shark *(Somniosus micro-cephalus)* swims through seas touched by glaciers. But most sharks live in water whose temperature is 68 degrees Fahrenheit or higher.[7] They also live—and attack people—in lakes and rivers of Australia, Borneo, Malaysia, Thailand, Africa, India, and Nicaragua. Sharks range in size from the dwarf dogshark (*Etmopterus perryi*), which can fit in the palm of a hand, to the huge whale shark (*Rhincodon typus*) and basking shark, which are more than fifty feet long. Sharks of about twenty species have attacked people, and only a few of those species are known killers.

An ISAF analysis of 1,165 attacks indicated that those at sea happened during daylight, particularly in late afternoon. Shore attacks peaked at about 11 A.M. and fell off until 3 or 4 P.M., when more attacks were recorded, falling off again around nightfall. Other research indicates that shark attacks coincide with the sharks' habit of seeking out prey in early light and twilight. But sharks, especially big sharks, eat when they want to eat. As a Mediterranean researcher remarked, "Sharks are erratic animals, and they go where they can find food."

Sharks swimming today are inheritors of an evolution-ary process that has left them little changed from their an-cestors of 350 million years ago. Unlike typical fish, sharks do not have internal bones, but instead have a cartilaginous skeleton. A shark's body is covered not with scales but with denticles, tiny teeth that give the shark a hide like sandpaper. Sailors, in fact, once used pieces of the hide for just that purpose.

Sharks have many senses, and an understanding of those senses is vital to an understanding of attack behavior. In a typical attack, each sense plays a role, giving the shark the information it needs for finding, tracking, stalking, and finally biting its prey. Besides possessing the familiar senses of sight, smell, hearing, touch, and taste, a shark has a complex electro-receptive sense that detects the electrical fields produced by animals, including human beings.

Sharks lack external ears, but their inner ears are powerful organs, able to perceive both speed and gravity. A shark can hear sounds—especially the pulsing, low-frequency sounds emitted by wounded prey—up to about half a mile. A shark's sensitive sense of hearing is augmented by a sense called the "lateral line," a network of fluid-filled canals just below the skin of the head and along the sides of the body. Pores along the canals are open to the water. The lateral-line system picks up low-frequency vibrations and sends data to the brain about the distance and direction of the vibrations.

Most sharks have a strange sensory system that appears as a number of pores scattered about the head. Each pore forms one end of a tube whose other end consists of a group of sensory cells called Lorenzini's ampullae, after the man who first described these organs in 1678. The word ampullae derives from their shape, which is similar to an *ampulla*, a narrow-necked bottle the Romans used in anointing themselves after bathing. Each ampulla is filled with a jelly-like substance that appears to react either to pressure changes or temperature fluctuations, or possibly both. Some scientists believe that the ampullae may bestow other senses: detection of changes in salinity and the ability to pick up weak electrical charges produced by prey hidden in the sand.

The shark's electro-receptive system can detect electric fields so weak that one scientist compared it to the electric field of a flashlight battery connected to electrodes spaced 1,000 miles apart. And the small signals produced within the weak field are detected against a large electrical background generated by the shark's own respiratory and muscle activity. Somehow, the shark's brain filters out its own electrical output while analyzing the signals outside its body. Sharks frequently seem to attack boats with metal hulls; such attacks may be triggered by detection of the boat's electric field. Similar fields also are sometimes given off by the metal cage used by divers and photographers in sharky waters.

Enhancing the hearing and lateral-line senses is the sense of smell. The shark's brain has been called a "brain of smell" because the biggest parts of the brain are the olfactory lobes. (The olfactory structure in the brain of the great white shark is larger and better developed than in any other shark.) Sharks, which have been observed following bathers who had merely scratched their legs, can detect the scent of prey one-quarter of a mile away. As zoologist A. D. Hasler has written, "We are concerned here with a sense of such refined acuity that it defies comparable attainment by the most sensitive instruments of modern chemical analysis."

Odor travels through the water to the olfactory pits, or nostrils, on the underside of the shark's snout. The pits, rarely used for breathing, are lined with a sensitive membrane that is usually folded into a series of ridges coated with scent-sensitive tissue. As the shark swims, a current of water constantly passes over this olfactory tissue. Since the swimming is essentially continuous, so is the flow of smell-messages being transmitted to its scent-oriented brain.

Sharks often attack each other, and there seems to be a tendency for large sharks to eat smaller sharks. All sharks appear to stay away from hammerheads, particularly the great hammerhead (*Sphyrna mokarran*). Hammerheads have their eyes and their nostrils on the edges of their odd heads, and this gives them an advantage over other shark species. The hammer shape increases the distance between ampullae, and this may increase hammerheads' ability to detect magnetic fields.

Experiments have shown that sharks can distinguish between amino acids, amines, and small fatty acids; these seem to be stimulating smells. Researchers have found that some sharks, through smell, can detect ten drops of liquefied tuna in a volume of water equivalent to the contents of an average swimming pool. Smells produced by carbohydrates and sugars do not seem to attract sharks. Blood certainly does, and in minute amounts. But H. David Baldridge, in his 1973 study, found only nineteen cases in which victims were bleeding before being attacked. He also discovered many cases in which the shark took a bite, causing profuse bleeding, and yet left without attacking again.

The shark uses each sense sequentially when it searches for prey. Wesley R. Strong, Jr., of the Cousteau Society, in experiments with great whites in Australian waters, proposed a "decision-making sequence" that begins with smell and ends with sight. Simultaneously offered a seal-shaped target and a square target, Strong's sharks overwhelmingly chose the seal. From depths of nearly sixty feet the sharks could discern objects on the surface as small as six inches in diameter.

Sharks' eyes are protected by a nictitating membrane that moves up instead of down, as eyelids do. The membrane protects the shark's eye, particularly from thrashing

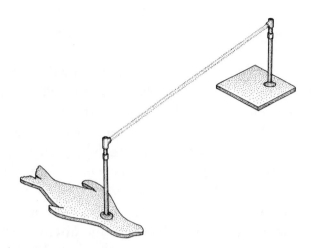

Visual discrimination array consisting of two black epoxy resin-coated plywood shapes of equal surface area, held apart by PVC uprights and a 2-m long clear acrylic crossbar.

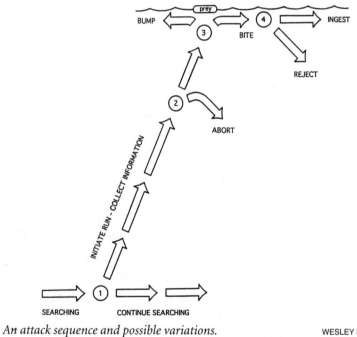

An attack sequence and possible variations.

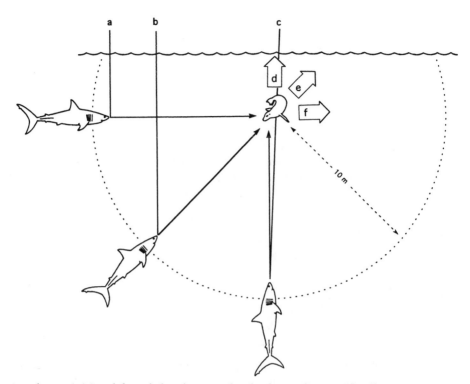

Attacks are initiated from below because the shark can distinguish silhouettes (c) better than images (a), and the route of escape for the prey is more limited (d).   WESLEY STRONG

prey as the shark eats. Some species seem able to discern colors, responding in experiments to light, bright colors. Researchers noticed a particular preference for a certain shade: the standard yellow of life jackets, which has become known among shark researchers as "yum-yum yellow."

The decision-making sequence begins when the shark makes a distant detection. Moving in closer, the shark decides whether to attack or veer off. If it attacks, it will bite or bump the prey. It will then make the final decision to eat or reject. This last judgment can mean life or death to a human being who is selected as the prey.

The shark tears into prey with razor-sharp teeth that never wear out. Because of the shark's powerful bite, its

Just before attacking, the snout and the lower jaw are in their normal resting position and the teeth are more or less parallel to the floor of the mouth. If the prey is small, the teeth do not need to be brought into action, and it can be swallowed immediately without the following sequence.

The snout is raised, and the depressing of the lower jaw permits a maximum opening of the whole mouth.

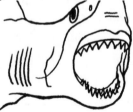

Without the snout changing position, the upper jaw itself turns forward and downward, exposing the upper teeth; the backward-angled direction of these teeth helps to get the prey into the mouth.

The snout is lowered, after the prey has been seized, allowing the upper jaw to return to its normal position beneath the skull. All these sequences follow one another in 1/400 of a second.

teeth often break off. As teeth become worn or lost, new rows of teeth come forward on a membrane from the inner surface. Behind the teeth in use there may be as many as seven reserve rows of replacement teeth. The lemon shark (*Negaprion brevirostris*) can replace a tooth in about eight days. Because of the structure of the jaws of a shark like the great white, the upper jaw extends forward so that the puncturing teeth of the lower jaw grab and hold the prey. The teeth in the upper jaw do the slicing.

How strong is a shark's bite? Answers are usually made in tons, based on the classic experiment performed in 1965 by James Snodgrass and Perry Gilbert. Using a "gnathodynamometer"' (bite-meter), wrapped in alluring mackerel, they tested the bite of tiger, lemon, and dusky sharks. In a formula based on measurements of the depths of indentations in the aluminum-and-steel bite-meter, they came up with a single tooth-tip pressure of three metric tons, or about eighteen tons per square inch. But, as marine biologist Rick Martin has pointed out, the Dental Science Handbook, published by the American Dental Association, gives bite pressures by humans as great as fifteen tons per square inch—83 percent as strong as the greatest pressure recorded thus far for any shark. "Having been bitten by sharks on several occasions (always my fault, I hasten to add)," Martin wrote, "I can attest that shark bites on humans are typically not very forceful, seeming threatening or exploratory rather than sincere attempts to inflict damage. Thus, sharks may well be capable of exerting even greater bite pressures than have been recorded for them."

Almost any large shark is a potential attacker. Three species in particular have been blamed for most attacks: the great white, tiger, and bull shark (see Chapter 10). These species probably are responsible for many or most "bump-and-bite" and "sneak" attacks. Most research into attacks focuses on great whites. But the ISAF has developed general conclusions based on attacks by all the species deemed dangerous:

- Most attacks occur near shore, typically inshore of a sandbar or between sandbars where sharks feed and can become trapped at low tide. Areas with steep drop-offs are also likely attack sites. Sharks congregate there because their natural food items also congregate in these areas.
- The most common kind of unprovoked attacks are "hit-and-run" attacks. These typically occur in the surf zone, with swimmers and surfers the usual targets. The victim seldom sees its attacker and the shark does not return after inflicting a single bite or slash wound. In most instances, these probably are cases of mistaken identity that occur under conditions of poor water visibility and a harsh physical environment (breaking surf and strong wash/current conditions).

"A feeding shark in this habitat," says an ISAF analysis, "must make quick decisions and rapid movements to capture its traditional food items. When these difficult physical conditions are considered in conjunction with provocative human appearance and activities associated with aquatic recreation (splashing, shiny jewelry, contrasting colored swimsuits, contrasting tanning, especially involving the soles of the feet), it is not surprising that sharks might occasionally misinterpret a human for its normal prey. We suspect that, upon biting, the shark quickly realizes that the human is a foreign object, or that it is too large, and immediately releases the victim and does not return. Some of these attacks could also be related to social behaviors unrelated to feeding, such as dominance behaviors seen in many land animals. Injuries to 'hit and run' victims are usually confined to relatively small lacerations, often on the leg below the knee, and are seldom life-threatening."

- "Bump-and-bite" attacks and "sneak" attacks, while less common than hit-and-run attacks, result in greater injuries and most fatalities. These types of attack usually involve divers or swimmers in somewhat deeper waters, but occur in near-shore shallows in some areas of the world. In bump-and-bite attacks, the shark initially circles and often bumps the victim before launching the actual attack. Sharks may also injure victims by bumping them vigorously, but most sharks move in cautiously when attacking.
- "Sneak" attacks occur without warning; the shark usually strikes again and again, biting repeatedly and inflicting grievous and often fatal wounds. ISAF researchers believe that this type of attack is "the result of feeding or antagonistic behaviors rather than being cases of mistaken identity." Most shark attacks on victims of air and sea disasters are bump-and-bite and sneak attacks.
- Many attacks seem to be assaults on people handling hooked or snared sharks or spear fishermen handling wounded fish. Through sight or sound, a shark may confuse swimmers or divers for prey.
- Sharks may attack from a territorial drive, with no intention to feed. (An analysis of 1,000 recent shark attacks showed that well over 50 percent of the attacks were not inspired by a desire to feed.) A characteristic swimming pattern called agonistic display usually precedes attacks inspired by territoriality. The shark shakes its head and swims erratically with a hunched back, pectoral fins pointing down, and snout pointing up.
- Up to 60 percent of shark attack injuries are slashes made by the teeth of the upper jaw. (This behavior is typical of courtship advances by some male sharks.)

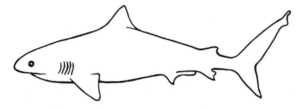

Non-aggressive shark.

- Great white sharks rush toward prey, attacking from beneath and behind. These sharks rely on stealth and surprise to prey on seals, sea lions, and other marine mammals. Some observers believe that after a great white shark bites its victim, it swims a short distance away, waiting for its victim to bleed to death. (If this happens in an attack on a human, he or she may survive if rescuers are nearby.)
- To reduce the chance of an attack by a great white shark, swimmers and divers should stay clear of seal and sea lion rookeries, or other known areas frequented by the sharks.
- Swimmers and divers at the surface are more prone to attack than divers beneath the water. At the surface, the silhouette of a swimmer or diver resembles that of a seal. Great white sharks may not be able to make the distinction. Researchers have also hypothesized that a surfer on a board so closely resembles a seal that sharks, particularly great whites, may strike after a moment of mistaken identity.

Shark giving agonistic display.

While on assignment for *National Geographic* magazine in False Bay, near Cape Town, South Africa, photographer David Doubilet set up a camera on a decoy shaped like a seal—and recorded a great white's airborne attack, a breaching maneuver provoked when a seal flees. But researcher Strong, commenting on such decoys, wrote, "It would be a disservice to surfers and divers to promote the notion that details of appearance [i.e., resembling pinnipeds in form or color] are even remotely as important to their safety as is their behavior based on knowledge of local pinniped and shark distribution patterns and behavior."[8]

- Sharks attack surfers more than any other group. In 1998, for example, 69 percent of the attacks were made on surfers; swimmers and waders accounted for 15.5 percent of the 1998 attacks, and divers 15.5 percent.

The ISAF focuses on unprovoked attacks. Investigation of sixty-five "incidents of shark-human interaction" throughout the world in 1999, for example, showed that fifty-eight incidents were unprovoked attacks. Cast out of the statistics were cases in which sharks were scavenging on bodies, usually drowning victims. Also deemed unprovoked were incidents involving divers or fishermen handling sharks and injuries to divers in public aquariums or research holding-pens.

The 1999 total of fifty-eight unprovoked attacks closely replicated the totals recorded in 1998 (fifty-four) and 1997 (sixty) and the decade's yearly average (fifty-four). During the early part of the 1990s, the number of unprovoked shark attacks grew at a steady rate, rising from thirty-seven in 1990 to all-time highs of sixty-two in 1994 and seventy-four in 1995. The 1990s had the highest number of attacks (536) of any previous decade, continuing an upward trend exhibited throughout the twentieth century.

"The number of shark attacks transpiring in a given year is directly correlated to the amount of human time spent in the sea," the ISAF reported. "As the world population continues to upsurge and the time spent in aquatic recreation rises, we might expect a gradual annual increase in the number of attacks. By contrast, near-shore shark populations are declining at a serious rate in many areas of the world as a result of over-fishing, theoretically reducing the opportunity for shark-human interactions. However, year-to-year variability in local economic, meteorological, and oceanographic conditions also greatly influences the odds of sharks and humans encountering one another. As a result, short-term trends in the number of shark attacks must be viewed with caution."

More than two-thirds of 1999 attacks occurred in North American waters—thirty-seven in U.S. waters and one each in the waters of Mexico and the Bahamas. Surfers and windsurfers were victims in 43 percent of the attacks; swimmers and waders accounted for 38 percent. Other attacks involved divers and snorkelers (11 percent), body surfers (2 percent), and kayakers (1 percent).

Four fatalities were reported in 1999, a substantial drop from the decade's yearly average of seven. The 6.9 percent fatality rate was the lowest yearly rate of the decade, well under the decade average of 12.7 percent. Two fatalities occurred in South Africa and single deaths were recorded from Australia and Saudi Arabia. Of the fifty-eight unprovoked shark attacks reported throughout the world in 1999, thirty-seven occurred in the United States, including twenty-five in Florida, making that state the global capital of reported unprovoked attacks.

"It's no coincidence that the fatality rate has been declining decade after decade," says George Burgess, director of the ISAF. "A big reason is dramatic improvements in the

quality and availability of emergency medical care throughout the world, which have boosted survival rates. We also
are seeing an increased awareness of how to avoid putting
ourselves in situations where we could get killed by sharks.
More enlightened media coverage and heavy use of the file's
Internet site have resulted in better informed marine recreationists."9

A Mediterranean Shark Attack File has also been created
to compile reports of attacks on humans and boats from
those waters. It is maintained in cooperation with the ISAF.
Herodotus and other ancient Greek writers described the
earliest recorded shark attacks from the Mediterranean. But
there are few modern reports. An analysis of Mediterranean
attacks from 1890 to 1999 showed thirty-four incidents and
nineteen fatal attacks.

In an attack in February 1989, a white shark attacked a
diver working on cables in the Ligurian Sea off Piombino,
Italy. The diver surfaced and began swimming to a support
boat. Witnesses said the shark circled him once and then attacked again, taking him below the surface. The body was
not found. In another 1989 attack off Marina di Carrara, a
surfer was on his board and urinating when a shark struck,
biting his right upper thigh. He survived. In 1993, a man
swimming off Playa de les Arenes, along Spain's Costa
Blanca, was attacked by a six-foot shark (species unknown),
which bit off the victim's toes.

The relative risk of a shark attack is very small. Bees,
wasps, and snakes kill more people than sharks do. In the
United States, the annual risk of death from lightning is
thirty times greater than that from shark attack. For every
1,000 drownings in the United States there is one shark attack; the ratio rises to 600 to 1 in South Africa, and 50 to 1 in
Australia. Here are some other relative comparisons, prepared by the ISAF.

Number of Attacks made by the American Alligator (*Alligator mississippiensis*)

State	Period	Number of Alligator Attacks	Number of Alligator Fatalities	Number of Shark Attacks	Number of Shark Fatalities
Alabama	??–1995	4	0	1	0
Florida	1948–1995	218	7	276	6
Georgia	1988–1995	5	1	1	0
Louisiana	1978–1995	1	0	1	0
South Carolina	1976–1995	6	0	9	0
Texas	1980–1995	2	0	12	0
TOTALS		**236**	**8**	**300**	**6**

FATALITY RATE: ALLIGATOR ATTACKS = 3.4%, SHARK ATTACKS = 2.0%   SOURCE: INTERNATIONAL SHARK ATTACK FILE-FMNH

State	Period	Number of Lightning Strikes	Number of Lightning Fatalities	Number of Shark Attacks	Number of Shark Fatalities
Alabama	1959–1990	244	79	1	0
California	1959–1990	69	18	59	6
Connecticut	1959–1990	79	13	1	0
Delaware	1959–1990	40	14	6	0
Florida	1959–1990	1155	313	180	4
Georgia	1959–1990	341	75	4	0
Hawaii	1959–1990	1	0	37	1
Louisiana	1959–1990	308	111	1	0
Maine	1959–1990	111	20	0	0
Maryland	1959–1990	230	111	0	0
Massachusetts	1959–1990	317	24	0	0
Mississippi	1959–1990	288	85	1	0
New Hampshire	1959–1990	66	6	5	0
New Jersey	1959–1990	158	54	5	0
New York	1959–1990	515	124	1	0
North Carolina	1959–1990	585	159	4	0
Oregon	1959–1990	25	6	8	0
Puerto Rico	1959–1990	34	28	1	0
Rhode Island	1959–1990	48	4	1	0
South Carolina	1959–1990	274	69	10	0
Texas	1959–1990	415	148	14	1
Virginia	1959–1990	201	43	1	0
Washington	1959–1990	24	1	1	0
TOTALS		5,528*	1,505*	336	12
Number per year		172.8*	47.0*	10.5	0.4

*Lightning data for coastal states only. In the entire United States during the period 1959–1990 there were 11,251 lightning strikes of humans resulting in 3,011 deaths (351.6 and 94.1 per year, respectively).   SOURCE: INTERNATIONAL SHARK ATTACK FILE-FMNH

Number of Injuries Associated with Home-Improvement Equipment (in 1996)

Equipment	Number of Injuries
Nails, screws, tacks, and bolts	198,849
Ladders	138,894
Toilets	43,687
Pruning, trimming, edging	36,091
Chain saws	13,458
Pliers, wire cutters, and wrenches	15,957
Manual-cleaning equipment	14,386
Power grinders, buffers, and polishers	13,458
Buckets and pails	10,907
Room deodorizers and fresheners	2,599
Toilet-bowl products	1,567
Paints or varnish thinners	1,549
U.S. shark injuries and deaths in 1996	18

SOURCE: INTERNATIONAL SHARK ATTACK FILE-FMNH

Number of Biting Injuries Occurring Annually in New York City

Biters	1981	1984	1985	1986	1987
Dogs	12,656	10,593	9,809	8,870	8,064
Humans	*	1,589	1,591	1,572	1,587
Cats	826	*	879	*	802
Wild rats	60	*	311	*	291
Squirrels	81	*	*	*	95
Hamsters	52	*	*	*	*
Rabbits	37	*	*	*	*
Raccoons	18	*	*	*	11
Horses	18	*	*	*	*
Gerbils	17	*	12	*	*
Laboratory rats	15	*	9	*	*
Monkeys	11	*	*	*	*
Snakes	8	*	4	*	*
Bats	7	*	4	*	*
Ferrets	5	*	5	*	7
Guinea pigs	5	*	*	*	*
Parrots	5	*	6	*	*
Blue jays	2	*	*	*	*
Spiders	*	*	2	*	*
Skunks	1	*	*	*	3
Parakeets	1	*	*	*	*
Opossum	1	*	*	*	*
Sea lion	1	*	*	*	*
Lion	1	*	*	*	*
Ocelot	1	*	*	*	*
Lion fish stabs human	1	*	*	*	*
U.S. shark injuries	12	14	12	6	13

SOURCE: INTERNATIONAL SHARK ATTACK FILE-FMNH

The fear of sharks is ancient and touches something deep within us. So deep was that fear in the hearts of sailors that many of them once believed it was good not to know how to swim. Better to drown than to die in the jaws of a shark. We are told that one of the twelve basic dreams that haunt our sleep is: "I'm swimming when a shark attacks me and takes a huge chunk out of my side."[10] The English language offers words for more than 120 kinds of fear, from acrophobia for fear of heights to zoophobia for fear of animals. And among the creatures that get their own fear words are sharks: galeophobia.

One way to dispel fear is to learn more about what you fear. In the pages that follow, there is much to learn.

CHAPTER 3

ATTACK:
On the Shore

Around St. Petersburg on Florida's Gulf Coast, people can swim every day right off the docks behind their homes. One of those daily swimmers, sixty-nine-year-old Thadeus Kubinski, of St. Pete Beach, jumped off his backyard dock one afternoon in September 2000. His wife, Anna, climbed down the dock ladder. As she entered the water, she heard him scream. In a moment his torn body lay face down in blood-stained water about four to five feet deep. She climbed up the ladder and went into the house to call 911. Kubinski was dead or dying as rescuers pulled him out of the water.

For hours, officials said they could not be sure that a shark had killed Kubinski. No one could ever remember any shark attacks in the area. But the right side of his body was rent from just below his underarm to above his hip. The shark also crushed Kubinski's rib cage and tore his liver. George H.

Burgess, director of the Florida-based International Shark Attack File (ISAF), was called in. A tooth removed from Kubinski's body was from a bull shark, estimated by Burgess to be nine feet long and 400 pounds.

People who jump or dive into the water make a splash, and records show that the sudden roiling of the water can attract a shark. Never had the phenomenon been more grimly demonstrated: The shark attacked the jumper, not the climber entering the water without causing a ripple. Also, as in many attacks, the water was murky and full of mullet and other fish that lure hungry sharks.

Mrs. Kubinski saw some turmoil in the water just before her husband jumped in. "That commotion," Burgess said, "very likely was the result of a shark chasing after, or actually feeding upon something, and that splash of the victim triggered a predatory attack from the shark. It was in there looking to find a meal, going about its normal existence. Quite frankly, the victim did not have a chance. The severity of the injury resulted in a very quick death."

Kubinski's death overshadowed all of the other thirty-four non-fatal attacks in Florida waters during the first eleven months of the year 2000—a record-breaking year. Fatalities are rare in Florida—Kubinski's death was the fifth fatality in twenty-five years. But horrifying attacks on swimmers in shallow water are not rare.

Garbage was drifting onto the shore at Atlantic Dunes Park in Delray Beach, Florida, and small fishes were splashing in the shallows. Ryan Welborn's mother decided it was time to take her five-year-old son out of the water and go home. Ryan was toddling around in two feet of water. Suddenly he started screaming.

"Get it off me!" the little boy cried, hitting at his leg. His mother grabbed him and lifted him from the water. His left leg was torn open at the knee. Lifeguards ran up, gave him first aid and called for an ambulance. No one had seen the shark. Ryan and his family were tourists from Georgia, on vacation in June 1999. They did not know much about the sharks of Florida. They did not know, for example, that in April a shark bit a fourteen-year-old boy while he surfed off Hobe Sound Beach, about thirty miles north of Delray Beach. Nor that in February another surfer was bitten on the hand while he was paddling off Hobe Sound Beach.

Surgery saved Ryan's leg. Ryan, physically and emotionally fine, has no fear of the water. He says he knows the shark did not mean to hurt him, and he tells everyone that he wants to learn about sharks when he grows up. Learning about sharks is a worthwhile ambition for anyone who swims in the sea.

The size and shape of the single bite on Ryan's leg showed that the shark's jaw size was about eighteen inches across, indicating a blacktip (*Carcharhinus limbatus*) or a spinner (*Carcharhinus brevipinna*). The spinner is an aggressive shark that has been blamed for attacks on divers and swimmers. It gets its name from its habit of pursuing schools of prey from beneath the school and then spiraling upward, snapping up prey, and sometimes leaping out of the water. The blacktip, also implicated in several attacks, feeds on small fish and stingrays, which are often found in shallow water.

Four months after the attack on Ryan, a thirteen-year-old surfer jumped off his board after riding a wave when a shark "bit my foot and then spit it out. My whole foot was in the shark's mouth." The attack happened at Fort Pierce Inlet State Park, about seventy miles north of Delray Beach. The surfer, Mike Sprague, got back on his board and turned around to paddle back to shore. The shark began chasing him. "It was pretty much waiting for me to get off my board," Sprague told a Palm Beach *Sun-Sentinel* reporter. The bite had severed one of the four tendons in his foot. Two other surfers were attacked off the park in the fall of 2000. Both received similar wounds on their legs and feet. One of the attacks came at dusk, a particularly dangerous time in waters that surfers share with sharks.

Painful bites on the legs and feet have become a routine form of shark attack along Florida's east coast. Usually, the shark takes one bite and disappears. But in one attack off Ormond Beach, north of Daytona, a shark bit twice, opening a fifteen-inch wound on the right thigh of a swimmer and an eight-inch wound on his right calf.

In one of Florida's nineteen attacks of 1998, a shark bit a thirteen-year-old boy off Delray Beach. The wound, on his right leg, required twenty stitches to close. A few days later, at Vero Beach, about eighty-five miles north of Delray Beach, nine-year-old James Willie Tellasmon was swimming close enough to shore for his parents to keep an eye on him. One moment he was stroking along happily. The next moment he was flailing his arms as if struggling to stay afloat. And then he disappeared.

Next morning, rescue divers found his body, headless and armless. Authorities blamed the attack on a tiger shark that had come upon the boy while pursuing migratory fish close to shore. Not since 1976 had a shark killed anyone near shore in the United States.

Fatal attacks are rare in Florida, but in recent years, non-fatal attacks along the east coast of Florida have numbered about fifteen to twenty a year. These attacks on swimmers, surfers, and divers are frequent enough to make Florida the shark-attack capital of the United States—and in some years the world capital. The twenty-five Florida encounters in 1999 accounted for 47 percent of all recorded attacks in the world that year. In 1996, there were thirteen attacks in Florida; in 1997, the number soared to twenty-five.

Usually, in Florida and elsewhere, the shark takes a bite and vanishes, an encounter classified as a "hit and run" attack. Many of these attacks occurred in murky or dirty water. A good example is the garbage-strewn water that Ryan's mother saw. In such an attack, the victim usually does not see the shark. Many researchers believe that a hit-and-run shark makes a quick investigation of a possible bit of food, finds the taste not to its liking, and sets out to find something more palatable. Sharks, like other predators, survive by developing successful search techniques.

The fatal attack at Vero Beach cannot be explained as hit-and-run. Commenting on the attack, Burgess said: "Under conditions of breaking surf, reduced visibility, and tidal currents, sharks apparently mistake the splashing of people's feet and hands at the water's surface for fish, probably because they have to make fast approaches to what they think are prey items in order to make a living." But, Burgess adds, "not all surf-zone attacks worldwide are explainable on the same basis. For example, white shark attacks in the surf in central California may simply represent a measured predatory event in which the shark considers the human a reasonable-sized food item. Alternatively, the white shark may mistake the dark wet-suited surfer as a sea lion or seal, normal food items in their diet."

Florida's number-one rating, Burgess points out, is explained by Florida's balmy beaches: "Everybody in the state is an hour away from the beach, and there is a large native population that is aquatically active, not to mention vast numbers of tourists who visit the water at least some time during their stay."

The August 2000 killing of Thadeus Kubinski at St. Pete Beach was the first fatal Florida attack since the death of Willie Tellasmon in 1998. And the boy's death was the first fatal Florida attack since 1988, when two were recorded: A shark killed a scuba diver in Biscayne National Park, south of Miami Beach. The other victim was a man swimming from a boat off Shell Island near Panama City. That place had known death by shark years before. On August 15, 1959, a scuba diver disappeared, never to be seen again. All that was found was his bloody, tooth-marked clothing and gear.

Florida's shark-attack record is one of the great untold stories of tourism. Because the attacks are rarely fatal, they tend to be given little media coverage and become known primarily to taciturn local officials and shark researchers. In December 1997, for example, an eight-year-old boy was swimming with a life vest in four-foot-deep water at Hollywood, Florida. Something struck him, slicing his left leg from knee to ankle. Initially, an "unknown predator" was blamed. For the tourist business, a moray eel or a barracuda

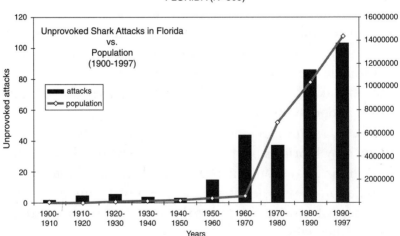

FLORIDA (N=305)

Unprovoked Shark Attacks in Florida
vs.
Population
(1900-1997)

ISAF

68

or a hungry bluefish would have been better than a shark. A lifeguard at Hollywood Beach called the "fish-biting incident" unprecedented. Prudently, officials closed several miles of beaches. Examination of the boy showed beyond a doubt that a shark, species unknown, had attacked him.

Similarly, when a Michigan man disappeared in 1995 while diving off the Florida Keys, some Floridians questioned whether a shark had killed him. When his pants, T-shirt, and weight belt washed up with bite marks on them, one expert identified this as evidence of an attack by a bull shark; another expert theorized that the man's body had been ravaged after he drowned. The ISAF listed the incident as Florida's twenty-fifth attack of the year.

"More attacks occur in Florida than in any state, country, or other geographical entity because so many people swim with sharks," says Burgess. The epicenter of Florida shark-attack country is Volusia County, the site of nine of Florida's twenty-five attacks in 1999, a typical ratio. (In 1998, it was fourteen out of twenty-two.) Palm Beach County (where the shark bit Ryan) was once the shark-attack capital of the state; between 1882 and 1997 there were forty-three attacks in Palm Beach County. As more people flocked to the beaches of Volusia, it won the title. Volusia is so much in denial as a shark-attack title holder that when county officials asked school kids to come up with a name for a new park, the satirical students came up with No Shark Park. The county's forty-seven miles along the central east coast include such tourist spots as Daytona Beach, Ormond Beach, and New Smyrna Beach.

By October 2000, Volusia County was well on its way toward a new yearly record, with ten attacks. Four of the attacks were at New Smyrna Beach, which ironically was calling itself "The World's Safest Beach," because sandbars running parallel to the shore theoretically keep out sharks. In July, a young woman and a girl were attacked the same day in separate incidents off New Smyrna. A nineteen-year-old woman said a three-foot shark sunk its teeth into her thigh and then let go. She was hospitalized. Two hours later, a shark bit a thirteen-year-old girl on her calf, producing a serious wound. The sharks were most likely blacktips.

Eight days later, off Ormond Beach, a shark twice bit a surfer, tearing a fifteen-inch gash on his right leg above the knee and then inflicting a smaller wound in the calf. Local lore was that the attackers were young sharks learning to hunt fish.

Volusia County's tenth attack of the year came when a small shark bit a man in waist-deep water, wounding the fingers of his right hand. Then, at New Smyrna Beach, came attacks number eleven and twelve—during a single afternoon. An eleven-year-old boy was bitten twice in the right foot as he swam in the surf. About two hours later, about a mile north, a two-foot shark grabbed the right hand of a twenty-three-year-old man bodysurfing in waist-deep water. The boy's wound required twenty-eight stitches.

By October, twenty-three people had been bitten by sharks in Florida waters, compared to twenty-five in 1999. Five people have been killed by sharks in Florida waters since 1975. No fatal attacks have ever been reported in Volusia County.

Also attracting surfers—and sharks—are the waves at Ponce de Leon Inlet near New Smyrna Beach. Sharks cluster around such inlets because "tidal flushing" draws small fish. Speaking of this area, Burgess observed, "Under conditions of breaking surf, reduced visibility, and tidal currents, sharks apparently mistake the splashing of people's feet and hands at the water's surface for fish . . . You've got four body parts doing their best impression of a mullet at the water's surface."

Florida, with its 1,277 miles of coastline, has at least forty species of sharks within its waters. Most of the sharks are usually considered not dangerous. For a long time one of those supposedly harmless types was the nurse shark (*Ginglymostoma cirratum*), a sluggish bottom-dweller—not to be confused with the gray nurse of Australia (*Carcharias arenarius*), which has been indicted in many fatal attacks.

Then in the summer of 1958 came two attacks that put the nurse shark on the list of Florida's biting sharks. A man was wading in water about three feet deep on a sandbar about thirty feet from shore off Sanibel Island on Florida's Gulf coast when he felt a sharp pain in his right foot. He yanked his foot out of the water and saw a seven-foot nurse shark clinging to it. At Siesta Key off Sarasota, a foolish diver grabbed the tail of a nurse shark five and a half feet long. The shark twisted and sank its teeth into the inner part of the diver's left leg, just below the knee. Both victims recovered without incident.

Within five weeks of that same summer, incidentally, there were two other attacks along a sixty-mile stretch of beach between Sanibel and Sarasota. At Turtle Beach on Siesta Key, Sarasota, a shark clamped its jaws around the left foot of a teenager wading near shore in murky water two and a half feet deep. The physician who saved the victim's foot said the wound looked as if it had been made by teeth "shaped like the teeth of a heavy saw." Nine miles north of the attack on the wading teenager, two young brothers were playing in water three feet deep only ten feet from shore when one of the boys screamed. His parents, aunt, and uncle ran into the water—so shallow that the shark's head, clamped to the boy's thigh, broke the surface. The boy struck at the shark with his left hand, slashing it on the shark's teeth. The boy's father pulled the shark by the tail while his uncle held the boy by the shoulders and tugged against the shark. The shark floundered, then slithered into deeper water and vanished. The boy was rushed to a hospital, where his leg was amputated above the knee.

Dr. Eugenie Clark, an eminent shark researcher whose marine laboratory was nearby, studied the attacks, interviewing victims, witnesses, and attending physicians. She believed that a tiger shark had become trapped between tides and, attracted by the vibrations made by the boys, had struck at a pale, untanned foot, which may have looked like a fish. She also suggested that the attack on the wading teenager "could conceivably have been the same species and possibly the same individual shark. The latter is considered doubtful, but . . . this could be an explanation for the unusual occurrence of these two unprovoked attacks so close together in time and location in an area where no similar attack had been reported in thirty-eight years."

Nurses that have bitten divers ranged in size from eighteen inches to nine feet, and when they latch on, their jaws snap closed like a Yale lock. Kevin Morrison, a teenager from Illinois, was scuba diving with his father near Marathon in the Florida Keys in April 1998, when he grabbed the tail of a two-foot nurse shark. It sunk its teeth into his chest. When he was taken from the water, the shark still hung on. In the ambulance to the hospital, medics left it clinging rather than risk further wounding by ripping it off. In the operating room, finally, a surgeon severed the shark's spine and, in death, it let go, allowing the physician to treat the wound. The boy recovered.

The ISAF does not count that incident in its statistics because it was a provoked attack. The ISAF's George Burgess put that one in a different file, marked "S for Stupid," he says. Burgess, recalling another example of a nurse shark's everlasting adhesion, tells the story of a man who was diving off Lantana, near Fort Lauderdale. The diver saw a piece of fishing line and, thinking that it might yield some lost fishing gear, pulled on it. Then, Burgess continued, "A three-foot nurse shark, which apparently had been hooked, came up and, after bumping him on the chest, bit his arm and re-fused to let go. His dive partner then attempted to spear the shark but the spear bounced off the tough hide of the shark and only made it thrash harder. The dive partner then grabbed his buddy and the shark's tail and dragged them to shore. After unsuccessfully trying to pry open the mouth, officer Pat Encinosa shot it once in the head and after it re-leased its hold, pumped two more rounds into the shark to make sure it would never swim again. Interestingly enough, the very next day the same officer shot and killed a dog while responding to a burglary call in a home, sparking out-rage from the dog's owners. Police Chief Ralph Meadows said both shootings were justified. Moral: Biting animals are not welcome in Lantana."

Florida is not the only East Coast state where shark attacks have been recorded. There have been victims off the beaches of Alabama, Georgia, North Carolina, South Carolina, and Virginia—along with the northeastern states of Delaware, New Jersey, New York, Connecticut, and Massachusetts.

For North Carolina, the year 2000 marked a drastic change in the state's experience with sharks. For 130 years there had been only sixteen confirmed shark attacks in state waters. Then, in 2000 there were three. One, attributed to a shark pursuing fish in the shallows, felled a twelve-year-old girl vacationing with her family on the Outer Banks. She was standing, playing in the surf when a shark bit her on the right calf, leaving a crescent-shaped wound that required more than 300 stitches. Sharks also bit surfers off Wrightsville and Holden beaches. Marine scientists speculate that changes in the course of the Gulf Stream may be luring schools of fish—and their shark predators—closer to the shores of beaches along the southern tier of the East Coast.

In the Gulf, Texas recorded ten attacks, none fatal, be-tween 1990 and 1999. Typical Texas attacks involve encounters between surfers and sharks as they share the same little patch of Gulf water. In June 2000, for instance, a shark, species unknown, bit the foot of a seventeen-year-old boy surfing off Corpus Christi. "The shark came up, bit in my skin, and shook a little and let go," he said. "I started paddling as fast as I could . . . hoping it wouldn't come around and take another bite out of me." In a classic hit-and-run, it did not.

Another June 2000 attack in the Gulf was nearly fatal. Chuck Anderson, forty-four, and Richard Watley, fifty-five, were swimming off Gulf Shores, Alabama, in a regular practice for a triathlon when Anderson felt something hit his leg. "You know, you bump into each other swimming out there sometimes. And sometimes a jellyfish will bump into you or something like that.

"But that weird feeling went into me," Anderson said as he began his recount of the attack in an interview with the *Mobile Register*. "As soon as it bumped into me, I kind of stood up in the water—I was probably in about ten feet of water—I brought myself up in the water and stuck my head down and that's when I saw the shark coming directly towards me.

"I don't know what anybody else's first reaction would be, but mine was to pull myself back. When I did, he snapped at my right hand and he took all my fingers of my right hand the first time he went by me. I kind of was able to push off. I know that both hands touched him and he kind of got my right hand. I started backpedaling, and I know I was up out of the water at that point, hollering to Karen [a third triathlon swimmer], 'Shark! Shark! Get out of the water! Tell Richard to get out of the water!'"

It was too late for Richard Watley to escape. The shark bit him on his right hip and right arm, inflicting deep wounds but not to the bone. At that point, the shark returned to Anderson. Watley would, meanwhile, make it to shore.

On the next pass the shark gnawed Anderson, leaving a pair of wounds about six inches apart. Then, as he started heading toward shore, the shark lunged again. "He got me by my right arm. When he got me that time, he rolled over and was thrashing. We went down to the bottom and that's how my knees got skinned up. He dragged me across the bottom. I assume we were in about eight feet of water.

"We came up out of the water and when we came up we were in waist-deep water. Evidently, he was working in toward the beach with me. I was fighting, trying to survive. The next thing I knew, and I don't know how we got there, we ended up on a sandbar that was about shin-deep. It was probably about fifteen yards off the beach."

Because the shark could go no farther, Anderson, six feet tall and 230 pounds, could stand over it and, using what strength he had left, pummel the shark with his left arm while shaking his right arm to get it out of the shark's jaw. "He was swinging his head back and forth and I was swinging at him, trying to get my arm out. I realized he couldn't come any farther toward me, but I couldn't get away from him. I just started working my arm up and down and finally it just broke off. That's probably the eeriest, worst sound I've heard in my life, my arm breaking. There was no great pain. I guess there was an adrenaline rush or whatever."

Anderson's right arm was so badly mangled that it had to be amputated above the elbow. He told the interviewer that he later dreamed about the attack. In his dream, he usually swims after the shark.

Four days after the attack on Anderson and Watley, a shark charged a twenty-two-foot boat just offshore in Pensacola Bay, about twenty-five miles east of Gulf Shores. People on board the boat, after spotting an eight-foot bull shark, shouted a warning to swimmers about twenty feet away and maneuvered the boat to put it between the shark and the swimmers. The shark then lunged at the boat, which was in water about six feet deep. It hit the hull, nearly ripped off the stern swim platform, and swam off.

The assault on the swimmers was Alabama's first confirmed and unprovoked shark attack in twenty-five years and only the second since 1900. In the 1975 attack, a shark grabbed a swimmer by the leg several miles from shore. The man survived with a wounded knee.

Told of the Anderson-Watley attack and the subsequent boat assault, Terry Henwood, branch administrator for the National Marine Fisheries Service in Pascagoula, Mississippi, tried the "rogue shark" theory, blaming an "aberrant, sick shark" that had become overly aggressive or deranged. This theory, which is no longer generally accepted by shark researchers, always comforts both those who fear sharks and those who admire them.

Researchers who speculate on East Coast and Gulf Coast near-shore attacks advance several possible explanations. After Florida recorded thirty-one attacks in 1995, theories focused on the weather. A string of hurricanes had driven huge waves along the state's eastern shores, luring more and more surfers, increasing the chances of encounters. Warm summer water carries more nutrients into the shallows, luring schools of fish and their predators, coastal sharks. Shallow-water attacks are surprisingly frequent. An ISAF analysis of attacks worldwide shows that more than 80 percent happen in waters five feet deep or less.

On the Fourth of July 1999, off Fort Pickens, at the western tip of the Gulf Islands National Seashore, a shark slashed the leg of a woman who found herself swimming in a school of small fish hugging the shore. The following spring, to the east, in Santa Rosa Sound, a fisherman was casting for speckled sea trout when he saw the sea churning about 220 feet out. In chest-high waders, he headed toward what he was sure were his prey. They were a shark's prey, too. Something banged into him, knocking him forward. He fled the water, sensing that a shark had just invited him out with the subtlety of a bouncer in a sailors' bar.

Theoretically, there are fewer sharks along both the East and Gulf Coasts. Over-fishing has drastically shrunk shark populations, and large sharks are scarce. The winning shark in Alabama's Deep Sea Fishing Rodeo averaged 615 pounds in the 1980s; in the 1990s the average weight was 247 pounds. But the bull shark, a shore-hugging species that is blamed for many of the attacks, is not hunted by commercial fishermen, who go after deep-water sharks. As a result, there are plenty of bull sharks along their western Atlantic range (from southern Brazil to North Carolina) and in the Gulf of Mexico, particularly off the Texas coast.

Farther north along the East Coast, from Delaware and Maryland up to the New Jersey coast, bull sharks occasionally appear near river mouths. Out to sea are several dangerous species, including tigers, hammerheads, and lemon shark. Great white sharks, once thought to be rare off East Coast beaches, are sighted with disturbing frequency, particularly off Montauk, Long Island, a popular port for shark fishermen. Chum lines for sharks, say local people, drift shoreward, bringing great whites with them. But attacks in Northeastern waters are rare.

The first recorded victim of a fatal shark attack in New England waters was a sixteen-year-old Massachusetts boy, Joseph Troy, Jr. On July 25, 1936, he was swimming about 150 yards off Hollywood Beach, just above Mattapoisett Harbor in Buzzards Bay, Massachusetts, when a shark suddenly seized his left leg and pulled him under. A courageous companion, Walter W. Stiles, who was ten feet away, swam to Troy's aid. When Troy, pummeling the shark with his hands, broke the surface, Stiles was at his side. The shark released Troy, but remained nearby in the bloody water while Stiles supported the youth and managed to get him into a boat. The shark did not charge Troy again, nor did it strike at Stiles. Troy died in a hospital five hours after the attack.

Almost exactly sixty years later, off Truro on Cape Cod, a shark attacked a man swimming in four feet of water. The wounds in his left leg required forty-six stitches. The attacker was identified as a six- to eight-foot blue shark (*Prionace glauca*). One of the most abundant oceanic shark species, blue sharks have two personalities: inquisitive and shy, especially around divers, and voracious around survivors of air and sea disasters. Although shark sightings are frequent around Cape Cod, attacks are almost nonexistent. The Truro encounter was the only one recorded in Massachusetts in the 1990s.

Waders and swimmers have far less to fear from sharks than divers or surfers do. But those who visit the sea by walking into it should be aware that they are sharing the sea with sharks. The Mediterranean has few attacks. Between 1899 and 1997, according to the Mediterranean Shark Attack File reports, there were sixty-six "reported interactions," twenty-one of which were fatal. Yet even with such a relatively mild shark experience, an Italian shark expert, Giuseppe Notarbartolo, speaks the frankest words about the relationship of sharks to their rarest prey: "Everyone says sharks like deep water. But it is a falsehood that is convenient for the tour agencies. In reality, the shark is a typical predator of river-mouths, and whose instinct is to approach the coast to strike. Luckily, it usually overlooks humans." A colleague, Corrado Piccinetti, head of the Marine Biology Laboratory in Fano, near Senigallia, adds: "Sharks are erratic animals, and they go where they can find food."

CHAPTER 4

ATTACK: California

On an August afternoon in 1998, Jonathan Kathrein, a sixteen-year-old surfer, was about fifty yards off California's Stinson Beach, riding the waves on a small plastic boogie board, when he felt teeth sink into his right leg. A shark was pulling him, screaming, into the sea. As Kathrein went under, he somehow managed to grab one of the shark's gill slits and yank. The shark let him go, and Kathrein surfaced. He struggled back onto the board before friends and lifeguards pulled him ashore. A helicopter flew him to a nearby hospital. He survived, with a foot-long gash in his thigh. Teeth marks in his wetsuit identified the attacker as a great white about eight feet long. Police quickly posted shark warnings at Stinson, but within hours after the attack, surfers and swimmers were back in the water. Never before had a shark attack been recorded off Stinson. After all, Stinson was safe.

Sharks have so often bloodied the waters of a certain area off California waters that surfers call the region "the Red Triangle." From 1952 to 1999, there were seventy-nine attacks recorded off the U.S. West Coast, eight of them fatal. Forty-one of the attacks were in the Red Triangle—encompassed by the sea from Bodega Bay south to the Farallon Islands (about thirty miles offshore and twenty-eight miles due west of Golden Gate Bridge); then back to the mainland near Santa Cruz, at the northern rim of Monterey Bay. Stinson Beach, although within the Red Triangle, was considered safe because shark-attracting seals were rarely seen off that popular surfing and swimming spot, and there had never been a great white attack recorded there. In fact the supervisor of lifeguards at Stinson said he had never even seen a dorsal fin in the twenty-three years he had been patrolling the beach.

There certainly were great whites some thirty miles away, because Peter Pyle, a shark researcher working in the Farallon Islands, later reported that on the day the great white attacked Kathrein, great whites attacked two surfboards placed in the Farallon waters in a study of shark behavior. But, after the Kathrein attack, most Stinson surfers decided that the attack was just a bit of aberrant conduct by one of "the men in the gray flannel suits"—bravado surfer-talk for great white sharks.

Then, on an August day almost exactly a year after the attack on Kathrein, a shark appeared about fifty yards off Stinson Beach. As the shark swam along, parallel to the shore, swimmers and surfers fled from the water, and lifeguards forbade them to go back in. "It's possible it's the same shark, because it's about the same size as last year's shark. But we can't say for sure," said John E. McCosker, a senior scientist of the California Academy of Sciences and a world authority on great whites. A seal was spotted in the surf, and McCosker surmised that "the seal was cruising the annual salmon run for a snack, which, in turn, draws the sharks, which want to dine on seal. A shark so close to shore isn't unusual, but typically sharks hunt underwater."

California divers and surfers know they share the sea with great white sharks, especially along certain parts of the coast. So, when Marco Flagg, an experienced, thirty-one-year-old diver, spotted a shark about twenty feet away, he quickly identified it as a great white and thought, *Gee, I got to see it without paying for a shark diving trip. It's just passing. It's not coming back or circling.*

Flagg was diving in June 1995 with two friends near Blue Fish Cove off Point Lobos, near Carmel and south of the Red Triangle. As he was preparing for his second dive of the day, a tourist asked him why he was diving. He told her that he was taking photos of great white sharks. When she asked him if that was dangerous, he sardonically replied, "No. If a shark gets aggressive I just punch him on the nose."

Flagg was on a scooter and wearing a DiveTracker, an underwater location device. He cautiously turned the scooter and headed toward the diving boat. "I did not want to rush to the surface because I knew that was where most great white attacks occur. I remained calm," he later told *Dive* magazine.

"About thirty seconds after the sighting," he continued, "I sensed something on my left. I looked down and saw a huge, gaping circle of teeth coming straight at me out of the murk. The thought of being eaten alive by a shark sounds nightmarish, but the speed of the thing meant all I had time to think was *Oh sheeeet* before it had me sideways in its jaws, clamped down like a vice. I felt an incredibly severe and dull pressure on my body, but no cutting. I was locked in the shark's jaws, facing away from it. It happened so quickly that there was no time to escape or struggle.

"As quickly as it had grabbed me, it let me go and swam away. It was so quick that I did not really appreciate the horror of what was happening. I was conscious of a lot of pain in my legs, and my mind was racing, thinking the shark had bitten one of them off. I felt to see if they were both still there, and they were. The relief was overwhelming. You think your life is going to flash before you when something like this happens, but it does not. I did not think about my family or anything like that. Instead I concentrated on getting back to the boat."

He reached the boat, jettisoned the scooter, weight belt, tank, and gear, and painfully managed to get into the boat. He did not remove his wetsuit because, he thought, *This might be all that was preventing my guts from spilling out.* Then he leaned over the side to haul in his gear—and fell in. He got into his boat again and started off to pick up his friends, who were diving nearby. Ashore, he collapsed. In the ambulance, still unaware of the extent of his wounds, he wondered whether he was going to live or die.

"At the hospital," he recounted, "the doctors stripped off my wetsuit and found cuts and abrasions—and that was all. I had to have seventeen stitches for cuts on my left forearm, leg, and lower abdomen. For an attack by a great white shark, my injuries were amazingly light." (It is thirty inches from the three-inch gash in his arm to the V-shaped puncture on his leg—the span of a single bite.).

Flagg, who owned a company that produced the DiveTracker and other oceanographic equipment, had made more than 300 dives around the world. "I have seen plenty of sharks," he said. "My philosophy has always been this: If it's not bigger than me, then I have no reason to fear it. I reckon the shark took a test bite, tasted metal, and spat me out. If it had not been for the tanks and the navigation unit, I would probably be dead." Bite marks on the

DiveTracker showed that it had almost certainly saved his life, acting as armor that had shielded his body.

As Flagg's description of the attack circulated among divers, some began to wonder what role his scooter had played. Did its sound or electromagnetic field attract the shark? Six months before, off San Miguel Island, Jim Robinson, an urchin diver, had been on a scooter when a great white zeroed in on him. The shark closed its jaws around him, killing him, just as he surfaced at his boat and passed the scooter up to a crewman.

Flagg doubted the connection. "My simple suspicion," he said, "is that it was hungry and I just happened to run across its path. Incidents such as mine are so rare that it's impossible to draw any meaningful conclusions. The shark did not attack the scooter, but my mid-section. From what I understand, the shark's final approach is guided by sensing electrical fields using sensors in its snout. And while it's true that a scooter emits a strong DC field, that field is uniform. I would suspect the animal is not attracted to field strength but to its variability, because many things in the water, such as dock and harbor structures, generate a DC field. This contrasts with a field generated by an animal, like one with a heartbeat."

A scooter's DC field is not necessarily steady, however. Most scooters have three speed settings, and during a dive a diver may frequently change speeds. Each setting produces a different DC field. More variances occur as the scooter's battery runs down.

McCosker contributed to the electrical-attraction debate by recalling that he once had had to release a healthy baby great white shark that had been repeatedly bumping into a certain spot on the wall of the Steinhart Aquarium's Roundabout tank. An electronics expert who examined the spot later detected there a very weak (about 0.125 millivolts) static electrical anomaly.

McCosker also remarked that while studying great whites along Australia's Great Barrier Reef he noted that they would "come up and mouth the shark cages in a funny way. Not attack them, but mouth them in a way suggesting it is part of a bioelectric stimulation. Have we demonstrated it? No. But let me put it this way: If a scuba diver forty feet down gets bitten, I would probably raise my eyebrows and ask, What gives? Because that's almost unheard of. But Flagg was forty feet down and holding onto a device pulsing an electrical DC field and making a noise, as it apparently did, that might incite a shark to mouth and bite, as it apparently did. That leads me to suspect that the scooter was probably contributory, but in ways we don't know. All the additional variables and attractive stimuli—sound, visual, electronic— complicate the issue. Sort of like *Murder on the Orient Express.* There are so many possible culprits." Whatever the scientific theories, many divers stopped using scooters, especially divers who, like Robinson, made a living harvesting sea urchins.

The attack on Flagg was not the first to occur in Monterey Peninsula waters. In 1981, Lou Boren was fatally attacked while surfing in Spanish Bay. Four years later, at Monastery Beach next to the Point Lobos Marine Reserve, Frank Gallo was about thirty feet underwater and about 150 yards offshore when a shark mauled him. He pushed the shark, which swam off as Gallo reached the surface. He called out a warning to his friends, who, ignoring their own safety, got him onto a diving mattress and towed him to shore, where they summoned help. Gallo, a paramedic and a competition scuba diver, was in superb shape and so survived a punctured right lung, and wounds—on his right shoulder, forearm, jaw, and neck—that required more than 600 stitches. In 1990, off the same beach, a shark gnawed a woman's leg, and then swam off. She also survived.

★ ★ ★

Native American coastal tribes encountered sharks close to the shores of what would become California. Members of the Pomo tribe said a prayer to guard themselves against sharks before they swam to outlying rocks on seal hunts.

Encounters remained unchronicled until the reporting of an attack in July 1926. A five-foot shark of unidentified species attacked a swimmer and his dog in San Francisco Bay, seriously injuring the swimmer. A boat launched from shore rescued him. The next reported attack came in 1950, this one off Imperial Beach in San Diego County. The victim was one of four swimmers treading water about twelve feet deep. The shark, probably a great white, came from behind, biting the swimmer on a leg and then attacking from the front, biting a leg as the victim kicked at it. The shark swam off. A lifeguard brought the man ashore. He recovered.

Coincidentally, in that same year the California Bureau of Marine Fisheries published a guide to local sharks that said the great white was "uncommon at best in our waters, and, since it rarely comes inshore, it is a negligible hazard to California swimmers." Two years after the guide was published, a shark killed another swimmer, and this time the attack was so thoroughly documented, there was no doubt that the killer was a great white.

Seventeen-year-old Barry Wilson was swimming off Pacific Grove on December 7, 1952, when something grabbed him. When he screamed, his cry was heard simultaneously by his friend, fifteen-year-old Brookner Brady, Jr. who was swimming nearby, and John C. Bassford, who was sitting on a rise directly above the beach. An instant before the scream, Bassford, an experienced diver, had noticed that the youth seemed to be frantically scanning the water around him. Then a large shark rose directly in front of him. As Bassford shouted a warning to Brady, the shark struck

Wilson. Bassford saw Wilson's body thrust straight out of the water.

Wilson pushed both his hands against the shark, trying to free himself. But he fell sideways, still clutched by the shark, and was pulled under. Blood gushed upward and spread on the surface, forming a circle about six feet in diameter. Wilson suddenly bobbed to the surface in the middle of the circle, screamed again, and began beating the water with his hands.

Now the shark appeared again, part of its back showing above the surface. It swept past Wilson, returned, then disappeared. Brady, who had seen the attack, swam about fifty feet to reach Wilson and began towing him to shore. Meanwhile, four members of the Sea Otter Club, a divers group, swam out to Wilson and Brady, bringing with them a large inner tube. Three of the Sea Otters were trained investigators: Sergeant Earl Stanley of the 63rd Military Police Platoon stationed at nearby Fort Ord; Robert Shaw of the 313th Criminal Investigation Detachment at Fort Ord; and Frank M. Ambrosio of the California State Highway Patrol. The fourth Sea Otter was John L. Poskus, a mathematics and physics teacher at Monterey High School.

The four men managed to get the tube around Wilson's body and up under his limp arms. As they struggled in the water with the bulky tube, Wilson suddenly lunged forward. Startled, Shaw looked around to see that a shark had violently pushed Wilson and then turned away. Shaw and Ambrosio clung to opposite sides of the inner tube, pushing it, while Poskus pulled it with a nylon rope he had attached to it. Stanley kept to the back of the tube, supporting Wilson's head.

Through rough seas, the men headed for a small breakwater pier. During the twenty-minute swim to the pier, the shark constantly hovered close by the rescuers and the victim. Again and again—usually when the men stopped to prop Wilson's slipping body back into the tube—the shark appeared. Never did it strike.

Wilson was dead when a waiting physician examined him the moment his body was carried up to the pier. The lower part of his right buttock and nearly all of the back of his right leg, from the thigh almost to the knee, was ripped away. His left leg bore deep slashes.

Evidence showed that the killer had been a great white, twelve to thirteen feet long. Rolf L. Bolin, an ichthyologist from Hopkins Marine Station in Pacific Grove, said the teenager had been bitten at least four times. "The corroboratory evidence of the witnesses," Bolin reported, "indicates the sequence: first, on the lower left leg from behind, which strike wounded and startled him; second, on the medial surface of the right thigh, when the shark approached him from in front, and, passing partially between his legs, lifted him high out of the water; third, on the upper left leg from the back and side, when Wilson struck in desperation at the water, and, finally, on the back and side of the right thigh, while he was being placed in the tube and when he was undoubtedly already dead."

The rescuers and Bolin were able to provide one of the most detailed descriptions recorded up to that time at the attack site itself. All the information the investigators assembled would later be seen as important elements in analyzing attacks. *Weather:* partly cloudy. *Water depth:* about thirty feet. *Water temperature:* around 55°. *Water conditions:* murky because of dirt washed into the sea by rain the night before and a heavy concentration of plankton. Surf was running to heights of about eight feet. *Underwater visibility:* six to eight feet.

There were no more shark attacks recorded in California until February 1955, when a spear fisherman diving in

Monterey Bay was grabbed about both ankles by a great white. It ripped off the ankle portions of the diver's wetsuit, tore off his right swim fin and a heavy wool sock, bit through his left swim fin, and swam off. Eight months later, a shark appeared near two divers swimming not far from shore off La Jolla, near the Scripps Institution of Oceanography. Hoping to positively identify the shark, a Scripps specialist in sharks, Arthur O. Flechsig, set out to catch it. The shark attacked his boat, leaving behind two teeth that gave a shaken Flechsig positive identification: a great white. Within two weeks, nine great whites were caught in the area. Now there could be no doubt that the 1950 state guide was wrong.

A scientist working in the 1950s and 1960s one day watched as a shark, undoubtedly a great white, seemingly pondered a possible attack on a scuba diver. His report is one of the earliest scientific accounts of shark attack-mode behavior: "The shark first appeared approximately 3 feet below the surface and moved directly toward the foot of the surface swimmer, who was wearing a black suit and green fins. The speed of the shark accelerated as it neared the flippers. When not more than $1\frac{1}{2}$ feet away, it turned abruptly down, as the diver pulled his flipper up in a recovery swim stroke. The shark swam in a circle of about 15 feet, dropping to a depth of 6 to 10 feet. On the second approach, it turned away at a distance of 2 to 3 feet as the diver clung to the skiff. After the diver and his partner had entered the skiff, a shark (believed to be the same one) surfaced nearby, but avoided the pier of the nearby Scripps Institution of Oceanography."[1]

There could be no doubt that great whites were appearing in California waters in increasing numbers. Tragic proof came again in April 1957.

Peter Savino and Daniel Hogan were swimming beyond the breakers of Morro Bay, near San Luis Obispo, when

Savino became tired and Hogan started towing him toward shore. A shark appeared, nudged Savino, and drew blood when it rubbed him with its sandpaper hide. "I have blood on my arms!" Savino yelled to Hogan. "We'd better get out of here!" They began swimming separately. A moment later, Hogan turned to see whether Savino was all right. Savino had disappeared, without an outcry, and was never seen again.

Two years later came what Californians called the Year of the Shark. On May 7, 1959, Albert Kogler and Shirley O'Neill were treading water about fifty feet off Baker's Beach, San Francisco, when Kogler screamed: "It's a shark! Get out of here!" But Shirley O'Neill stayed. As she later recounted, "It was just blood all over—I knew I couldn't leave him—he just kept screaming and screaming. I could tell the fish was chewing him up. It was a horrible scream. He was shouting, 'Help me! Help me!' I grabbed for his hand, but when I pulled, I could see that his arm was just hanging on by a thread. So I grabbed him around his back. But it was all bloody and I could see the insides." She towed him to shore. He died that night.

Less than a month later, on June 14, Robert Pamperin, a husky, thirty-year-old aircraft engineer, was diving for abalone about fifty yards off La Jolla with another diver, Gerald Lehrer. Suddenly, Pamperin rose high out of the water. His faceplate had been torn off. He screamed once. "I was swimming about fifteen feet from Bob," Lehrer said later. "I heard him calling, 'Help me! Help me!' I swam over to him. He was thrashing in the water, and I could tell he was fighting something underneath . . ."

In the next instant, Pamperin went under. Lehrer peered underwater through his faceplate. The water, though bloodied, was remarkably clear, and he saw his friend's body in the jaws of a shark, estimated by Lehrer to be twenty feet long. "It had a white belly and I could see its jaws and jagged teeth," Lehrer said. "I wasn't able to do anything more." Lehrer, wanting to warn other swimmers, swam to shore, where several stunned bathers witnessed the attack. Pamperin's body was never found.

Eight days after the Pamperin attack, a twelve-foot shark was caught off Catalina Island, about sixty miles north of La Jolla. In its belly was a man's watch, too badly deteriorated to be identified. It could not have been Pamperin's, for he had not been wearing a watch. Had it come from a corpse or a victim? Now shark-conscious, the chief of San Diego life-guards said that during the three months before the attack on Pamperin three people had disappeared in the area, and their bodies had never been found. Were they also victims of sharks?

Before 1959 ended, there were three more attacks in California. A hammerhead shark (*Sphyrna mokarran*) slashed a spear fisherman's left leg about 300 yards from where Pamperin had been devoured. Off Malibu, a shark raked a swimmer's left arm from wrist to elbow. And a great white bit a diver's swim fin, "shook me like a dog shakes a bone," and then released him, unharmed. Dr. H. David Baldridge, who had recently begun supervising what was then called the Shark Attack File, described 1959 as a "peak year," during which fifty-six attacks were reported through-out the world.

In California, public officials asked for some explanation for the shark boom. Oceanographers reported a rise in water temperatures off the coast of California in recent years. But no scientist could offer any answers to the officials' ques-tions: Why had sharks suddenly appeared off California? Why had those specific people been attacked? And what about that lifeguard's remark: Was it possible that people who had disappeared were in fact victims of shark attacks?

CALIFORNIA (N=96)

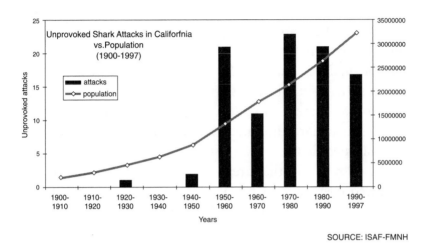

SOURCE: ISAF-FMNH

To get the answers, scientists began a research effort that still goes on. From their observations in California have come not only ideas about the comings and goings of great whites but also unprecedented close-up observations of shark predation. By watching how sharks attacked their natural prey, scientists were able to produce scenarios that showed parallels to attacks on human beings. The epicenter of research is found in the Farallon Islands. In Native American legend the desolate, rocky isles were known as "the islands of the dead." Scientists have another name for the Farallons: "a white shark hotspot," a place so teeming with great whites that, after a series of non-fatal attacks there, sports divers have essentially abandoned the islands to the sharks, the pinnipeds, and the scientists.

Shark researcher Peter Klimley is one of those scientists. Klimley, a University of California professor, works out of the Bodega Marine Laboratory north of San Francisco. Klimley uses a Zodiac inflatable boat to ferry himself and other researchers to and from a research skiff tied to a buoy in a shark-watching bay. One day, while the skiff bobbed in large swells "like a large fishing jig" (in Klimley's words), a shark bolted toward the empty boat and attacked it. If anyone doubts whether sharks attack boats, just ask Klimley. But he believes that sharks do not actively seek human victims. And he believes that human beings entering California's waters should be aware of the sharks around them, particularly the great white, the shark that wounds and kills people more than any other species.

Klimley thinks that great whites sample unusual or unexpected prey, such as people, by first taking a bite. If that taste is satisfactory, they keep on eating; if not, they swim off. Klimley and two other scientists videotaped, above and below the water, 129 white-shark predatory attacks on northern elephant seals and California sea lions in the Farallons.[2] In a typical attack—dubbed "feeding bout"—the sea explodes as a shark hits a seal underwater. Next, the seal appears in a widening blot of red as it bleeds to death. The shark then leaps out of the water and seizes the seal in its jaws. Neither the shark nor the seal is seen again.

Another researcher is Peter Pyle of Point Reyes Bird Observatory, who alternates annually between studying the birds of the Farallons and the sharks of the Farallons. The switchover comes in the fall when juvenile elephant seals haul out on the islands. Sharks prowl around the rocky ledges as the young seals struggle ashore. Sometimes the waves wash them back in the sea, and the sharks are waiting.

When a shark strikes, Pyle and Scot Anderson, a shark biologist, head for the kill site in a fourteen-foot boat. They lower underwater cameras and photograph the sharks eating their prey. From scars—probably inflicted during a food-fight misunderstanding—the scientists can identify the sharks. They have given the sharks names, such as Cut Dorsal and Notched Lobe, and have repeatedly watched them eat, sometimes consuming a seal (about 400 pounds of food) in about ten bites. Great whites seem to prefer elephant seals over sea lions, probably because the seals are loners that move slowly or, motionless on the surface, are literally sitting targets. The seals, which stay together and move swiftly, are more likely to spot a hunting shark and escape. African herd animals use the same many-eyes strategy against hunting lions.

As researchers analyze the great white's attack strategy for getting a seal, they see the act beginning as the shark launches a swift strike from below and takes a large bite, which usually causes death from loss of blood. Sometimes, however, the prey veers at the last moment—or the shark's aim is slightly off—and the seal escapes, either cleanly or raked by teeth. Researchers have seen many seals with scars testifying to such a near-death experience.

Most seals and sea lions suffered fatal wounds on their lower bodies. Sea lions usually survived the shark's first strike, unless that first strike decapitated the sea lion. The observers never saw a prey animal attacked on the surface.

Translating their observations from marine mammals to humans, the scientists compared a representative attack on a pinniped to an actual attack on a commercial abalone diver. A shark grabbed the diver as he paused about twenty feet below the surface to clear his ears. As the diver described the attack, "the shark swam up from underneath, seized me, carried me down for five to seven seconds, and suddenly let go and swam off." The diver, bleeding profusely, struck the shark with a club. Elephant seals are big enough to struggle successfully, surviving though scarred. And, like an elephant seal that fights as it is carried underwater by a shark, the diver had a similar experience—surviving with scars.

The observers also saw sharks sample an animal and then reject it, presumably as unappetizing. Unwanted meals included a brown pelican (*Pelicanus occidentalis*) struck from below. Hurled into the air, the bird bled and died from the strike. But the shark did not feed on it. Sharks also turned down rotting pinniped carcasses. Other observers had noticed that sharks bite but do not consume jackass penguins (*Spheniscus demersus*) and sea otters (*Enhydra lutris*), which are not eaten, though they sometimes are beheaded.

The scientific conclusion: "The birds, sea otter, and human are composed mainly of muscle tissue, whereas pinnipeds and cetaceans possess a great deal of superficial fat tissue. Sharks may prefer energy-rich marine mammals in favor of energy-poor prey." Sharks, probably for the same reason, selectively feed on whale blubber but not on muscle layers. "Fat," Klimley points out, "has twice the energy value that muscle does."

If that reasonably explains what sharks do as predators, why are the sharks there in the first place? Recent research by Klimley and his colleagues shows that white sharks are drawn, every summer and fall, to feasts offered by the seasonal arrival of seals and sea lions to waters off central California.[3] In summer the sharks feed on seals and sea lions as far north as Oregon and occasionally the Gulf of Alaska; in fall, the sharks head south to prey upon pinnipeds living on offshore islands. Female white sharks migrate to southern California to give birth, an energy-draining event that presumably leaves them ravenous.

During the El Niño years of abnormally warm water, when both white sharks and their pinniped prey were found farther north, researchers noted a sharp increase in white shark predation. Great white shark populations seem to be increasing along the coasts of California and Oregon in concert with the booming populations of seals and sea lions, whose numbers have been growing since they gained federal-imposed sanctuary under the Marine Mammals Protection

Act in 1972. The law made it illegal to hunt pinnipeds. Fifteen elephant seals were living within the Red Triangle in 1961. There were 5,000 by 1984, and the population began rising at the rate of 5 percent a year.

Another population is also increasing: divers, surfers, windsurfers, and ocean-going kayakers. And that means more encounters with sharks. Those California encounters, researchers discovered, resembled unprovoked attacks reported in Chilean, South African, Australian, Japanese, and Italian waters. Great white attacks, they observed, were "typically centered where pinnipeds are abundant, such as nearshore rocky outcrops and islands and often near the entrances of rivers."[4] These are prime danger zones for human visitors.

Warnings of danger are not always heeded. California's recent attacks seem to follow a pattern: A shark bites or mauls a victim, who reaches shore and is saved by prompt and skilled medical attention. Divers and surfers may be venturing into sharky waters because, at least subconsciously, they know that expert emergency care is almost always available if the men in the gray flannel suits ruin a perfect day. Divers and surfers around Point Lobos knew there were seals in the area; Flagg saw some just before the shark grabbed him. And most of them knew that the seals attract hungry great whites. Recent victims like Flagg live to tell their shark tales because of modern rescue techniques and modern medical skills.

Recreation once meant refreshment of the spirits after toil—Isaac Walton's "calm, quiet, innocent recreation" of fishing, for example. But many who seek recreation in the sea today are looking for thrills. In the Red Triangle, the thrill involves statistics. Of the seventy-nine attacks recorded between 1952 and 2000, forty-one were in Red Triangle waters. The odds favor the human over the shark. As researcher Scot

Anderson has observed, "California averages about two attacks per year, with a fatality once every five years. Statistically speaking, more people are killed by pigs in Iowa."

Abalone divers are not recreationists. They work the waters around the Farallon Islands, risking their lives for what could be a small fortune on a good day. They are not quite as foolhardy as they may appear. About 90 percent of all shark attacks happen at the surface, and most of the others take place between the surface and the sea floor. Once at the floor, a diver is relatively safe from attack.

"The first key to white shark safety is spotting him before he spots you, or at the same time he spots you," a diver told a Discovery Channel interviewer. "The minute he loses the element of surprise, we feel like that's a big factor, and the key thing again is to stay on the bottom, stay low to the rocks, climb into a hole if there's one nearby. Don't go anywhere. The guy who swims to the surface is going to get bit for sure." That diver carried a handgun modified to work underwater and, he hoped, capable of killing a shark within ten feet.

"We consider the springtime to be the relatively safe time of year," the diver said, "and we've always been somewhat lax. Up until this last month, I've never seen a shark at the Farallons in the springtime, not one. On this day, as I worked my way through a kind of flat, wide open bottom, and worked my way out into deeper water, like what would be thirty-five or forty feet for us, I saw a flash. I said, *That was a white shark.* Then I said, *No, that wasn't a white shark, whitey's not out here this time of year.* And then I looked down and picked an abalone, and I looked up and he was coming straight at me. This thing was huge. It was like laying on the street and having a station wagon drive over you.

"Normally, I would be getting the gun out at that point, and be ready to shoot it, if it got real close and got real aggressive with me. But it didn't come back, and I waited for about five minutes, and it didn't come back, and it didn't come back. I worked my way back to the boat, just hugging the bottom real close. I still didn't see it, still didn't see it . . . And when I got under the boat, I took my knee out from under the rock and made the fastest free ascent in the history of mankind. I happened to come up right at the ladder. And I pretty much walked on water the little distance I had to go, and then climbed up the ladder. I remember taking the regulator out of my mouth when I hit the deck. It was full of white foam, and I realized my mouth had gotten completely dry, and I kind of was just slobbering this white foam.

"I'm afraid of white sharks. I guess I'm not afraid enough to stop what I'm doing. I'm cautious. But I feel like we've achieved some kind of working relationship. We've achieved kind of a harmony where I can continue to work the areas that I'm working. The shark's looking for specific circumstances, and as long as I stay out of those situations, I'm going to be safe."

One abalone diver's luck ran out one day in September 1995, when he was surfacing after a dive in Shelter Cove, north of San Francisco. He was just putting an abalone in his diving bag when he felt a shark bite his left leg. "It pulled my leg and foot out of the water," he recounted. "I saw the shark's mouth with its ugly teeth. It was awful. I couldn't believe it." Abruptly, the shark swam off. The diver's partner and other divers got him ashore and to a hospital, where physicians took three great white teeth out of his leg and closed the wounds with fifty staples.

It happened again in August 1996 when another abalone diver found himself about ten feet above a great white, which was swimming in the same direction as the diver. Suddenly, the shark lunged upward, biting the thirty-five-year-old diver on the upper body. The shark took him to the surface—much as it would a seal that had been caught below—

and inexplicably released him. The demonstration of prey-taking and prey rejection happened in the heart of shark territory: off Tomales Point, at the northern tip of the Point Reyes Peninsula. The diver, bleeding heavily, swam about twenty yards to his boat, from which his friends radioed for help. Ashore, he got medical help quickly and survived.

Ten months before, at Dillon Beach, not far from the abalone diver's attack site, a great white grabbed a surfer by a leg and flipped him and his surfboard over, then quickly released him, leaving him with a mauled leg. He was able to paddle to shore and get treatment for wounds not considered serious.

Kayakers are the newest members of California's shark-endangered population. And, like the surfers and the divers, kayakers have learned about the sharks of California.

A boat was sailing off Channel Islands Harbor, about forty miles north of Malibu, in January 1989 when a crew member saw the body of a young woman floating on the calm sea. A summoned Coast Guard craft retrieved the body and took it ashore, where a coroner examined it. The body, he said, bore "a classic shark bite"—a wound that had removed a piece of flesh nineteen inches wide from the front of the woman's left thigh. She had also suffered several other wounds, including a "defensive-type" bruise on the back of her right hand. That injury conjured up a woman trying to ward off a shark.

"The lungs did not show any of the classic findings of drowning," the coroner reported. "This was about as likely a fresh bite case as I've ever seen." She was bitten, he believed, before she died.

This "gorgeous young girl," as the coroner described her, was eighteen to twenty-six years old, had short brown hair, and was wearing a blue and black Spandex swimming suit, with a blue and black zip-up jacket. The published description added that she had ear studs and wore a ring on her right hand. Not a swimmer or a surfer, the coroner deduced. He guessed that she had been a windsurfer.

He was wrong. Near the shore in the area where the body was found, searchers discovered a kayak paddle. At Ventura, just up the coast, the surfers kept surfing. "It's just one of those things you live with when you go surfing," one of the surfers told a *Los Angeles Times* reporter.

John McCosker, the shark researcher, said attacks were "entirely predictable" on anyone venturing far from shore. The kayaker—if that was what the unidentified woman was doing—was paddling through an area filled with sharks drawn to the Channel Islands, a breeding ground for sea lions and seals. "A shark looks up and sees a silhouette from something like a kayak, thinks he's got a big elephant seal, and swims up to take it."

Two fifteen-foot kayaks were found, lashed together, about five miles offshore, south of where the body was found. The underside of one of the kayaks bore abrasions and had been holed three times. Experts who examined it said a great white had probably attacked it.

When the body was identified as Tamara McAllister, a twenty-four-year-old UCLA graduate student, the mystery nearly ended. She and her boyfriend, fellow graduate student Roy Jeffrey Stoddard, twenty-four, had put their kayaks into the sea north of Malibu. They planned to paddle north about a mile and a half to Paradise Cove and return. Somewhere offshore they had tied the kayaks together, possibly to go for a swim, a common practice of kayakers. Whatever happened next will never be known.

There were not enough clues to determine whether a shark struck while the young man and woman were in the kayaks or in the water. The attack on Tamara McAllister was a characteristic great white hit-and-run. Stoddard's fate was not known because his body was not found.

The next kayak attack came in November 1992 when two paddlers chose to venture into what was undoubtedly the best place along the central California coast to confront great whites: Año Nuevo, a tiny island twenty-three miles north of Santa Cruz. Not only was Año Nuevo well within the Red Triangle; it was also an elephant seal rookery that one shark researcher compares to a supermarket for great whites: "It's stationary, it's open twenty-four hours a day, and it's full of things they like to eat." Like the Farallons to the north, Año Nuevo is a magnet for pinnipeds and their hungry predators. From December to March, about 8,000 northern elephant seals haul up on the bleak island, and massive males—called beachmasters—fight over female harems.

The two kayakers were Ken Kelton and Mike Chin. Although an experienced whitewater kayaker, Chin was paddling out to the open ocean for the first time. Kelton paddled a red kayak eleven and a half feet long; Chin's sixteen footer had a blue deck and a white hull. In the story Chin told on the Internet, the two circled the island, "gawking at the seals," then crossed the shallow channel between the island and the mainland, where seals also haul out. As they dawdled, looking for likely landing sites, Chin was about thirty or forty feet behind Kelton.

"I don't remember if it was sight or sound that first caught my attention," Chin wrote. "I vaguely recall hearing a thump & perhaps Ken saying 'What the . . . ???' " Chin saw something yanking and splashing at the stern of Ken's kayak. "Even though I couldn't yet see the shark in these first 1–2 seconds, I somehow knew exactly what was happening. I believe in this initial contact, the shark was mainly placing his jaws on the boat. In the next 3–4 seconds, the shark lunged horizontally out of the water with the boat clamped in his jaws, his belly skimming the water surface. I saw a dark dorsal fin, and the profile of the shark's immense bulk, dark on top turning to silver on the sides & fading to white on the belly. . . . It seemed that half the shark's length cleared the water, causing the stern to disappear, and it seemed that the shark had merged with the kayak/Ken. The shark seemed at once horrible, beautiful, powerful, terrifying & graceful.

"There was a rush of water like that of a breaking wave as the shark surged forward, up, & finally down. It seemed that the dorsal fin was towering over Ken's head as I finally lost sight of him amidst the spray. I was sure that I had just watched him die. After the shark submerged again, he abruptly let go and vanished; we never saw him again. Unbelievably, Ken was alive, unhurt, and still upright. Two thoughts were flashing through my head: white sharks rarely hit a victim more than once, and even more rarely do they attack rescuers.

"I paddled up nervously, scanning the water beneath my boat, slapping the water with my paddle, striving to not look like an injured seal. Ken yelled, 'What *was* that??!!' Somehow the humor of Ken not immediately realizing what had happened escaped me at that moment. I yelled back, 'Shark!' "

After a few moments of indecision—paddle seaward or shoreward?—Kelton landed his water-filled kayak on the mainland. There was a bite seventeen inches across a foot and a half behind the cockpit where Kelton had been sitting. At the waterline were several three- and four-inch gashes.

Not quite a year later after the Kelton attack, Rosemary Johnson went kayaking in another area known to be swarming with seals—and, of course, great whites. Johnson, in a blue kayak, paddled, with three other kayakers in separate boats, off the Sonoma coast, near the mouth of the Russian River. River mouths are a notorious rendezvous for sharks feeding on food items that float into the sea. Russian River has an added treat because seals haul out along the shore here. Johnson was on the ocean side of Arched Rock, a local landmark, when a white shark hit her kayak, lifting it out of the water and hurling Johnson out of the kayak. Confused, she thought she had hit a rock. The other kayaks sped to her side, got her into a kayak—hers had a large hole in it—and paddled to shore. She had not been injured. The shark was not seen again.

An analysis of seventy-four attacks along the U.S. West Coast[5] showed that twenty-six attacks involved surfers (one in Washington, ten in Oregon, fifteen in central and northern California); and twenty-nine attacks involved divers from the same California areas. A close look at the fatalities shows that kayakers and swimmers died at a much higher rate than divers or surfers. Counting Stoddard as an attack casualty, of four kayakers who encountered sharks, two died. Of the five swimmers in the attack analysis, three died, compared to two of the twenty-nine divers and one of the twenty-six surfers. The probable reason is that swimmers tend to be solitary and often may not be able to get immediate help, as congregating surfers do.

There's something else. Surfers in southern California usually chose long, broad beaches, where there may be sharks but not pinnipeds. Along the coasts of northern California, Oregon, and Washington, surfers often chose places where there are pinnipeds and sharks. And on a board a surfer can look like a pinniped. Attacks again and again appear to be instances of mistaken identity, or perhaps it is a matter of territory—whose sea is this anyway?

CHAPTER 5

ATTACK: Hawaii

Bruce C. Brown and his girlfriend Robyne Knutson were treading water, looking for whales, about three hundred yards off Kaanapali on the island of Maui when he heard Robyne scream and saw her body move, as if tugged by some underwater source.

"I saw a shark's head clamped on her right upper thigh," Brown said later. He kicked at the shark, which let go of Robyne and swam off. Part of her thigh had been torn away. Brown was trying to pull her to shore when the crew of a nearby catamaran saw the couple, radioed for a rescue squad, and picked them up. The prompt rescue and medical aid undoubtedly saved her life. Gauging the thirteen-inch bite on her leg, a biologist estimated that the attacking shark was about twelve feet long.

That shark struck on March 5, 1999. Three days later, an eighteen-year-old man was surfing on a body board off

Kealia Beach on Kauai in shallow, murky water. He felt a shark bang into his right leg and swim away, leaving him with a cut on his calf surrounded by a large bruise. The attack did not amount to anything, but it was the second in three days. And in Hawaii, where shark attacks have a long history, any brush with a shark summons up grim statistics: In the 1990s there were three times as many shark attacks in Hawaii as there were in the 1970s.

Ten days after the attack on the body surfer, a honeymoon to Hawaii ended tragically. A newlywed husband reported that a shark attacked his wife as their rented kayak was swept out to sea off Maui. The thirty-nine-year-old husband, Manouchehr Monazzami-Taghadom, said that he and his twenty-nine-year-old wife, Nahid Davoodabai, got out of the kayak and were trying to swim ashore, pulling the kayak, when the shark struck, biting off one of her arms.

Monazzami-Taghadom said he got back on the kayak, pulled his wife onto it, and tried to stop her bleeding by tying a tourniquet around her injured arm with the tie from his swim trunks. His wife died in his arms, he said. The kayak drifted across the Alalakeiki Channel to Kahoolawe, a small island long used as a bombing range. There, according to the *Honolulu Star-Bulletin*'s account, he found a telephone in a military bunker and called for help. The kayak was later found, but not Nahid Davoodabai's body.

Three attacks in such a short time carried Hawaiian memories back to a series of attacks that began a decade of drastic change in Hawaii's shark-attack toll: twelve in 1970–1979; twenty-four in 1980–1989. Those figures are from the National Marine Fisheries Service, the most reliable source of shark-attack statistics in Hawaii, where "official" data is highly influenced by the conflicting interests of tourist, diver, fisherman, environmental, and shark-welfare constituencies.

The best way to gain an understanding of those interests is to go through the records of attacks, back to the event that forever altered Hawaii's long coexistence with sharks. From 1886 to December 13, 1958, there had been sixteen known shark attacks in Hawaiian waters, and only five had been fatal. Then came the attack of December 13, 1958, when everything changed.

Billy Weaver, fifteen years old, was swimming with five friends in the surf off Lanikai, a long, wide stretch of beach east of Honolulu on the island of Oahu. The boys caught a wave, and in their tumbling excitement they did not immediately notice that Billy, who was on an air mat, had missed the wave. One of the boys saw him slide off the mat and momentarily disappear. Then he bobbed to the surface screaming for help. "There was blood all in the water and his leg was cut off," one of the boys said later. They tried to keep Billy afloat and get him ashore. He slipped from their grasp and, as he sank beneath the water again, they saw a shark move in toward him.

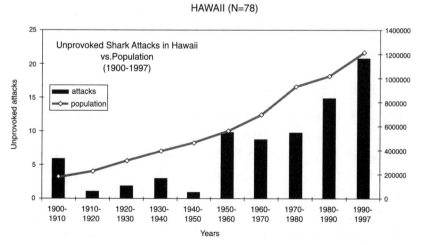

HAWAII (N=78)

SOURCE: ISAF-FMNH

The boys rushed to the shore and set off a massive search for Billy. Men in several of the search boats saw a large shark. Then, wedged in a hole in the reef off the beach, about seven feet beneath the surface, was Billy's body, the right leg gone to the knee.

Community leaders and government officials met and decided to mount an attack on the sharks that menaced the island of Oahu. Two days after Billy was killed, a research vessel was sent to Lanikai, where it caught three tiger sharks and two sand tiger sharks (*Eugomphodus taurus*). That was only the beginning. A Billy Weaver Shark Control Fund was started to finance the catching and destruction of sharks menacing the inshore waters. Fundraisers went from house to house on Oahu. As an added inducement, a merchant offered a twenty dollar bounty for any shark caught in Oahu's inshore waters, and a jewelry company said it would pay a quarter for each shark tooth that a hunter brought in. A boat was chartered to circle Oahu and catch sharks. During the yearlong campaign, 697 sharks were captured and killed; in the females killed was a total of 641 embryos. At least nine species were taken—including a sixgill shark (*Hexanchus griseus*), a species never before recorded in Hawaiian waters, and the second bramble shark (*Echinorhinus brucus*) ever caught in those waters.

On February 17, 1990, Roy T. Tanaka was scuba diving and spearing in water forty feet deep about 200 yards off the Kaneohe Marine Corps Air Station on Oahu. His tank, backpack, dive light, and mask were later seen on the bottom. Next day, a helicopter spotted his body, its right arm gone. As the helicopter hovered over the body, one shark fled, but a larger one remained, gnawing on the body until the searchers retrieved it. (In a similar incident a few months before, rescue divers trying to recover the body of a scuba diver left the water after a shark appeared and began feeding on the body.)

The grim 1990s continued with more attacks on surfers: A shark grabbed the left leg of a man sitting on his board off Waialua, Oahu. A similar attack inflicted a bone-deep wound on the left leg of a surfer while he sat on his board 350 yards from shore at an Oahu site known as "Shark Country." And another: A surfer about 100 yards off Maili Beach on Oahu was sitting on his board when a shark bit him on the right calf, inflicting five- and seven-inch wounds.

November 1991 brought two more incidents, one definitely an attack, the other almost certainly an attack. On November 19, a man, described as a strong swimmer in good physical condition, was swept into the sea by a large wave while fishing off Maliko Point, Maui. Next morning, divers found his shorts and shirt, both with large pieces torn away. Bite marks indicated that a twelve-foot tiger shark had attacked him from his left side.

There was no doubt about the next incident. On November 26, Martha J. Morrell and Louise Sourisseau were snorkeling off Olowalu, Maui, at the edge of a reef, about fifty yards from the end of an old pier that jutted from the beach at Martha Morrell's beachfront home. A shark, eight to eleven feet long, passed by Louise Sourisseau, scraping her right calf and grabbing the other woman by the right arm, pulling her under. Louise Sourisseau suffered only a scraping wound. Physicians who examined Mrs. Morrell's recovered body said the shark took her right leg at the hip, nearly all of her left leg, and her right forearm.

Three months later, surfer Bryan Adona disappeared after heading out on his board at Leftovers, a surfers' spot near Waimea Bay, on the north shore of Oahu. His left swim fin and his board were later found. The board bore the teeth marks of what appeared to be a tiger shark; a sixteen-inch, crescent-shaped piece of the board was missing. The last person to see Bryan Adona alive reported sighting a large shark shortly after the two of them had paddled out toward separate breaks at Leftovers. People on shore also reported seeing a large shark in the vicinity.

In March 1992, Jude Chamberlin was body-surfing, alone, off a spot known as Cannon's on the north shore of Kauai. A leash on her ankle tethered her to the board. Suddenly, she felt her board lift. As she turned, a tiger shark's jaws closed over her legs. "Sick with fear, Jude watched in a trance as the terrible jaws bit down on her legs," Greg Ambrose wrote in his account of her ordeal.[1] "Although her mind was buzzing with terror, one small corner of her brain wondered in fascination why she couldn't feel the hooked teeth tearing into her flesh. The answer came in a lightning bolt: One of her surfboard's three fins must have stuck in the tiger's bottom jaw, preventing the shark from biting through her board and chewing off her leg." The shark shot off, holding the board in its teeth and pulling her behind. In a moment, the tether slackened and she realized that the shark had let go of the surfboard. Trailing blood in the water behind her, she made it to shore, with only a cut on her foot. When she dreams of sharks, she dreams that she is fighting them.

Then came similar attacks on surfers only three weeks apart in the waters of Oahu. Rick Gruzinsky, riding the waves about 120 yards off Oahu's North Shore, felt a jolt under his surfboard. Out of the sea came a shark that clamped down on the surfboard. While Gruzinsky held onto one end of the board, the shark bit off the other. Gruzinsky reached shore bruised and scratched by the jagged edges of the chunk the shark bit off his surfboard, just missing his legs. Aaron A. Romento was not as lucky. While he was body-boarding with friends at Keaau Beach Park, a shark, passing by other surfers, bit his right leg in three places and then vanished. Romento, bleeding heavily during his agonizing paddle to shore, died on the beach, despite immediate first aid. Surfing publications began calling 1992 "the Year of the Shark," and after Romento's death, the *Honolulu Advertiser* ran a story about the ideal conditions at Keaau Beach Park—a bright, sunny day; the surfer only thirty yards from shore; the water only four feet deep. The headline read: IT SHOULD HAVE BEEN SAFE. Resort developers hired fishermen to secretly set long-lines baited for sharks in waters off developments, in the hope of getting rid of any sharks that might scare off an investor. An important tourist-promotion organization, the Maui Visitors Association, succeeded in thwarting plans for plans for an international shark fishing tournament on the island.

Sometimes a shark is only a suspect, as in one case during that awful year of 1992. In August, a man fell from a cliff on Maui. When his body was recovered the next day, the left arm was gone and there were wounds described as shark bites; the autopsy report said that the wounds "appeared to be post mortem." So, no shark-attack casualty for the official record.

Surfers were again the victims in 1993–1994. A week before Christmas in 1993, Daniel McMoyler went surfing in large waves off Waipio on the island of Hawaii. He never returned. On January 11, 1994, human remains washed ashore. With the aid of scientists at the U.S. Army Central Identification Laboratory in Hawaii, the remains were identified as McMoyler's. Other experts, examining the fragment of a shark tooth in a bone and grooves along bones, blamed an eight-foot tiger shark. Twenty days later, Jim Broach was surfing in twenty- to thirty-foot waves off Oahu's north shore when he disappeared. His wetsuit and board were later found. A kayaker reported seeing remains, but they disappeared before they could be recovered.

Two other surfer attacks of the 1990s: A surfer was enjoying the waves at a spot off Maui called Paradise when a tiger shark grabbed his right calf, its teeth sinking to the bone. As the shark tried to pull him under, the surfer fought him off and reached shore with wounds requiring more than 200 surgical staples to close. In another attack, a shark seized the right foot of a surfer off Oahu's Malaekahana State Park and began working its way up his leg. The surfer drove the shark off, hitting it so hard that he tore a tendon in his fist. In the hospital, a physician dug a tiger shark's tooth out of a bone in his right ankle. In October 1999 a shark off the western shore of the Big Island attacked a sixteen-year-old surfer. The shark grabbed the surfer's right arm, badly damaging it. But he was able to pull away and paddle to shore with his left arm.

Early in the 1990s the state legislature created an ocean advisory task force—an up-to-date version of the 1958 shark massacre. Supposedly, the task force was to merely investigate shark attacks and start an educational campaign. But an unspoken mission of the task force was to find sharks. At least twenty tiger sharks were officially killed in a 1993 hunt, and volunteers slew at least thirty more; the final unofficial total was fifty-eight. One night, off the coast of Waikiki, hunters dropped an anchored line with twelve hooks baited with freshly killed tuna. They hoped to prove that no tiger sharks lurked off Hawaii's most famous bathing beach. The following morning the hunters found only a five-and-a-half-foot sandbar shark, a member of the most abundant species in Hawaiian waters, a species never implicated in an attack. John Naughton, a member of an ocean advisory task force, called the result of the hunt "eventful for us because there was no big tiger shark on the line; that's the last thing we wanted to catch."

Hawaii's all-important tourist industry—and the tourists who read newspaper stories about attacks—were relieved. Surfers, however, criticized the task force for claiming there was no shark problem after only one overnight hunt. The surfers said they were seeing more tiger sharks than ever before. And, of course, sharks were seeing more surfers than ever before. Environmentalists and pro-shark animal rights activists also disapproved of the hunt, as did many native Hawaiians whose ancestors revered the tiger shark as *Aumakua,* a god.

As the old century gave way to the new, Hawaii endured another wave of attacks. Between March 1999 and October 2000 there were twelve attacks in Hawaiian waters. One of the attacks particularly startled state officials. In November 1999, a fifty-one-year-old tourist from Rhode Island was swimming with her nephew about 300 yards offshore near the Kona Village Resort on the island of Hawaii, which Hawaiians call the Big Island. A shark, ignoring the nephew, bit her on the right buttock. She cut her fingers fighting off the shark. A boatman, hearing her cries, snatched her from the sea. A helicopter got her to a hospital. That was the third Big Island attack of 1999. The other victims were surfers who escaped with painful bites. There had not been a confirmed Big Island shark attack in twenty-five years, and that 1972 incident was relatively minor: An eight-foot shark bit a spear fisher on the arm. (Of the many shark attacks in Hawaii's waters since 1900, none of those in Big Island waters was fatal.)

Maui Island was the site of two serious attacks in 2000. In August, a shark attacked a fifty-three-year-old French tourist who was windsurfing about three-quarters of a mile off Kanaha Beach Park. Jean Goenvec was sitting on his board, his legs dangling, when a shark bit his left leg. He made a tourniquet out of a line on his rig and sat on his board. About a half hour after the attack another windsurfer saw the injured man and sped off to get a lifeguard. Water-safety officers closed the beach and posted twenty shark-attack warning signs, most of which were quickly stolen.

In October, a fifty-six-year-old California tourist was snorkeling off Otowalu on Maui, when a shark that was believed to be a tiger, grabbed her about the body—a type of attack that is almost always fatal. But the shark, which bit her twice, appeared to be "mouthing" her and did not inflict any serious damage to internal organs. A kayaker who was paddling about seventy-five yards from the woman told the *Honolulu Advertiser* that he had seen a splash and then "a big gray thing." He heard her scream and paddled to her aid. Her daughter, who was swimming nearby, was not attacked. (This behavior, where a shark singles out one victim and ignores everyone else, is a frequent phenomenon.) The kayaker towed the woman ashore while her daughter swam behind her. The woman, who had large wounds on her back and hip, survived. The attack came nine years after a tiger shark killed a woman who was snorkeling near the same site, off Camp Pecusa, a recreational site owned by the Episcopalian Church.

Naughton, speaking for the task force, told the *Star-Bulletin* that the attack on the swimming and snorkeling tourists seemed to be typical of the kind of shark attacks occurring in Hawaii: A shark attacks a person who is isolated and swimming or surfing alone or with another person in the early morning or evening hours. Only one of a pair is attacked.

As usual, tiger sharks were blamed for the attacks. Of the forty-odd species of sharks found in Hawaiian waters, tiger sharks are the most aggressive and the most likely suspects in attacks. Other dangerous Hawaiian sharks—the Galapagos shark (*Carcharhinus galapagensis*), gray reef shark, and scalloped hammerhead (*Sphyrna lewini*)—have not been indicted for any attacks.

Under scientists like Naughton, the task force moved from hunting sharks to learning more about them. The scientists could show that previous rampages against sharks had not reduced the risk of attacks. A tiger-tagging program began. Researchers set research, rather than killing, lines. They were baited with fish-market scraps, at dusk, just off Honolulu. At dawn the following day the researchers returned in a small boat, identified, measured and determined the sex of captured tigers. They also took a tissue sample from each shark, "for genetic fingerprinting," tagged them, and surgically implanted acoustic transmitters about the size of a beer can.

Studies of the travels of more than 130 tagged tigers showed that they swam farther than ten miles offshore along a similar course in the first twenty-four hours after their release; in the next forty-eight hours they remained far offshore. "These results," says a report on the program, "may suggest that tiger sharks have extremely large home ranges and that control programs are unlikely to be effective in catching sharks responsible for attacks as these individuals may move beyond the fished area within hours of the incident."

Tiger sharks, which can grow as long as twenty-one feet, are the biggest sharks encountered in most Pacific reefs. As apex predators, they eat fish, seals, turtles, rays, other sharks—and just about anything else. The list of what has been found in their stomachs includes coiled wire, license plates, lumps of coal, boat cushions, and human remains. A fourteen-footer landed at Durban, South Africa, had inside it the head and forequarters of a crocodile, the hind leg of a sheep, three seagulls, two (unopened) two-pound cans of green peas, and a cigarette tin.

Sharks—*Aumakua,* the guardian spirit—are woven into Hawaiian history and culture. There is even a special word for sharks that eat people: *niuhi.* Practical knowledge from the culture has emerged, known to native Hawaiians and visitors wise enough to learn a bit about where they are. Tradition, for example, says that A*umakua* does not want people to enter the water at sunrise and sunset. Nor should they swim near the mouth of a river or a stream, especially after a rain. Those are good rules anywhere, especially in Hawaii.

Visiting tourists and surfers full of bravado often do not know the local lore. Nor do many know a theory of biologists who have studied Hawaiian attacks: Sharks do not usually venture into an area where there are many people in the water—such as popular surfing sites (rather than "secret places" loners keep to themselves). Sharks, at least in Hawaii, more often attack surfers or swimmers who are in the water alone or in pairs. "We have far more people in the water off Oahu, but most of these attacks happen on Maui, Hawaii, and Kauai," says Naughton. "Tigers, for such big animals, are rather timid. They seem to be shy of a lot of activity. When they do attack, it seems to be one or two people by themselves."

For many who enjoy themselves far off Hawaiian shores, the well-trained lifeguards along the beaches are only symbols of security. Windsurfers who sail miles from shore are absolutely on their own. The windsurfers in Hawaii call the great waves "Jaws," and that is also the name for the place where the legendary big waves—some with faces sixty feet high—break on the north shore of Maui. In the waves themselves there will be no sharks. But beyond the line where the waves are born, sharks sometimes trail solitary windsurfers.

One windsurfer told of being hit suddenly as he sailed along at high speed. His board spun out and a shark grabbed a leg. Holding onto his booms with one hand, he pushed at the shark with his other. The shark let go, and the windsurfer sailed to shore, where he was taken to a hospital. He identified the attacker as a gray reef shark, not a tiger.

Two other windsurfers, deciding to get away from the crowds, found a remote stretch of sea off Maui. One of them noticed that the water was murky and said, "This is perfect water for sharks." Seconds later, a relatively small ten- or twelve-foot tiger shark grabbed one of his legs and tried to pull him under. He drove off the shark by beating it on the side of the head. He then luckily caught a wave and surfed in to shore, his leg badly gouged. Prompt medical aid saved his leg.

Tourist-conscious Hawaiian officials stopped formally collecting and reporting information about shark attacks in 1996. (But officials still offer a number to call if you see a shark bigger than eight feet: On Oahu, call 58-SHARK. On neighboring islands, dial 1–800–468–4644, then dial SHARK.)

The *Honolulu Star-Bulletin* took up the task of listing shark attacks and published a table that compared decades:

	1990–1999	1980–1989	1970–1979
Oahu	16	7	2
Maui	12	4	6
Kauai	6	7	2
Big Island (Hawaii)	1	4	2
Molokai	1	2	0
Total	36	24	12

SOURCE: *HONOLULU STAR-BULLETIN*

There are usually two or three shark attacks in Hawaiian waters each year, with surfers and spear fishers the most likely victims. Attacks have been increasing since the 1950s—as have users of Hawaii's beaches and waves. Oahu beaches alone attract about 17 million people a year. Researchers believe that a major reason for the increase in attacks is a change in recreation patterns. Kayakers, canoeists, and windsurfers are seeking solitude by heading far from the crowded shore. "Instead of being one hundred or two hundred yards off the beach," says one researcher, "they are one or two miles away."

George Balazs, a research biologist with the National Marine Fisheries Service in Honolulu, has meticulously studied 118 Hawaiian attacks, using books, newspapers, autopsy reports, and correspondence with victims and witnesses. He lists forty-eight as fatal and assigns four possible causes to each fatal attack:

- ten fatalities *directly* attributed to shark attack.
- six fatalities *likely* attributed to shark attack.
- twelve fatalities *likely* attributed to another cause (drowning, etc.) besides shark attack. Indications of shark attack may actually be post-mortem mutilation or dismemberment by shark or sharks.
- twenty incidents in which he could not make a definite opinion because of a lack of information. "Although mutilation and/or dismemberment by sharks had occurred," Balazs writes, "fatality may have been directly attributed to shark attack, or may have resulted from another cause. This category also includes an absence of any witnesses or the absence of sufficient body remains or medical evidence to determine cause of death by autopsy."

Balazs, for example, lists this case in the "no definite opinion" category: On April 5, 1943, a small boat or canoe swamped about three miles off Maui; one of the four occupants did not make it to shore. On April 29, remains of the man and his "brightly colored swimming trunks" were found in the stomach of a sixteen-foot shark caught in a turtle net, along with a piece of a newspaper dated March 25, 1943.

Balazs also tries to find similarities between attacks, particularly on surfers. Two cases stand out for having parallels. August 19, 1993: Reggie Williams is paddling seaward in murky water near Iao Stream at Paukukalo, Maui. About fifty yards from shore a large shark knocks him off his surfboard. He scrapes and bruises the right side of his body. The shark's bite leaves a thirteen-and-a-half-inch crescent etched by teeth marks in the surfboard.

August 29, 1996: David Nanod, Jr., is body-boarding about fifty to one hundred yards from shore in murky water at Paukukalo, Maui, near Iao Stream in an area known as Big Left's. A shark bites him on the right calf and rips it; the wound is a foot long. Nanod punches the shark and then kicks it when it lets go. About twelve surfers are nearby. Surfing friend Kamuela Hamakua stays with Nanod in the bloody water. As another surfer, Yansi Casis, describes the attack, the shark came up from underneath, grabbed Nanod, thrashed him a couple times, let go, circled, and darted off. "The incident was over in ten seconds or so," Casis says.

What makes surfers so vulnerable? They take risks, often violating a fundamental warning to stay out of murky waters, particularly near the mouths of streams. Some surfers believe that they will be safe if they stay away from sea turtles,

Balaz's Analysis of Attacks in Hawaii

Activity	Fatal	Nonfatal	Total
Swimming/Snorkelling	8	15	23
Spearfish while snorkeling	1	5	6
Scuba diving	3	1	4
Spearfishing with scuba	2	0	2
Surfboarding	2	13	15
Body-boarding	2	3	5
Body-surfing	1	2	3
Windsurfing	0	1	1
Surfing on air mattress	1	0	1
Fell into sea or swept out to sea	16	0	16
Fell off boat or boat capsized	3	1	4
Net fishing	0	3	3
Crabbing	1	2	3
Other types of fishing	2	1	3

a favorite shark food. A popular surfer theory is that sharks mistake them for turtles. George Balazs will have none of that theory. "We have specifically gone to places in Hawaii that are the best sites for turtles, and in all those years of diving, we have never once, I have never once, encountered or even seen a tiger shark," he told a Nova interviewer. "Any object in the water at or near the surface could be liable to be snapped at by a shark. You don't have to look like a turtle in order to be eaten by a predator."

CHAPTER 6

ATTACK: South Africa

For South Africans, those 107 days will always be known as "Black December," the time of the tragic series of attacks that began the nation's long history of dealing with sharks. First viewed as a pitiless enemy, then as a mysterious opponent, during that long history the shark would eventually become, incredibly, a ward, protected by an unprecedented law. The metamorphosis from villain to poster animal was accomplished by the great white shark. It was not the shark responsible for all of the South African attacks, but it became the symbol of our slow awakening responsibility as stewards of every creature, even those that occasionally eat us.

December 18, 1957. At the resort of Karridene, south of Durban, sixteen-year-old Robert Wherley was body-surfing in water that came up to his chest. The Umngazi River empties into the sea here, but few people in 1957 knew that

sharks gathered at river mouths. Wherley felt something—
seaweed, he thought—touching his left leg. In rapid succes-
sion, he next saw a shadow, bloodied water, and a dorsal fin.
"It was only then," he said later, "that I realized what was
happening. I saw the shark coming at me and there was
nothing I could do. I tried moving sideways, but it was no
good. There was this jarring shock as the shark grabbed my
leg. I surged through the water as it swam with me in its
mouth."

Wherley pummeled the shark with his fists. The shark
shook him and abruptly released him. The shark had taken
his leg, bitten off at the knee. He body-surfed to shore and,
unaware that he had lost his leg, tried to stand. People on
the beach reached him as he fainted. He survived.

Two days later, at the resort village of Uvongo to the
south, Allan Green, a fifteen-year-old, was standing on a
sandbar about thirty yards out. Between the swimmers on
the sandbar and the shore was a channel. The swimmers
were plunging into the three-foot waves that were breaking
across the channel. Then, someone in the crowd heard a cry.
As a large shark's tail lashed the water, Green stumbled
backward and vanished for a moment. When he appeared
again, the shark was gone but he was struggling in the
bloodying surf. Some of the swimmers, in panic, splashed
through the channel to shore. Others stood frozen, too terrified to flee.

Someone started a human chain that stretched to shore,
and Green was passed from hand to hand. By the time he
reached the beach, he was dead, his right arm, chest, and abdomen bearing huge wounds.

Some vacationers began checking out of nearby resorts.
Others saw no reason to react to a tragic freak accident. As
newspapers spread the story of two attacks in three days, a
third one was just over the horizon at Margate, another re-

sort farther south. And the phrase Black December would be born.

Vernon Berry, a twenty-three-year-old motorcycle enthusiast, was heading for Cape Town to compete in a race. He and two friends stopped off at Margate for a day at the beach. If the hundred swimmers at Margate were worried about the previous attacks, they did not show it. People on vacation usually don't read newspapers. A man was running down the beach, shouting. As he came closer, people could hear what he was saying: "Shark!"

A vacationer perched on a rock near shore saw the shark. It seemed to be heading toward Berry. The man stood up and relayed the warning to Berry. Too late. The shark churned the water, seized Berry, and began pushing him violently. Witnesses said they seemed to somersault through the reddening shallows. Berry's friends reached him as the shark disappeared. He was on his back, floundering. "Oh, my God! Just look at me!" he exclaimed, then fainted. His right arm was little more than bone. His right thigh, abdomen, and buttocks had been torn away. He never regained consciousness.

Resort owners, residents, and municipal officials declared war against the sharks. The Tuna Angling Club hooked shark-rigged lines to kites so the hooks would reach beyond the breakers. Shark spotter planes skimmed along the shore looking for sharks and warning swimmers if sharks appeared.

Early in the afternoon on the next-to-last day of Black December, a spotter plane flew over Margate. A few moments later, a group of vacationers—fourteen-year-old Julia Painting, two other relatives, and an adult friend, Paul Brokensha—dove into the surf for a last swim before heading home. About 2,000 other vacationers were on the broad beach. Julia was standing in waist-deep water when a shark suddenly was on her. It bit off part of her left buttock, whirled, and returned, taking her left arm off at the shoulder and slashing her left breast. Brokensha courageously splashed to her side and took hold of the shark's tail. It brushed him aside. He came back, striking the shark and pulling at the girl. The shark swam off. Unconscious, she was rushed to a hospital. Physicians and nurses had never seen wounds like these. There was no blood available, so the physicians and nurses gave up their blood, alternating between transfusion and operations. Miraculously, she survived.[1]

The mayor of Margate closed the beaches to swimmers, divers, and surfers. The Margate council set a bounty for all sharks caught off Margate. A South African Navy minesweeper patrolled the southern coast, dropping depth charges and hand grenades to kill any sharks that might be lurking in the shallows. The dead-shark count was eight, but no one knows how many sharks were attracted to the thousands of fish killed by the explosions.

Bloody December had ended. But on January 9, 1958, at another resort at the mouth of another river—Scottburgh, thirty miles south of Durban—the overwhelming number of vacationers stayed on the sands. Among the twenty or so in the surf was Deryck Prinsloo, a forty-two-year-old man. He was standing in water up to his thighs.

The surf was murky. So no one saw the shark until it closed its jaws over his buttocks and hurled him out of the water. It swiftly returned: a bite that ripped out a large chunk of his left thigh, leaving his leg hanging by bloody shreds. Then another bite, taking away more of his buttocks and his right thigh. He was dead on arrival at the hospital.

Now the panic was on. Holiday celebrators began leaving hotels. People still remember the jarring news broadcasts, the thousands of cars in the worst traffic jam South

Africa had ever seen. Cars were backed up for miles, especially where there were one-lane bridges. Hotels went bankrupt.

In search of an immediate defense, authorities turned to nets. Back in 1907, Durban had responded to a spate of attacks by building an offshore anti-shark net, a semicircular mesh barrier about 100 yards in diameter. The surf pounded it, and it was in constant need of repair. Finally, in 1928, it was torn down. Most people agreed that it had done its job. Attacks fell off sharply. When a new deadly time began again on Durban beaches—twenty-one attacks between 1945 and 1951, seven fatal—Durban once more tried nets, this time basing the design on the highly successful net system guarding the beaches of Sydney, Australia.

Resorts hastily set up nets and launched an advertising campaign touting them as providing swimmers with a dependable protection against sharks. The campaign was aimed at assuring vacationers in advance of one of the big holiday periods of the year: Easter vacation. Easter would come on April 6 in 1958, and as it neared, the deluge of vacationers began to arrive at the resorts, convinced that the nets would shield them.

On April 3, Nicolas François Bandenhorst was already enjoying the holiday. The twenty-nine-year-old man was swimming face-down with a mask and flippers in chest-deep water at Port Edward, about 100 miles south of Natal. Near him were his brother Andries and a friend. When he cried out, swimmers started a stampede for shore. Instinctively, they knew the cry meant a shark was among them.

The shark struck once. Brandenhorst's wife and children watched in horror. Then, as the shark came back for a second strike, a black man—who, by the rules of apartheid, should not have ventured onto the beach—dove into the surf and pulled what was left of Bandenhorst out of the sea. The shark had taken both arms, his right leg, and a large piece of his abdomen.

The exodus began again from resorts along the eastern coast. But some beach goers were determined to get what they had paid for, and so the shores were far from deserted. At Uvongo, where a shark had killed Allan Green four months before, local authorities had put up a net barrier. Two days after Bandenhorst's death, a crew went out at low tide to repair the surf-battered Uvongo nets.

Fay Bester, a twenty-eight-year-old mother of four, had taken her children to Uvongo on her first holiday since her husband was killed in a motorcycle accident eleven months before. The widow and the children joined about 500 others who were drawn by curiosity to the nets. Because it was such a hot day, she left the sand flats to stand in knee-deep cool water where a river mingled with the sea. Moments later, a shark slammed into her, knocking her down. Then the shark spun around and encircled her waist with its jaws. Shaking her vigorously, it raised her out of the water. The shark, which vanished as swiftly as it had materialized, had nearly bitten her in half.

In the 107 days between the first Black December attack and Easter, five people had been killed.

Amanzimtoti, the most dangerous beach in the world, is also one of the most beautiful. The broad carpet of perfect sand stretches for miles. The Indian Ocean is a brilliant blue. Tourists looking out at that vista probably do not notice something else in the seascape: Jutting out of the sea are the buoys marking the location of the anti-shark nets. The nets are even mentioned in the tourist promotions for this South African resort, the "Gateway to the South," sixteen miles south of Durban.

One of the scenic attractions of Amanzimtoti is a promontory known as Inyoni Rocks. The beach courses along to the rocky outcrop and then continues, a smooth seam between sea and shore. Within a 700-yard stretch of shore dominated by Inyoni Rocks there have been at least eleven shark attacks, a record unmatched by any other strand of beach in the world. Little is known about the first three recorded attacks in the 1940s, except the fact that all were fatal. As more thorough record keeping began in the 1960s, the first details of an Inyoni Rocks attack were chronicled. It happened on April 30, 1960.

Sixteen-year-old Michael Hely was about thirty feet from shore, in water less than ten feet deep, when he felt something brush his legs. He thought that it might be tendrils of seaweed. Then a shark seized his right arm and pulled him under the murky water. With his left hand he groped for the shark's eyes and instead stuck his hand into the side of the shark's mouth. His left index finger was jammed between two serrated teeth, and as he pulled it out the teeth stripped the finger of all flesh and muscle, down to the bone. The shark released him for a moment, but struck again, this time tearing open his abdomen. Somehow the teenager made it to the beach, with his intestines hanging out. Lifesavers summoned a physician who started working on Hely twelve minutes after he emerged from the sea. He survived.

Nine months later, fifteen-year-old Michael Murphy and several pals were swimming about 400 yards south of Inyoni Rocks. When the others went in, Murphy dawdled to body-surf in water about six feet deep. In one bite a shark ripped his left leg from the thigh to the calf. Again a local physician arrived quickly. But the leg was so grievously damaged that it had to be amputated.

That is how the shark nets came to Amanzimtoti. Seven months after the attack on Murphy, two shark nets were installed off the beach. Experts on shark netting—an old skill in South Africa—decided that a third one was needed. It went up a few months before the next attack.

This time it was another teenager. Fifteen-year-old Errol Fourie was swimming backwards in murky water on an April day in 1963 when a shark slammed into him so hard that the boy was hurled out of the water. The shark did not strike again. Fourie swam rapidly to shore, where lifesavers found on his left buttock a large bite that had removed skin and some muscle near the surface but was not life-threatening. A physician took him away in a car.

Now more nets went up, and for eleven years Amanzimtoti was free of attacks. Then one day strong seas swamped the net buoys. The next day, January 7, 1974, as high waves continued to break about 300 yards off the beach, an off-duty lifeguard plunged into the waves to body-surf. A shark bit his right leg and swam off. The lifeguard first tried backstroking to shore so that he could see the shark. Realizing he should be swimming as fast as he could, he flipped over and quickly reached the beach. There he did what his training had taught him to do: He applied finger pressure to the femoral artery until his colleagues took over. He fully recovered.

A month later, because the nets had not been serviced for several days, officials banned swimming in the murky sea. But Damon Kendrick, an off-duty lifeguard, decided to wash the sand off his body. Once in the water, he could not resist doing some body-surfing. He was a few feet from shore. A friend in the water with him let out a shout after being bumped by a shark, which headed for Kendrick. The shark shook him for about two seconds and pushed him onto the shore.

"I pushed myself backwards up the sloping beach holding my injured leg up in front of me," Kendrick later recounted. "Only then did I know what had happened, and my mind did not want to accept what I was seeing. Great strips of skin and muscle hung like old rags from where my calf muscle used to be. Blood spurted and dripped from my leg and formed a river of blood in the sand."

In those two seconds Kendrick had been bitten three times. The first bite severed the fibula—the thin outer bone of the leg—at the ankle. The second sliced into the fibula near the knee. The third cut away calf muscle and part of the fibula. The bites also scraped the tibia, the other leg bone, leaving clues to the attacker: a great white with a jaw about seven and a half inches wide. The wounds were so severe that Kendrick's leg had to be amputated below the knee.

The next attack, not quite a month later, also came on a day when officials banned swimming because they believed that conditions were similar to those on the day that Kendrick had been attacked, and they did not want to take any chances. The attack on the foolhardy, twenty-one-year-old surfer only damaged his board.

A few days after the first anniversary of the attack on Kendrick, a friend, Bretton Russel Jones, sixteen years old, decided to try some morning surfing near Inyoni Rocks. Again swimming had been banned (turbid water, large swells). Jones wiped out on a wave, scraping his left knee. He was bleeding slightly when he swam closer to the Rocks—and felt something bump his toes, then grab his right leg. *Somebody is playing with me*, he thought. But he lifted his leg—and: "I couldn't believe my eyes when I saw a shark's head clinging to it. It suddenly began to thrash and pulled me partly into the water." He held onto his board with all his strength and pulled his leg from the shark's jaws. "I felt a strange sensation; it felt as if I had pulled my foot off." He lifted his leg and saw a bloody stump. He paddled in, not feeling any pain, a phenomenon reported by many victims right after an attack. On shore, a tourniquet from a surf-board leash staunched the blood.

Shark experts believe that a shark had been attracted to the yellow sock tied around his right ankle with the board leash. The shark bit that ankle. Jones twice tried to pull out his foot. The first time the shark's teeth tightened and, as Jones pulled, the shark stripped off flesh to the bone. On the second tug—"he shook me like a dog"—the shark chopped off the foot, which disappeared with the yellow sock. There was little left of his leg below the knee. It was amputated, just as Kendrick's had been.

The Amanzimtoti attacks inspired a scientific search for possible natural triggers. The investigation showed that prior to at least five of the attacks, large schools of anchovies and other species of fish had appeared around the Inyoni Rocks. Scientists speculated that sharks had followed the anchovies close to shore and were preying on them. When the sharks happened upon other possible prey—human limbs in turgid waters—they sampled the new food. In the five attacks that were analyzed, the shark took one bite and did not return. "This shows," writes T.S. Wallett,[2] "that after the first bite the sharks concerned found their victims sufficiently unappetizing not to want to return to finish their meal."

Few sharks were caught in Amanzimtoti nets, compared to the shark count at several other netted beaches. This may mean that sharks do not ordinarily lurk off Amanzimtoti's shore. But, lured close in by a sudden appearance of small prey, the sharks come. And they go when the anchovies or other fish prey leave. At places where more sharks are net-ted, sharks are finding dependable meals all the time.

As scientists began to study the ecological setting for shark attacks, they were baffled by the apparent effective-ness of the meshing as a shark barrier. After taking a hard look at the Durban meshing, David H. Davies, director of the council of the South African Association for Marine Biological Research, concluded: "There is no really satisfactory explanation for the success. Although the nets extend for a considerable distance parallel to the bathing beaches, they do not form a continuous wall, and at all times sharks are able to penetrate the area between the beach and the nets by swimming between separate nets or round the ends. Sharks have been found to have been gilled on either side of the nets when traveling both toward and away from the beaches. The only reasonable explanation for the success of the set-net system seems to be related to the already established fact that it is possible to reduce a shark population by systematic netting. This has been shown in commercial shark fisheries in various parts of the world. . . "

Davies began a systematic study of attacks, looking at every aspect, especially water and weather conditions.[3] One of his first case studies was devoted to an attack at Amanzimtoti: A young man swimming in six feet of water was attacked about thirty feet from shore. He was bitten once, on the left leg, which had to be amputated.[4] Looking back at the carnage off Amanzimtoti, Davies concluded, "At the present rate of incidence on humans, this section of the east coast of South Africa is one of the most seriously affected areas in the world."

At the same time the surfing beaches of South Africa became known throughout the world. As increasing numbers of surfers discovered South Africa's big waves, shark attacks also increased. The attacks were so frequent that lifeguards were equipped with special first aid kits known as Feinberg Packs, named after the physician who had developed them. Davies had said in 1963 that shark attacks were unlikely when the water temperature was less than 69 degrees. But now surfers and divers wear well-insulated wetsuits, and no longer was temperature a factor in attacks.

In a study of forty-one attacks in which the surface sea temperature was known or estimated, 65 percent of the attacks took place in chill waters (less than 69 degrees). That same study, by Marie Levine of the Shark Research Institute,[5] looked at where swimmers, surfers, and divers were when they were attacked. Her report, based on sixty-three attacks between 1922 and 1994, focuses on attacks by great whites. She interviewed 1,200 people—victims, witnesses, physicians, lifesavers, and others involved in rescuing and treating the victims—to produce one of the most comprehensive analyses of recent times.

The study showed that two-thirds of the swimmers were fifty yards or less from shore and in water less than six feet deep when they were attacked. Most of the surfers were more than fifty yards offshore when the shark struck. Of the twenty-one divers attacked, only one was hit below the surface. This is a consistent finding of researchers all over the world: You are safer under than on the water.

Most sharks attacked in murky waters. Rivers were in flood. Sewage or other waste matter was in the water. Fourteen attacks happened in kelp beds, on a reef, near an estuary, or near an upwelling of cold water. Fifteen took place near pinniped rookeries or haul-out areas. And in nineteen cases, shoals of fish were nearby or some kind of fishing was going on. All of these environmental factors have been seen in attacks outside South Africa. But South Africa has grimly unique geography. A shark-attack map of South Africa, created by Levine, shows forty-three white shark attack sites, from the KwaZulu-Natal coast southward to the Eastern Cape and Western Cape provinces, then around the tip to Melkbossstrand. There are few attacks along the Atlantic coast, where the water is cold.

"Achieving insights into shark attacks is by no means the same as discovering means of preventing attacks," Levine wrote. But, she added, "we have learned some ways of lessening the risk of an attack: high-risk area and seasons can be identified, and recreational use of the sea can be restricted when the risk of shark attack is highest."

In 1998, not long after Levine wrote that, a series of attacks on surfers in South Africa's southern resorts led politicians and resort operators to once again appeal to scientists to find ways to stop shark attacks. The victims included Neal Stephenson, South Africa's national bodyboarding champion. He had been surfing with friends at Keurbooms on the southern Cape coast, when a shark selected him for an attack. The massive bites destroyed his right leg and tore up his left foot. His right leg was amputated above the knee.

In another attack, a great white mauled twenty-year-old Anton Devos as he body-boarded off Gonubie Point, near East London, about 400 miles south of Durban. The shark bit Devos' hands and right calf, severing a main artery in his left thigh. He died from loss of blood. Two weeks after the attack on Stephenson, sharks, believed to be great whites, bit but did not seriously injure two other Cape coast bodyboarders. Adding to the total was a fatal attack at a so-called "safe beach," where there had not been a fatal attack for thirty years.

Most surfers reacted with bravado. "Everyone knows there is a shark risk," said one. "But we are in greater danger of being in a car smash on the way to the beach." When a shark hit a surfer so hard that he flew through the air, however, surfers fled. It happened in a surfing paradise, Jeffrey's Bay at Port Elizabeth, near the tip of Africa. Witnesses said terrified surfers cut their feet and hands on razor-sharp reefs in their frantic exit. The surfer, an American on his first visit to Jeffrey's Bay, said the shark struck from behind and catapulted him out of the water. It was the second shark encounter at Jeffrey's Bay in a week.

Surfers got another jolt in July 2000 when a cameraman caught on video an attack on a South African surfer, fifteen-year-old Ainslie Shannon. Just as he is taking off on a wave, a twelve-foot great white lurches forward and throws Shannon over the back of a breaker. A second shark is seen nearby. The video (with digitally enhanced close-ups) was later telecast throughout the world. One viewer said these were the "most frightening shark attack images since the movie *Jaws*." The shark bit Shannon's right hand, severely damaging the flesh and exposing bone. Physicians reattached a severed middle finger. The shark, which struck at a beach near East London, seemed to come from the shallow water on the front side of the wave, where surfers always believed they were safe from attacks. Instead of coming from the deeper water, the shark lunges through the break and the white water. The video also confirmed that great whites strike without warning, for no one in the video sees the shark before the strike.

When 1998 ended, the International Shark Attack File declared that South Africa had more attacks in 1998 than had been recorded for many years: seventeen, more than three times the five-per-year that South Africa had averaged during the previous ten years. Most South African attacks occur during the summer months when the beaches and surf lure thousands of vacationers. But the worrisome attacks of 1998 came in the winter—a direct result of the all-weather clothing and equipment of modern divers and surfers.

Why the surge in attacks?

The Natal Sharks Board, the official maintainer of South African shark nets and the leading South African authority on attacks, admitted it was stumped.[6] The board, which investigates every shark attack on the South African coast, dismissed the popular suggestions. *El Niño:* has little influence on the south and east coasts, where most of the attacks took place. *Localized increases in coastal water temperatures:* no evidence that shark attacks took place in these bodies of warm water. *Increased shark-dive tourism:* None of the operations were near where the attacks happened. The board felt that great white sharks were probably responsible for most of the attacks, adding that the great whites were probably "investigating" rather than hunting. Proof of this came from the fact that most of the attacking sharks made only one strike, then disappeared. The board has a caring attitude toward the great white, as does South Africa itself, which in 1991 became the first nation to make the great white a protected species. The board, in an attempt to "put the threat into perspective," pointed out that in twenty years, sharks killed nine people while, in 1996 alone, eighty-five people drowned at sea.

The board, looking back over thirty-five years of attack records, found some patterns.

- At first, most victims were swimmers in KwaZulu-Natal, but the shark nets greatly reduced the number of attacks.
- In KwaZulu-Natal there were more attacks in the late afternoon than at any other time of the day, even though most people swim in the heat of the late morning and early afternoon. "This," said the board, "is presumably related to the nocturnal activities of many sharks that venture inshore to feed. Shark attacks have

often taken place in very murky waters when the rivers come down in flood. Zambezi sharks [known elsewhere as the bull shark (*Carcharhinus leucas*)] find these situations extremely attractive and they have been responsible for many attacks in water no more than waist-deep."

- In recent years, surfers and spearfishers have been attacked far more often than swimmers. This is because their wetsuits enable them to stay out longer and venture farther offshore. Noting several attacks in which spear fishers were bitten while heading for the surface, the board analysis said that the sharks undoubtedly were attracted by fish blood and the irregular vibrations of a struggling fish after it has been shot. There was only one attack on a scuba diver, who was fatally attacked while he was swimming on the surface.

Shark attacks in South African waters 1990–1998

| | Cape | | KwaZulu-Natal | | Netted beaches |
	Total	Fatal	Total	Fatal	
1990	4	1	0	0	0
1991	2	0	1	0	1*
1992	1	0	2	0	0
1993	4	0	2	0	0
1994	9	1	0	0	0
1995	3	0	1	1	0
1996	3	0	1	0	0
1997	5	2	0	0	0
1998	15	1	0	0	0
Total	46	5	7	1	1

*Angler fishing from surfski, legs dangling in water; foot bitten by four-foot shark immediately after a fish was boated. The nets provide limited protection against small sharks of this size.
SOURCE: INTERNATIONAL SHARK ATTACK FILE

- Fatal injuries have decreased because of improved medical treatment and the equipping of lifeguards with a specially designed first aid kit, known as the Shark Attack Pack.

And what of the rest of Africa? While the 1998 South African attacks were capturing headlines in that country, an attack in Mozambique made the press, probably because newspapers were on the alert for any shark news. On a remote area of the Mozambique coast, 110 miles north of Maputo, the capital, Wilma von Molendorff and her fiancé, Johan Preller, had been diving on a reef. When they were finished diving, they boarded their inflatable dinghy and began to motor to shore. About a mile and a half from shore, the outboard motor stalled and would not restart. So they decided to swim ashore, towing the dinghy on a long rope. About 500 yards from shore, Wilma swam back to the dinghy to take a Global Positioning System reading. Before she could get into the dinghy a nine-foot shark, species unknown, swam up, bit her chest and stomach and severed her left forearm. The shark was still holding her when Preller reached her and punched the shark's snout until it released her. By the time he got her into the dinghy, she had bled to death.

During the colonial era—and on into modern times—there have been few reports of shark attacks unless the victim was white. No one knows the actual number of Indian Ocean attacks beyond South Africa—along the coasts of Mozambique, Tanzania, and Kenya, and off the shores of Madagascar. Many attacks in these places go unreported because of poor communications, governmental indifference, or the realization that sharks are bad for the tourist business, especially in countries that desperately need the money.

In 2000 came an indication of how deadly the Indian Ocean can be. Officials in Dar es Salaam, Tanzania, said that during the year there had been five fatal attacks along the Coco Beach coast area of Dar es Salaam. The fifth victim was a university student whose body was not found. "We have lost five residents this year, and we cannot still keep silent," said Yusuf Makamba, regional commissioner of Dar es Salaam. "We kindly ask residents to stop frequenting Coco Beach until further notice." The ban was not enforced, and the pressure to keep the beach open reflected the tension between the demand for safety and the demand for tourist income.

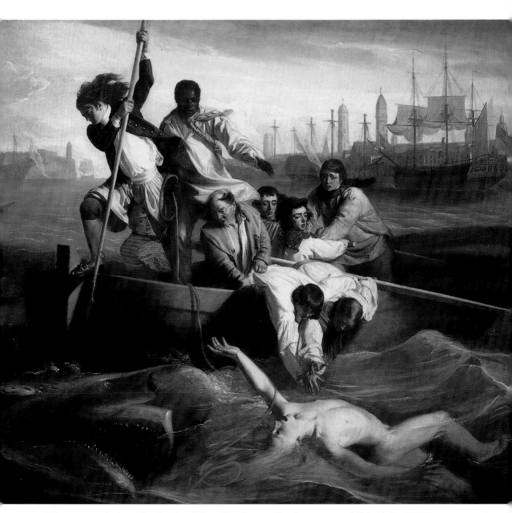

Watson and the Shark, *by John Singleton Copley, was exhibited in 1778, proving the reality of shark attacks. The subject, Brook Watson, was fourteen when a shark in Havana Harbor took his right foot. Years later, Watson, then Alderman of London, commissioned the painting. He also put a shark in his coat of arms.* Ferdinand Lammot Belin Fund, Photograph © 2001 Board of Trustees, National Gallery of Art, Washington.

Dangerous Sharks

These are the sharks to beware of, beginning with the white shark, star of *Jaws* and the shark responsible for ten to twenty of the thirty or so fatal attacks reported in the world each year. These three species perpetrate most of the attacks classified by researchers as "bump and bite" and "sneak."

White Shark (Carcharodon carcharias). **Maximum Size:** *25 feet; 2,658 pounds recorded.* **Also known as** *the great white shark, white pointer (Australia and South Africa), and white death (Australia).** **Distribution:** *worldwide.*

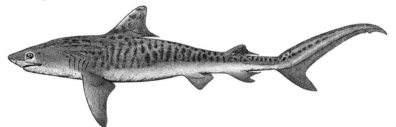

Tiger Shark (Galeocerdo cuvier). **Maximum Size:** *18 feet.* **Distribution:** *All tropical and subtropical seas; frequently in temperate seas.*

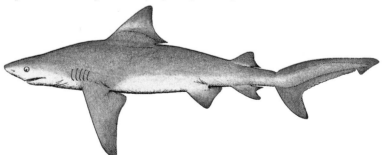

Bull Shark (Carcharhinus leucas). **Maximum Size:** *11 feet; average adult male about 7 feet.* **Also known as** *cub shark, Ganges shark, Nicaragua shark, river shark, Zambezi shark, shovelnose, slipway, square-nose, Van Rooyen's shark, freshwater whaler, estuary whaler, and Swan River whaler.* **Distribution:** *All tropical and subtropical oceans and seas, especially along shore; also in some rivers and lakes.*

*Dangerous sharks known as whalers in Australia and New Zealand are members of the family Carcharhinidae. Some have universally accepted scientific names, such as the dusky whaler shark or whaler shark *(Carcharhinus obscurus)* and the copper shark or bronze whaler *(Carcharhinus brachyurus)*. But many sharks called "whalers" are white sharks or bull sharks.

A kind of attack labeled "hit and run" happens so quickly that surviving victims cannot identify the attacker—unless it happens to be the great hammerhead. Other sharks that hit and run include the shortfin mako, the fastest swimmer of all the sharks, and the oceanic whitetip.

Great Hammerhead Shark (Sphyrna mokarran). ***Maximum Size:*** *Largest of the hammerhead sharks, known to reach 18.3 feet and grow to more than 20 feet.* ***Distribution:*** *Along coasts and well offshore; often found in passes and lagoons of coral atolls.*

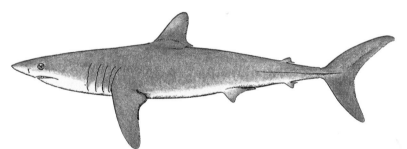

Shortfin Mako Shark (Isurus oxyrinchus). ***Maximum Size:*** *13 feet.* ***Also known as*** *mako, blue pointer, bonito shark.* ***Distribution:*** *Worldwide in temperate and tropical seas.*

Oceanic Whitetip Shark (Carcharinus longimanus). ***Maximum Size:*** *13 feet.* ***Distribution:*** *Worldwide warm oceanic water, usually far from shore, from the surface down to a depth of about 500 feet.*

Divers and spear fishermen have had hostile encounters with these three. The silky is a large, aggressive shark. Nurse sharks, though sluggish, can inflict a painful bite. Blue sharks are suspected of feeding frenzies at air and sea disasters.

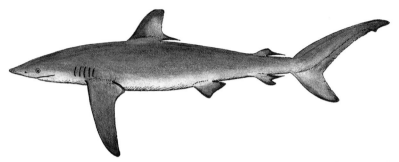

Silky Shark (Carcharhinus falciformis). **Maximum Size:** *14 feet.* **Distribution:** *Worldwide oceanic and coastal waters.*

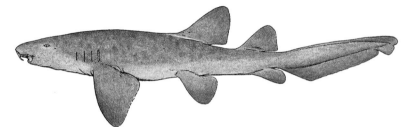

Nurse Shark (Ginglymostoma cirratum). **Maximum Size:** *14 feet; usually smaller.* **Distribution:** *Bottom-dwellers in the western Atlantic and eastern Pacific; common in coral reefs. Not to be confused with a large, very dangerous shark, the Australian gray nurse shark* (Carcharias taurus).

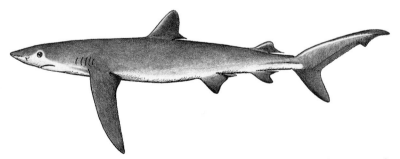

Blue Shark (Prionace glauca). **Maximum Size:** *12½ feet.* **Also known as** *the blue whaler.* **Distribution:** *All temperate and subtropical seas.*

© CHRIS FALLOWS

A great white shark soars out of the sea after snatching a pinniped in the spectacular conclusion of a hunt off Seal Island in South Africa. Some researchers believe that great whites may strike surfers on boards from below because the silhouette looks like that of a seal.

© CHRIS FALLOWS

A blue shark darts into a school of anchovies. Ceaseless hunters far at sea, blue sharks often congregate to feast on dead or dying whales.

Above: A great white feeds on an elephant seal off Año Nuevo in 2000 (Pelagic Shark Research Foundation). Below: The "seal" is an eight-foot plywood decoy and the shark is a great white, nosing the object to investigate it. Similarly, sharks sometimes nip at humans, then swim off without a lethal attack. (Pelagic Shark Research Foundation.)

CHAPTER 7

ATTACK: Australia

In Australia, when police report a shark attack, the verb usually is not "attacked" or "seized," but "taken," as in *taken by a shark*. It has the sound of a dark tale: Some malevolent force takes away an innocent victim, never to be seen again. For Australians, one of those dark tales began early on the morning of December 17, 1967, when Prime Minister Harold Holt plunged into the surf at Portsea's Cheviot Beach, a sea-battered peninsula that forms an arm of Port Phillip Bay. Sharks—great whites and what Australians call bronze whalers—prowled those wild seas.[1] People said later that the water became turbulent just before he disappeared. And a police officer, summoned to the beach, went to a hill and looked through binoculars. "I thought I saw something pink in the water," he said, "but I couldn't see what it was and I couldn't be sure."

Holt's body was never found. People speculated that he had committed suicide, that he had contrived his own disappearance. There was even a wild story that he had been a spy and had been spirited away by a Chinese submarine. All the government would say was that "there has been no indication that the disappearance of the late Mr. Holt was anything other than accidental" and that "his last movements followed a routine domestic pattern, his demeanour had been normal, and despite his knowledge of the beach, the turbulent conditions (high winds, rough seas and rip tides) overcame him."

Investigators said that his body was not found because it had been carried out to sea, or had become wedged in rocks, or that the body was lost during "an attack by marine life." Officially, no one said he had been taken by a shark. But there had been that "something pink in the water," and everybody knew that sharks in Australia have a habit of swimming off with the body, or part of the body.

Four months before Holt's disappearance, a shark— probably a great white, called by Australians a white pointer or a white death—had taken a spear fisher. The attack was in the waters of the state of Western Australia, near Jurien Bay, about 150 miles north of Perth, in the epicenter of western shark attacks. Twenty-four-year-old Robert Bartle had gone to Jurien Bay for a spearing competition with Lee Warner, a twenty-six-year-old fisherman, who, like Bartle, was a spear fisherman with an eye on the national championship. They had been in the murky water for about twenty minutes. Warner told the *Australian* what happened next:

"The shark came out of the blue like a rocket and grabbed him when we were about eight feet down. It moved so fast that by the time I looked back it had Bob in its mouth and was shaking him like a leaf. I dived straight down. It was directly below me. I put a spear in the top of its head, but it had no effect. The shark broke Bob in half and rose up at me.

"I only had an empty five-foot gun, and I tried to hit the shark in the eye. It began circling, keeping about eight feet away. Its body looked about five feet thick, and it was an enormous length. By now I was swimming in a cloud of blood."

Warner spotted Bartle's loaded spear gun and aimed for an eye. He missed. The shark kept circling him.

"I was stuck in this big cloud of blood," he continued. "I knew Bob was dead. . . . I swam backwards fast. The blood was obscuring my vision. After about ten yards I got out of the blood. From 150 yards I could look back and see the blood, and the shark. . . ."

Ashore, Warner got a boat and, with others, returned to the spot where he had seen the shark with Bartle's legs hanging from its jaws. They saw the rest of the body—and the shark, which slowly swam away.

That was one of the more than 560 recorded shark attacks during the nineteenth and twentieth centuries in Australian waters. The twenty-first century continued the grim record. During two deadly days in September 2000, along the coast of South Australia, sharks snatched two surfers. The first attack was off Black Point, near Elliston on the Eyre Peninsula. The surfboard was recovered, but the surfer's body was not found. The day before, a surfer was pulled off his surfboard by a white pointer at Cactus Beach, also in the state of South Australia. "I just saw a flash of red as the wave came over and then it was all over," a witness said. The surfer was on his honeymoon. Sharks struck fatally twice in November 2000, taking a diver clinging to his upturned boat off Ceduna, South Australia, and a swimmer in shallow water off Perth.

Australia's sharks are not just unseen shadows in the sea. They are a visible presence and have their own locally recognized season—along Australia's East Coast, the shark season usually runs from November to March, the southern summer. During the later months of summer and early autumn, warm ocean currents bring fish close to shore, followed by the sharks.

In the warm waters around Moreton Island, just off the Queensland capital of Brisbane, the pilchards (as Australians call sardines) come to spawn and the sharks come to feast. In some years so many sharks gather at Moreton Island that the beaches must be cleared of people. The sharks slash and slither in the shallows, their feeding frenzies churning the sea. White sharks live in the waters off six of Australia's six states. And, although the Northern Territory is not white shark territory, there have been attacks in those waters, especially off Cape York Peninsula, which juts into Torres Strait. Australian great whites were the sharks of *Jaws*, which did its real-shark filming off aptly named Dangerous Reef in the state of South Australia.

Dangerous sharks can be seen along much of Australia's coast, especially from the air. To keep an aerial eye on them, volunteers fly a shark patrol on weekends and holidays along popular beaches. When sharks are spotted, the flying lifeguards warn off the swimmers and buzz the sharks to drive them away. Often, though, people, especially surfers, do not heed the warnings. Once, the spotters saw eight sharks swimming in the breakers on beaches protected by nets. Surfers were warned, but placing their faith in the nets, they surfed on.

Recent research has analyzed modern attacks, showing that fifty-two of them were by great whites, and twenty-seven of those were fatal. In the United States, researchers have advanced a "bite-and-spit" thesis, noting that great whites often take a bite and swim off, leaving a victim wounded but alive. In the Australian analysis, 26 percent of the victims were consumed or taken away.[2] The other principal attackers—whalers and Australian nurse sharks—are about as deadly. In Australia, about one out of every three attacks ends in death. Worldwide, the fatality average is about 15 percent.

Elsewhere, particularly in the United States, swimmers are assured that shark-attack deaths are far, far more rare than deaths by lightning. That rhetoric does not work as well in Australia, where, in the 1980s, sharks killed eleven people, lightning killed nineteen people, and bees killed twenty, statistically putting all three causes at about the same degree of risk. (In 1977, when announcing Australia's decision to protect great whites, Environment Minister Robert Hill used the same bees-and-lightning mantra.)

In terms of sharks, bees, and lightning, there was no reason to believe that the twenty-first century would be any different than the previous one. But Australian officials certainly hoped so, because the Olympic Games were coming to Sydney in 2000. Sydney's vast and picturesque harbor would be the site for Olympic sailing events and the swim leg of the Olympic triathlon.

But, on one of the final days of the twentieth century, Glen Cowdrey, a triathlon athlete, was on his surf ski, training off Sydney's Maroubra Beach, when a ten-foot Australian gray nurse shark knocked him into the water. Two other gray nurses hovered nearby. Calmly, Cowdrey returned to shore and reported the sharks. This set off an alarm that closed the beach, sent helicopters aloft to warn people and seek sharks, and created a public-relations nightmare for Olympic-minded officials.

Australians are used to seeing sharks and hearing about attacks. But after competitors from other countries read the globally reported attack, they were not as calm as Cowdrey—especially competitors from landlocked countries. Sydney Olympics officials announced that divers on underwater scooters would patrol the harbor during the Olympic test event at the 1,500-meter swim course in the Sydney Harbor. None of the competitors was taken.

Sydney's war against sharks traces back to the 1930s, when attacks stained the waters around the port. A great sweep of land and estuaries form one of the world's great natural harbors. It is also an alluring place for dangerous sharks.

There had been terrible days in the days before nets. There seemed to be no way to ward off the sharks, let alone understand their ways. In 1919, about the time surfing began to sweep into Australia, Victor Coppleson, a Sydney surgeon, began a study of attacks, particularly in his city. As he pieced together what would become the earliest long-term record of shark attacks, he found clusters of attacks around Sydney, including six fatal and two non-fatal attacks at the city's most popular beaches.[3]

A double attack, for example, came two days before Christmas 1934, at Brisbane Water, a boating and swimming vacation spot north of Sydney. Fourteen-year-old Roy Inman dived from a jetty in front of the cottage where his family was staying. He was following his twelve-year-old sister, Joyce, who had dived in moments before. At that instant, Joyce screamed. A shark was streaking toward her. She kicked vigorously, and felt a sharp pain from the shark's abrasive hide as it sped past her and took her brother. His head appeared for a moment and he was able to scream. His mother, sitting on the cottage porch, saw him go down in reddening water.

Roy's twenty-six-year-old sister, Kathleen, ran to a boat and pushed off toward her brother. Joyce was swimming to the jetty. She saw her brother—and then the shark, which struck Roy again, carrying him off. She kept poking the oar into the water, hoping to strike the shark and force it to release her brother. Finally, she had to give up.

"Roy was seized by the monster and it dragged him down," she told the Sydney Morning Herald. "Before I reached him the shark had grabbed him again and pulled him below the water. It was terrible. The boat was right over the shark and it was just covered with blood. It disappeared. I did not see it again. Other boats came over, but we could not find him."

Coppleson believed that "rogue" sharks were responsible for the clusters of attacks in Sydney. Attacks, he noted, were occurring in sequence. He felt that the theory that best fit the facts he found was that each cluster was the work of a rogue shark that had staked out a stretch of shore and waited for its next victim. The idea paralleled the Raj India belief that tigers, after tasting human flesh, became rogue tigers that hunted exclusively for humans. Shark researchers of recent years have dismissed the rogue theory. But it prevailed in the 1930s, when the people of Sydney were looking for an explanation for the blight on their shores.

After a fatal attack at Bondi, one of Sydney's most popular beaches, a boat swept the waters for the rogue. Instead, the boat caught twenty-nine sharks off Bondi on a single day. One of them was a fourteen-foot tiger shark. It was caught in the first line of breakers, a favorite spot for surfers.[4] Sydney's problem was not rogue sharks; the problem was too many sharks.

Sydney officials set up a Shark Menace Advisory Committee, which recommended that a "systemic and continuous meshing programme" be inaugurated along Sydney's beaches. Critics called the meshing idea "a stupid, futile waste of money," and not until 1937 were the first anti-shark nets set up outside the breakers athwart the probable paths of sharks. From December 1, 1939, to

December 1, 1940, the nets snagged 751 sharks. The following year, 705 were caught. Sydney beaches had become safe
from sharks. Elsewhere, along unprotected beaches, sharks
took at least one swimmer a year.

During World War II, when no one could be spared to
mind the nets, the sharks returned.

For a January picnic in 1942, four people headed out in a
motorboat to Middle Harbor, moored near a landmark
known as Egg Rock, and had lunch on a rocky ledge along a
shallow shore. After lunch, three of the picnickers slipped
into the water, two staying close to shore. Zieta Steadman,
twenty-eight, ventured about ten feet out. One of her companions, Frederick Bowes, called to her, urging her not to go
out so far. As she turned toward shore, she suddenly
screamed and threw up her arms. From the boat, someone
saw what was happening and shouted, "Shark!"

Bowes grabbed an oar and tried to drive away the shark,
says the *Morning Herald* account of the next moments. The
shark, as it repeatedly struck Zieta Steadman, "was throwing
itself out of the water and lashing the surface with its tail."

Seeing the shark pulling its victim farther out, Bowes
jumped into the boat and headed for the shark, hoping to
ram it. The shark eluded the boat. Bowes left the tiller,
leaned over the side of the boat, and tugged Zieta by her
long black hair. Bowes, who weighed 210 pounds, "had to
use all his strength to free the upper part of the body. So
great was the force he had to exert that the young woman's
hair bit into his hands. He saw the remainder of the body
disappear into deep water."

Eleven months later, eight teenagers set out in two boats
for Ironstone Point, another picnic spot in Middle Harbor.
Denise Rosemary Burch, fifteen, was doing the dog paddle
in shallow water when she screamed and was dragged off by
a shark, whose jaws were clamped around her legs. One boy

grabbed an oar and tried to drive off the shark. Others threw sticks and stones. The shark disappeared as the remains of Denise's body floated to the surface.

Denise, her mother, and her sister had been evacuated from Hong Kong before the British colony fell to the Japanese in December 1941. Her father and brother were prisoners of the Japanese.

Sharks eluded the nets again in 1955 in two attacks within nineteen days. Off Balmoral Beach a gray nurse shark killed a teenager who was spear fishing. The next attack came nearby in Sugarloaf Bay when a shark struck a twenty-five-year-old swimmer, so ripping his legs that he bled to death in the water. The shark did not make a second strike. This was the eighth fatal attack in Sydney Harbor since 1919.

In January 1960 came another. Theo Brown was on the beach in Middle Harbor, near the Killarney picnic reserve. He was watching thirteen-year-old Ken Murray, who was diving in water about eighteen feet deep a short distance from shore. Brown saw the boy surface and rip off his facemask. Gasping, he did not answer to a hail. Then Brown saw something red spreading in the water. He screamed at Ken's brother Gary: "Keep out of the water! Ken's been attacked by a shark!"

At that moment, Brown later wrote, "Time ceased to exist. I didn't know I had moved until I was at Ken's side dragging him through the water and then onto the beach. The water was red with blood. Blood was streaming down the wet sand, and it seemed to be everywhere."[5]

The boy's right leg "had been torn away above the knee, and the shattered bone was protruding through the remaining flesh." Brown put Ken into a fisherman's boat and held a towel around him while the fisherman rowed to a boatshed, where an ambulance arrived. The boy survived for a week, finally succumbing when marrow, released from the shattered bone, formed a blood clot that lodged in the brain and shut down the respiratory system.

An attack that inspired new defenses against shark came during the Christmas-to-New Year's holidays in 1961. At Mackay, in Queensland, a shark took eighteen-year-old Margaret Hobbs, an eighteen-year-old schoolteacher who had gone to the beach with her fiancé, twenty-four-year-old Martyn Steffens. As the young man and woman stood in waist-deep water, a shark lunged at her, tearing off her right arm at the shoulder and, in another strike, her left arm above the wrist. In the fury of the attack, Stiffens, trying to aid Margaret, had his right hand mauled. His arm was amputated above the wrist in the same hospital where Margaret died after a desperate attempt to save her life. The double tragedy shocked the nation.

Along the Queensland coast, beaches closed and aircraft patrolled the deserted shore, reporting an unusually large shark presence close to the coast. Queensland and New South Wales—the states of Australia's east coast—were notorious as shark-attack country. The attacks on Margaret Hobbs and Martyn Steffens led to the hasty building of a defense network of anti-shark netting along Queensland beaches.

Sydney remained free of attacks until January 28, 1963, when, in a poignant sequel to the 1961 tragedy, another engaged couple encountered a shark. Marcia Hathaway, a Sydney actress, was standing in murky water thirty inches deep about twenty feet from shore in Middle Harbor. A shark, thrashing in the shallow water, took her by the right leg and turned, as if to pull her out to sea. Marcia's fiancé, Frederick Knight, grabbed the shark, straddled it and, with fists and kicks, fought to free her.

"The water was stained with blood, and I never thought I would get her away from it," Knight told the *Sydney*

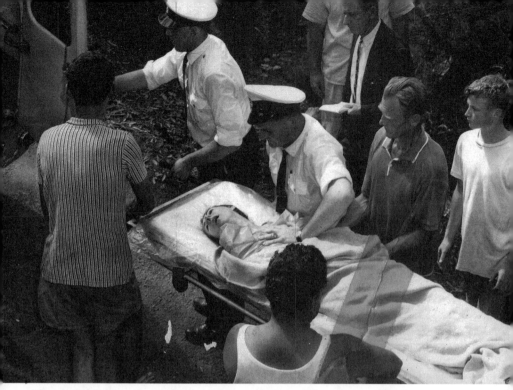

Marcia Hathaway after the attack in January 1963. Although she was in less than 30 inches of water, the shark nearly tore her right leg off, and she died from blood loss before reaching the hospital.   JOHN FAIRFAX HOLDINGS LTD

Morning Herald. "I think at one stage I had my foot in its mouth. It felt soft and spongy." Knight believed that the shark struck her leg twice, almost ripping it off. After a nightmare journey—from beach to rowboat to cruiser to land to an ambulance that broke down—she died before finally reaching a hospital.

The attack stunned Sydney, which had transformed itself from a city notorious for shark attacks to a citadel that protected people from sharks with an elaborate array of nets. All that could be done was to improve the nets and improve the warning system so people would leave when a shark was sighted.

Events in the run-up to the 2000 Olympic events showed that the nets and the warnings were not enough. First came the attack on the triathlon athlete. Then in March 2000 a shark knocked a woman out of her racing scull in Sydney water and, ignoring her, attacked the scull. The next day, nearby, a shark overturned a schoolboys' rowing scull and bit it, forcing the boys to swim to shore. No one was injured in the strange scull attacks. But a shark did bite a man on the leg while he was swimming at a beach near Sydney's luxury suburb of Mosman. A newspaper helpfully noted that a ten-foot whaler caught near Sydney years back had a large capacity. Its stomach contents reportedly included eight legs of mutton, half a ham, the hindquarters of a dog, and 300 pounds of horseflesh.

Then in July, on a beach on the Gold Coast north of Sydney, near "Surfers Paradise," a shark grabbed the leg tether of twenty-six-year-old Andrija Rojcezic, dragged him, bit him, and let him go. Rojcezic was surfing about 100 yards out to sea, away from a patrolled area, when the shark struck. Bleeding from a twelve-inch gash on his left calf, he screamed. A lifeguard raced out with a board, getting him medical aid in time to save his life. It was the first attack in thirty years along a shore whose beaches are lined with nets. Each year they snare about 150 sharks, mostly tigers and bronze whalers.

Hoping to head off panic, officials closed Gold Coast beaches, cancelled a junior surf carnival, and stopped a sand-pumping project that may have been improving the beaches but was also making the waters murky, a prime factor in attacks. The general manager of the Gold Coast Tourism Bureau gave his professional assessment of the attack: "It would appear to be that in the murky waters the shark has opened its mouth and found the leg of the odd surfer. As tragic as it is, it really is one of those freak occasions."

Meanwhile, to counter the shark publicity, Sydney Olympic officials commissioned a study by John Paxton of the Australian Museum and John West of the Taronga Zoo, which supervises the Australian Shark Attack File and contributes data to the International Shark Attack File. "Australia, and especially Sydney," said the report "have largely unwarranted reputations as high risk areas for shark attacks"—a remark that does not define high risk. Although the Paxton and West report said the risk of shark attack in the harbor was "virtually nil," it did list some protective measures that Olympic officials might want to consider, especially if there were a sudden rise in water temperature.

The suggestions clearly indicated what kind of defenses would be needed to try to make Sydney—or any other place in Australia—sharkproof. For example, commercial shark fishers would have to be commissioned to catch sharks in the area. This in a nation whose states have made the great white a protected species. Sharkproofing would also mean scuba divers wielding electric Protective Oceanic Devices (PODs—see Chapter 11) and inflatable boats with motors, presumably to lure sharks toward the electric fields set up by the motors.

In fact, there is no defense against sharks except common sense. The Australian Shark Attack File (ASAF) has developed several theories about shark attacks. These theories are basically in line with those developed by American researchers: "Some attacks may be purely an inquisitive testing of an object, some may be territorial, others may be related to the invasion of the shark's personal space by the human. Other theories include curiosity (i.e. just testing an object with their teeth to see if it is edible), or the shark may have been disrupted during its breeding behavior." And the ASAF promulgates rules that generally follow those laid down by American researchers.

In John West's exhaustive study of Australian great whites,[6] he mentions the two basic attack theories—"bite and spit" and "let it bleed to death"—and says that his statistics confirm neither thesis. More than half of the victims in his study received only one bite and in nearly 70 percent of the Australian attacks the shark did not return after its last (or only) bite.

Other researchers offer a chilling third theory: human beings are novelty food items.

Many times the body is not found after an Australian attack. As an example: Twenty-two-year-old Tony Donoghue went windsurfing in Hardwicke Bay, off Yoke Peninsula in South Australia, on May 29, 1999, and was never seen again. Searchers found a shredded wetsuit, scratched sailboard, and torn harness. "There's no doubt he was taken by a shark," a police spokesman said. In Australia, the lack of a body usually suggests devouring, not drowning.

George H. Burgess and Matthew Callahan of the International Shark Research File, in a worldwide study of white shark attacks,[7] noticed that in 32.8 percent of attacks the shark bit more than once—"including many instances in which victims were wholly consumed." Perhaps, they argue, "humans are treated somewhat differently than natural food items, because they are novelties in the domain of the white shark; as such, they may elicit more cautious secondary attack behavior." This gives the victim a chance for a frantic escape—into a boat, rescue by others, medical aid. Natural prey animals do not get that kind of a chance. "Another plausible explanation, which is also applicable to both hypotheses of predatory strategy," they continued, "is that we mainly are observing failed or poorly executed attacks on humans (or natural prey) when we see those that are released; those not released may represent successful attacks."

The sharks that attack people in Australia—whites, whalers, and tiger sharks—are big and extremely competent. One of the mysteries of Australian attacks is why these sharks don't kill far more people than they do.

A very unscientific explanation arises from stories about Australian survivors. Perhaps at least some of them are too tough to kill. The most famous survivor is an Australian diver, Rodney Fox, who was competing in a spear fishing tournament in 1963 off Aldinga Beach, about fifty-five miles south of Adelaide, when he felt jaws close on his chest and back, hurtling him through the water with the impact of the strike. He drove his fist at the shark's eyes. But his arm slipped into the shark's mouth, tearing his hand and arm to the bone. The shark swam off, then charged again. "I looked down and saw that great big jaw rising at me through a cloud of my own blood," Fox recalls. In the second strike, the shark pulled him down. When Fox bobbed to the surface, the shark lunged again, this time grabbing the fish line on his waist. When the line snapped, Fox was free.[8] (Contest rules later were changed so that divers no longer had to wear their shark-attractant fishes.) Someone in a boat, who noticed the blood in the water, came over and picked Fox up.

His thick neoprene wetsuit held in his guts. The shark had punctured a lung and ripped open his ribcage and stomach. The flesh had been stripped from his arm. It took 462 stitches to sew him back together. He lived to win the South Australian team spear-fishing championships again and become consultant to Steven Spielberg for the movie *Jaws*, supervising the filming that was done in Australia. He has devoted his life to studying and protecting great whites.

One of Fox's friends, Brian Rodgers, had been attacked by a great white off Aldinga Beach two years before. A shark closed its jaws on his left leg. Rodgers tried to hit the shark in the eye—a punch all Australian sea adventurers seem to know. But he missed, jamming his arm into the shark's mouth and tearing his arm open. The shark let go and swam off. Rodgers fired a spear into the shark's head and it swam off again, this time permanently. As he struggled to shore, a boat picked him up. With prompt surgical treatment and more than 200 stitches, he was saved.

In 1964, another Australian diver, twenty-nine-year-old Henri Bource, leader of a Melbourne rock 'n roll band, was diving off at Lady Julia Percy Island, a volcanic island near Port Fairy, at the tip of the state of Victoria. Bource, diving without scuba equipment, was swimming with the seals when they swiftly vanished. Seconds later, a great white hit him, pulling him down and ripping off his leg. The shark swam off.

"Suddenly there was a swirl of water and clouds of blood," another diver told the *Morning Herald*. "I heard Henri scream. Then I saw his leg floating in the water. It was the most horrifying sight of my life." People on the diving boat pulled him up. As someone applied a tourniquet, he managed to tell everyone his blood type, which was radioed to shore. Two physicians were waiting when the boat reached the dock.

He was soon back in the water. Four years later, another shark attacked again, only this time all the shark got was the artificial leg.

Not everyone is a survivor. A year before Rodney Fox bested a shark, sixteen-year-old Geoffrey Corner lingered in the water after other divers had left the water during an outing at Caracalinga Head, South Australia. As Corner swam along the surface, propelling himself with his swimming fins, a shark seized him. Witnesses said that the shark had been circling around other swimmers before the great white grabbed the boy's right leg, shook him violently, and abruptly released him. In one of several accounts of the attack, Jon Wadrop, said he and Brian Kennington, seeing blood spread on the dirty, wind-whipped water, swam from shore toward the blood.[9] About 100 to 200 yards out they found Corner. A physician who examined the body said the shark, in a single bite, had removed much of his right leg and slashed his left leg.

The awesome power of the great white's bite was gruesomely demonstrated in three attacks of unspeakable horror. In March 1985, thirty-three-year-old Shirley Ann Durdin was snorkeling for scallops with her husband, Barry, and a family friend, off a stretch of beach north of Port Lincoln, at the eastern edge of the Great Australian Bight. Abalone divers also worked in the area, where sharks were known to hunt.

The three were in water about seven feet deep and headed for shore, where her three sons and daughter watched them. Then she was gone. Fishermen set out in boats to find her. They saw her headless torso and, with a lunge, the shark took that. Her body was never found. She is one of the victims that in researcher John West's words, were "wholly consumed."

One day in June 1993, Theresa Cartwright, a national celebrity as the mother of six-year-old quadruplets, set out for the coast of Tasmania in a diving boat with her husband, the quadruplets, and her eleven-month-old baby. Accompanying the family were two other divers. They hoped to dive among the seals around King Island, about fifty miles off Tasmania. There are not many places on earth more isolated than that.

In the early nineteenth century, when the British maintained prison colonies on Tasmania, hardy prisoners managed to escape from a colony at the end of a narrow peninsula. They would slip into the sea, swim past the area patrolled by guards and watchdogs, then wade ashore and creep through the bush, eventually finding freedom at friendly hands. To stop the escapes, the governor of the colony ordered that garbage be dumped daily in the waters along the peninsula. Lured by the daily meals, sharks began to appear in the waters of the escape route. After prisoners learned the reason for screams in the night, the escape attempts stopped.

In modern times, Bass Strait, the 150-mile passage between the Australian mainland and Tasmania, was thought to be the southern limit of Australian shark attacks. In January 1959, a shark seized and killed a Royal Australian Navy sailor several hundred yards off Port Arthur in southeast Tasmania. Five days later, another attack was reported off Port Davey to the southwest. By 1963 there was no doubt that Tasmanian waters were dangerous. The seals there, as everywhere in the world, attract sharks. And there were seals aplenty around King Island. Only, divers said later, the seals were out of sight on the day that Theresa Cartwright went down. That is an ominous sign, as Henri Bource had learned.

Two divers had already reached the sea floor when Theresa Cartwright was still having some kind of trouble with her air supply. Finally, she did a backward roll off the boat and, after giving the OK sign, began to descend. No one knows exactly what happened next. Her husband saw a reddening cloud spread in the sea alongside the boat. Police later said that she had been torn in half.

In that same month of June 1993, another spouse was taken by a great white. John Ford, a thirty-one-year-old scuba diver on his honeymoon, was diving near Byron Bay, 400 miles north of Sydney, with his twenty-nine-year-old bride, Deborah, when a shark appeared. As the shark rocketed toward them, John Ford pushed his wife aside. The shark took Ford in its jaws and swam away.

A short time later, a fishing boat netted a sixteen-foot great white that rammed the boat several times and dragged it nearly four miles out to sea. As it broke free, it disgorged remains believed to have been John Ford.

Keeping Australia's sharks in perspective:

Human Deaths in Australia 1980–1990 inclusive

Activity	Total Deaths	Average/Year
Crocodile Attacks	8	0.7
Shark Attacks	11	1
Lightning Strikes	19	1.7
Bee Stings	20	1.8
Scuba Diving Accidents	88	8
Drownings/Submersions	3367	306
Motor Vehicle Accidents	32,772	2979[10]

Compared to fatalities from any other form of water-related activity, the number of fatal shark attacks, from all reported shark encounters in Australia, is extremely low. During the period 1968–1991, in New South Wales alone, 121 rock fishermen were swept off the rocks and drowned and thirty-seven surfboard riders drowned. In that same period, thirty-two shark encounters were recorded with only one fatality reported.

Attacks and Deaths by Region[10]

State	Total Attacks	Fatalities	Last Fatal Attack
New South Wales	211	69	1993 Byron Bay
Queensland	203	68	1992 Morton Island
Victoria	30	7	1977 Mornington Peninsula
South Australia	40	19	2000 Cactus Beach
Western Australia	51	10	1997 Geraldton
Northern Territory	10	3	1938 Bathhurst Island
Tasmania	18	8	1993 Tenth Island, Georgetown
Total	563	184	

155

CHAPTER 8

ATTACK:
In River and
Lake

About fifteen miles up the Ramu River, on the northwest coast of Papua New Guinea, a shark seizes and kills a teenage girl who is washing clothes at the riverside. Next day, a shark takes into its jaws a young man swimming across the same river. In a Mozambique river twelve miles from the sea, a fisherman works on his prawn net in five feet of water. Out of the water comes a shark that takes off an arm. When the fisherman falls, the shark takes off the man's head. In the Limpopo River a shark appears and carries off a swimmer. Forty miles up the Rewa River on the island of Suva in the Fijis, a shark attacks a group of waders.

And in Australian rivers–

157

In November 1921, Herbert Jack, carrying his eight-year-old son, George, on his back, wades out to his dinghy moored near a bank of the Bulimba Reach, a sweep of the Brisbane River in Brisbane, thirteen miles from the sea. Just one step from the dinghy, a shark grabs Jack's right hip. He beats the shark off and turns for the riverbank. The shark lunges again and Jack slashes his arm as he tries to fight it off. George slips from his father's back and, taken by the shark, disappears into the river, never to be seen again.

In January 1934, at East Hills, on the Georges River, in New South Wales, twenty miles from the sea, fifteen-year-old Wallace McCutcheon dives into the river to retrieve a tennis ball. As he swims back to shore, a shark hits him, but the force of the strike is not enough to injure the boy. When he reaches shore, his friends are screaming and pointing toward several large sharks that have ascended the river.

Nine months later, on New Year's Eve in 1934, nineteen-year-old Richard Soden is racing several other boys across the Georges River, about two miles upriver from East Hills. Soden, a strong swimmer, is in the lead. Suddenly, he disappears. The other boys see a large dorsal fin. Soden bobs to the surface and his friends pull him ashore. His left leg is so ripped open that he bleeds to death before they lay him on the riverbank.

Not quite four hours later, three miles upriver from where Soden was killed—some twenty-five miles from the sea—thirteen-year-old Beryl Morrin and several other children are playing in four feet of water no more than ten yards from the riverbank. Beryl screams and thrusts her arms out of the water. Both of her hands are gone. Swift application of tourniquets saves her life, but the shark's swift bite has so mutilated her arms that both must be amputated, one below the elbow, the other above.

The shark of the rivers is the bull shark, a large and formidable shark feared in the sea but little known as a marauder in lakes and rivers from Africa to the United States. Most of the world's isolated river and lake dwellers, who have always known and feared this shark, have had little contact with the world outside their villages. Not much, if anything, is reported in the Western media when an African woman vanishes while washing at a pool in the Zambezi, or an Indian bathing in the Ganges is never seen again. And few people in the West even realize that sharks can kill in rivers and lakes. River sharks are a very local peril. We know the names of the Australian victims because they lived in Australia. Elsewhere, there are no names in the reports that trickle out from the dark rivers.

For a long time no one knew about the river sharks. British medical officers, toiling at the ragged edges of Empire, discovered them during the Victorian era. Usually amateur naturalists as well as physicians, they saw the sharks as a scientific curiosity. They treated the sharks' victims and wrote the medical reports. Among them were people on the Hooghly River, a branch of the Ganges in northeastern India. In the *Indian Medical Gazette,* a physician reported in 1880: "At Pannihattu, Barrackpore, Dackhineshwar, Barahonagore, Kashipur, and Chitpur down to Baug Bazar Ghats more than 20 persons have been severely bitten by sharks this year. Almost all were fatal." Think of that litany of remote, unknown places; think of unchronicled attacks decade after decade; and wonder exactly how many times a year do bull sharks strike, not only along bleak seacoasts but also in the dark rivers of unnoticed lands. One estimate puts the number of unreported attacks in third-tier nations at 1,000, and many of these are riverine.[1]

One relatively recent report tells of the death of five people and the mauling of thirty others by sharks from July to

September 1959 near the mouth of the Devi River in northeast India. On the Ganges itself, there is no reliable count of attacks or deaths or desecrations. Sharks go up the Ganges to get easily obtained food. This consists mostly of corpses cast into the river for burial in sanctified waters. Sharks also regularly devour living men, women, and children. Pilgrims bathing in the sacred waters of the Ganges sometimes must fight off sharks during their devotions. Sharks have struck down as many as twenty river bathers in a single year, killing half of them.

The great naturalist of India, Frances Day, said in *The Fishes of India* (1878) that the river shark "seldom loses an opportunity of attacking the bather." Sharks "are found all along the coasts of India, but their carrying off of human prey is not a common occurrence. The most savage species appear to be the ground sharks of the river. . . . This is one of the most ferocious of Indian sharks, and frequently attacks bathers even in the Hooghly at Calcutta, where it is so dreaded that a reward is offered for each that is captured." One of the sparse records tells of four attacks on the Hooghly in a month; two unnamed Indians died and two survived. So prevalent were the Ganges River sharks that they were recognized as a species, *Carcharias gangeticus.* That name has been abandoned, for now we know the Ganges predators are only opportunistic bull sharks that have expanded their domain to include rivers and lakes.

At another outpost of empire in recent times, a British soldier stationed at Ahvāz, Iran, decided to wash his ambulance in the Karun River, ninety miles from the sea. He took off his shoes and socks and climbed down into the water, which was about a foot deep. As the soldier started to wash the ambulance, he felt something seize his right ankle and pull him off balance. Thrashing in rapidly reddening water shallower than a bathtub, the soldier began fighting for his

This picture, taken in 1901, is thought to be one of the only images of a shark attack in existence. Though not verified, the reactions of the onlookers give credence to the photo's authenticity.

life against a shark. He lashed out with his fists and was bitten repeatedly. Then, as suddenly as it had appeared, the shark disappeared, leaving behind a man with a gouged right leg, his right arm torn open, his left hand and forearm raked by the shark's sandpapery hide.

That British soldier was one of twenty-seven men, women, and children attacked in the Karun River near Ahvāz from 1941 to 1949. The brief records (preserved in the epic 1963 worldwide list of Leonard P. Schultz and Marilyn H. Malin) show that a fisherman died near Ahvāz, and that an anonymous Gurkha soldier, fighting with an unnamed British unit, survived an attack at the junction of the Tigris and the Euphrates.

During that record-keeping period, Allied military authorities maintained one of the earliest sequential records of
riverine attacks in an isolated area. The records showed that
about half of the Karum attacks were fatal. Most of them
began just as with the ambush of the soldier: a lunge at the
ankles in very shallow water, close to shore. The record of
attacks in the 1940s is buttressed in a report on fishes of the
Persian Gulf, by H. Blegvad, a Danish marine biologist:
"Every year several people, especially children, fall victims
to these sharks. I think the big sharks do not find the same
abundance of food in the rivers as in the sea; this may ex-
plain why they are more voracious in the fresh water than in
the sea, where the pearl divers do not fear the sharks."

The Karun River, like the shark-prowled Euphrates and
Tigris, empties into the northern end of the Persian Gulf. A
pelagic shark would have to travel from the Arabian Sea, up
the Gulf of Oman, into the Persian Gulf, then across the
Persian Gulf and up the mouth of the Karun just to begin its
journey to Ahvāz. But the sharks of the rivers appear to be
longtime residents, objects of legends and even worship. In
Baghdad, some 350 miles from the sea, legend says sharks
come to feast upon the city's melons. In Khorramshahr, below Ahvāz on the Karun, the story goes that the sharks linger
under the date palms to eat the dates falling from the trees.

The shark is one of the powers of Lord Krishna:

I am the Divine Life Spark, in all beings. I am the
Creator, the Protector and the Destroyer of all
Beings. I am Vishnu among the Twelve Adityas, the
Sun among the luminaries, Indra among the Gods,
Mind among the senses, Intellect among the beings,
the Ocean among the reservoirs of water, OM among
words, Time among the instruments of measure-
ment, Lion among the beasts, Shark among the

fishes, the Ganges among the rivers, the Beginning, the Middle and the End of all Created Things. (*The Bhagavad-Geeta*, Chapter 10)

There is nothing mythical about the river travels of the bull shark, the only shark species known to live in the salt water of the sea, the brackish water of estuaries and river mouths, and the fresh waters of rivers and lakes. Bull sharks have been spotted hundreds of miles up the Mississippi River and in the Atchafalya River of Louisiana.

A large shark washed up near Marlboro, New York, in 1925, apparently the victim of a steamboat hit-and-run. The shark was not identified at the time; it may have been a bull. Eight years later, New York City police put its own force on shark alert and sent a warning to communities along the Hudson as far north as Poughkeepsie. The alarm followed the sighting of at least one shark by several fishermen in the Hudson, six blocks west of Times Square. Apparently there are enough fish to keep the bull sharks in U.S. rivers on a non-human diet, for there are no significant modern reports of attacks in American rivers.

In the summer of 1960, so many sharks were reported in the Delaware River that Delaware state police patrolled river beaches, warning startled swimmers and water-skiers to get out of the water. At least one shark, a seven footer, was caught off New Castle, Delaware, about thirty miles from the mouth of the river. It was not identified, but it probably was a bull. Bull sharks have been caught in the Chesapeake Bay, one at the mouth of the Patuxent River. In the United States, bull sharks are suspects in attacks close to shore along Florida's east coast, where they happen upon human legs and arms while pursuing schools of food fish. They have been seen far inland in the roadside canals of south central Florida, and in Tampa Bay on Florida's Gulf coast.

Bull sharks with various local names have been found in the Miraflores Locks of the Panama Canal, where the waters of numerous lakes mingle with the waters of two oceans, in Guatemala's Lake Izabal and Rio Dulce, in Lake Maracaibo in Venezuela, in many east coast rivers in Central America, and as far as 2,400 miles from the sea in the Amazon River system. In Asia, bull sharks live in the Saigon River of Vietnam, the Perak River in Malaya, and in lakes and rivers of the Philippines and Fiji Islands.

In Africa, where the bull is called the river shark or the Zambezi River shark, it is known as a killer of crocodiles and hippopotami, and it is rightfully feared along many rivers hundreds of miles from the sea. Attacks on swimmers, once attributed to the great white shark, were undoubtedly made by Zambezi sharks. In a six-month period during 1961 bull sharks were blamed for three attacks in the mouth of the Limpopo River and another 150 miles up the river. An entry in Schultz's list gives a location on the Limpopo for an attack on "child (African)," who survived.

River-dwelling sharks, assigned to the genus Glyphis, are among the rarest of sharks. A Glyphis found in the Ganges River grows to seven feet and has been blamed for attacks that may well have been made by bull sharks. In 1997, researchers[2] found a Glyphis of unknown species in the Kinabatangan River in Northern Borneo. Until that fish turned up, Leonard Compagno, curator of fishes and head of the Shark Research Center at the South African Museum, could only examine a few museum specimens, most of them collected in the nineteenth century. "We have very little idea of the geographic distribution of these sharks, much less their general biology," he said. "They show up like ghosts, few and far between, in a handful of scattered localities." Among those localities are the lakes and rivers of Malaysia, Thailand, and Borneo, all places where attacks have been reported. Until more is learned about the Glyphis sharks, however, bull sharks will continue to get the blame.

Lake Nicaragua, the vast lake of that Central American country, has a breed of sharks notorious for attacks on people who live along the lake's shores. The sharks are looked upon locally as sharks unique to the lake, killers that take at least one swimmer or wader or fisherman a year. Villagers say that every family along the lake has lost at least one member to the shark. In a poor nation ravaged by hurricanes and torn by a long civil war, the death of an occasional lake dweller is left unrecorded. So there are no recent reports of attacks. In the spring of 1944, a single shark attacked three persons near Granada, the lake's principal town. Two of the victims died. Numerous dogs have been devoured by the sharks, which are locally renowned for their voracious appetites. Fishermen say the sharks will readily seize meat bait.

In the 1940s and 1950s, when there was a great demand for shark-liver oil and shark hides, Lake Nicaragua fishermen caught countless thousands of sharks. A woman who caught sharks for a living reported in 1953 a catch of 2,008 in six months. A fisherman at the same time told of catching nearly 7,000 in eight months. The men, workers in the region's only industry, went out in dugout canoes with hand lines and caught sharks six or seven feet long weighing 200 or 300 pounds. Many fishermen did not come back.

The shark boom ended when demand for oil and shark leather slackened. The sharks may also have been fished out. A new market—fins for shark-fin soup—revived the shark industry in recent years. But it is a chancy trade, pitting desperate men against fewer and fewer ferocious sharks.[3]

The sharks have been known for centuries, but only in recent years has the mystery of their freshwater existence been solved. A Spanish historian in 1526 wrote about them, these puzzling oceanic sharks in a seemingly landlocked lake. Ephraim G. Squier, an editor, diplomat, and archaeologist who went to Nicaragua in 1849 as U.S. *chargé d'affaires* to Central America, said the sharks abounded in the lake. "They are called 'tigrones' from their rapacity," he wrote. "Instances are known of their having attacked and killed bathers within a stone's throw of the beach at Granada, and I myself have repeatedly seen them from the walls of the old castle, dashing about, with their fins projecting above the water." In their encyclopedic study of the shark, *Fishes of the Western North Atlantic,* ichthyologists Henry B. Bigelow and William C. Schroeder in 1948 confirmed the existence of the shark, which, they wrote, is "reputedly a danger to bathers, as well as to any dog that may venture into the lake." They cited reports of fatal attacks in which victims lost legs and arms.[4]

The lake shark was given the scientific name *Carcharhinus nicaraguensis,* on the assumption that, while it resembled the bull shark (*C. leucas*), in its landlocked existence it had to be an individual species. Over the years, geologists and biologists worked on theories about the way sharks could get into Lake Nicaragua. Now most scientists believe that the huge lake— 45 miles wide at its widest and 110 miles long—does indeed have a pathway to the sea via the winding, rapids-laced, 130-mile-long San Juan River, which flows into the Caribbean on the eastern coast of Nicaragua. There are sharks in both the San Juan and the lake. Local people distinguish them as *visiantes,* white-bellied visitors from the sea, and *tintoreros,* "dyers" because they have brownish bellies from life in the lake.

A close shark relative, a sawfish of indeterminate species (genus Pristis) also lives in Lake Nicaragua. It has a narrow, elongated snout that looks like saws with wide-spaced teeth.

The sawfish wields its weapon to snare fish, not people, as far as is known.

There is a story told around the shores of Lake Nicaragua. Long ago, after elaborate funeral ceremonies, Indians once hurled bodies into the lake, bedecked in jewels and gold ornaments. They were consigned to the sharks, apparently to appease them, for their voracious appetites were as well known then as now. A Dutchman fished for the sharks, ripped them open, and stole the sacred sacrificial jewelry and gold. He had harvested a fortune, so the story goes, by the time the Indians discovered his desecrations and killed him. His body was not thrown to the sharks, of course. He was not good enough for that. Instead, the Indians set fire to his house and cut his throat, adding to the victims of the Lake Nicaragua sharks.[5]

CHAPTER 9

ATTACK at Sea

I t is one of the grimmest reports in the battle-action archives of the U.S. Navy: "All bodies were in extremely bad condition and had been dead for an estimated 4 or 5 days. Some had life jackets and life belts, most had nothing. Most of the bodies were completely naked, and others had just drawers or dungaree trousers on—only three of the 28 bodies recovered had shirts on. Bodies were horribly bloated and decomposed—recognition of faces would have been impossible. About half the bodies were shark-bitten, some to such a degree that they more nearly resembled skeletons."

The report was written by the commanding officer of the U.S.S. *Helm,* a destroyer that sailed into bloodstained waters and snatched from the jaws of sharks the bodies and the survivors of the cruiser *Indianapolis.* Her legacy is not only what she did in World War II but what was done to her men by sharks.

On July 16, 1945, the *Indianapolis* departed San Francisco for a ten-day, 5,000-mile voyage. Traveling unescorted, she carried components for the first atomic bombs to the U.S. base at Tinian, the takeoff point for the dropping of the atomic bombs on Hiroshima and Nagasaki. After unloading her cargo, on July 28, again sailing alone, she made a brief call at Guam and then headed westward for Leyte in the Philippines. At 12:15 A.M. on July 30, two torpedoes, fired by a Japanese submarine, struck her. She capsized and sank within minutes. There was no time to send an SOS. In those few moments, hundreds of survivors managed to plunge into the oil-slicked water.[1]

Of the more than 1,190 men aboard, about 880—many of them badly burned, maimed, and wounded—made it alive into the sea in the early minutes of Monday, July 30. One of the men in the water, Woody James, a twenty-two-year-old sailor from Alabama, remembered that at first the sharks merely circled around, not striking anyone in his group. That was July 30, the first day, when the men in the water thought that help was inevitably on its way. Neither he nor any other survivors knew that U.S. Navy officials at Guam and Leyte did not realize that the *Indianapolis* was missing. The men—and the sharks—would be in the water for a long nightmare.

Another man in the water, Patrick Finneran,[2] told what came with the dawn: "One by one sharks began to pick off the men on the outer perimeter of the clustered groups. Agonizing screams filled the air day and night. Blood mixed with the fuel oil. . . . It was a terror-filled ordeal—never knowing if you'd be the next victim." Survivors said they saw sharks by the hundreds, most of them swimming just below their feet, some of them rising to take a victim.

Both James and Finneran remember the third day, Wednesday, August 1, most of all. Numerous sharks—hundreds, by several estimates—swam amid the men, dorsal fins cutting through the blinding sun-glare of the oil. "By the third day," Finneran later wrote, "lack of water and food, combined with the unrelenting terror, began to take its ef-

170

fect on the mental stability of the men. Many began to hallucinate. Some, many who had taken in seawater, went slowly mad. Fights broke out. Hope faded."

"You'd hear guys scream, especially late in the afternoon," James remembered. "Seemed like the sharks were the worst late in the afternoon. . . . Then they fed at night too. Everything would be quiet and then you'd hear somebody scream and you knew a shark had got him."

By then, men around him were fighting and "going berserk." So he and a buddy tied their life jackets together and "kind of drifted off by ourselves."

On the fourth day, Thursday, August 2, the sharks were among them still. Many survivors clustered in groups, knowing now that the sharks picked off loners. The sharks also took the easiest prey, the corpses. Survivor manuals, if anyone could remember them in the delirium of blinding sun and desperate thirst, said it was safer to remain still. *But would that make you look like a corpse? Or did the manual say you should fight the sharks when they came close?* When they had the strength for it, men did kick and splash when a shark came into view. And, in a swift, sensible assessment of shark behavior, men kept together. Those who swam off were doomed to drown or be eaten.

At first, men took precious lifejackets off the corpses and pushed them off as lures for the sharks. As their strength waned, they were too weak to dispatch the corpses. And so the sharks kept coming among them, taking the living with the dead. Oil still covered everyone, but as the sea carried off patches of oil, men could look into the clear water and see the sharks swimming beneath their feet.

During the night, and now during the day, men were swimming off to die, sometimes in the jaws of a shark, sometimes because their minds and bodies had surrendered to the sea. At dawn one man noticed another floating down facefirst in his lifejacket. The sailor nudged him, thinking he was asleep. The head and torso flipped over. From the waist down there was nothing.

Later that morning, a Navy aircraft on routine patrol spotted some survivors. Thinking that a plane had gone down, the patrol craft radioed for a rescue craft to drop life rafts and set up a recovery operation. No one at the Navy's two Pacific headquarters yet officially knew that the *Indianapolis* had gone down and that there were hundreds of men in the sea. Responding to the rescue call late on the afternoon of August 2, Lt. Robert A. Marks, flying a Catalina PBY, spotted a long oil slick and many black, bobbing heads. He took the amphibious aircraft down to about 100 feet and began dropping life rafts. Then one of his crewmen saw sharks attacking the men in bloodstained water and shouted the news to Marks. He knew he had to save those men immediately.

PBYs were not rated to land in heavy seas. But he went into a power-on stall—tail low, nose high to keep the propellers from churning the waves—and put the plane down between swells, popping a couple of hull rivets. Sharks were attacking nearby men as Marks wove through the clusters, picking up the loners he judged to be most vulnerable. Men died swimming to the plane, but it slowly filled, and men were lashed to its wings. By nightfall, Marks's PBY had fifty-six survivors in it and on it.

Shortly after midnight, the destroyer *Doyle* arrived and took Marks' men on board. Other ships were arriving. The rescue of the *Indianapolis'* men had begun, on the fifth day of their ordeal. One of those ships was the destroyer *Helm*. At dawn, when the *Helm*'s men began looking for survivors, they saw that the sharks were still there.

"From one to four sharks were in the immediate area of the ship at all times," the *Helm* report says. "At one time, two sharks were attacking a body not more than fifty yards from the ship, and continued to do so until driven off by rifle fire."

The *Helm* was recovering not just the occasional survivor but body after body. "For the most part," the report says, "it was impossible to get finger prints from the bodies as the skin had come off the hands or the hands lacerated by sharks. Skin was removed from the hands of bodies containing no identification, when possible, and the Medical Officer dehydrated the skin in an attempt to make legible prints. All personal effects removed from the bodies for purposes of identification, and the Medical Officer's Reports are forwarded herewith in lieu of the Bureau of Medicine and Surgery and the Personal Effects Distribution Center, Farragut, Idaho, on the assumption that such effects will be assembled from all ships recovering them. After examination, all bodies were sunk, using two inch line and a weight of three 5"/38 cal. projectiles. There were still more bodies in the area when darkness brought a close to the gruesome operations for the day. In all, twenty-eight bodies were examined and sunk."

The destroyer *French* made a similar report about the bodies: ". . . appeared to have been partially eaten by sharks . . . very badly mutilated by sharks . . . Body clad in dungaree trousers only. Badly mangled by sharks . . ." The search went on for six days. Of the 800 men who had gone into the water after the sinking, 318 had survived, and two of them would die soon after rescue.[3]

The "shark-infested Pacific," as war correspondents inevitably referred to that theater of war, was indeed well sharked, with at least 150 species, not including bottom-dwellers. The deep water where most survivors found themselves is the habitat of one of those species, the oceanic whitetip shark (*Carcharhinus longimanus*). Whitetips, large and aggressive, are the chief suspects when survivors disappear at sea. Whitetips live in deep water, prefer seas with temperatures around 70 degrees, and are rarely found near land (except for mid-ocean islands like Hawaii). There are probably more whitetips in the sea than any other species of large sharks. Blue sharks may out number them in places. No one knows the true population size of either species.

Whitetips are persistent predators, reluctant to leave a potential meal. Two eminent shark researchers cited their personal experience with the whitetip's stubborn attitude: "Once, while bailing bloody water from a dory, we time after time hit an attracted whitetip on the head with an oar. This backed it off a few feet, but it would soon again swim up to the dory and get another drubbing."[4]

Reports of shark attacks came sometimes, but not always, after the sinking of a U.S. warship in the Pacific. Such reports followed a battle off the Savo Islands, for example. In that battle, Japanese warships sank three U.S. heavy cruisers and one Australian heavy cruiser in less than an hour on the night of August 8–9, 1942; a badly damaged U.S. destroyer went down after an air attack on August 9. More than 1,500 men were lost. Sharks killed countless survivors in the oil-covered water.[5] After the Savo battle, lookouts aboard the destroyer *McCalla,* searching for survivors, noticed that bright aluminum powder cans, being used as lifebuoys, were luring sharks. Crewmen drove off the sharks with rifle fire.

After the torpedoed cruiser *Juneau* sunk off Guadalcanal on November 13, 1942, a shocked nation learned that the dead included five brothers. The five Sullivans, united in heroic death, became a symbol of patriotism at war bond rallies. But what happened to the *Juneau*'s men was not fully disclosed. Four of the Sullivans did go down with their ship, along with about 600 of the some 700 men aboard. The eldest brother, George, was one of about 100 men who went over the side and awaited rescue. But, like the men of the *Indianapolis*, the *Juneau* survivors faced a long ordeal. For eight days, sharks picked off man after man. No one knows who died of what, but George Sullivan almost certainly was taken, dead or alive, by a shark. When rescue ships arrived eight days after the sinking, they found ten survivors. The sharks were still there.

Reports of sharks did not follow the battle of Okinawa in April 1945, when Japanese kamikaze bombers sank dozens of ships and sent hundreds of men into the sea. Those waters, far to the north and west of battles earlier in the war, may not have been hospitable to whitetips. But sharks—among them tiger sharks and great whites—abound around Guadalcanal, Savo, and other islands of the Solomons. Native people long had worshiped sharks, made myths of their behavior, and often offered their dead to the sharks that lived in the islands. Presenting the dead to sharks was a chilling precedent for the taking of wartime dead.

Sharks still are a natural part of life in the Solomons. When the Solomon Islands became independent in 1978, the nation's new green and blue flag was emblazoned with frigate birds, a crocodile, and a shark.

Elsewhere in the seas of World War II, sharks frequently added their victims to the casualties of war. On November 28, 1942, a German U-boat torpedoed the troopship *Nova Scotia* in the Indian Ocean off South Africa. Most of the 1,000 men aboard safely abandoned ship. But they floated close to a shore notorious for shark attacks. Only 192 men survived, and many of the recovered bodies were legless. One of the survivors told David H. Davies, an authority on South African sharks, how one of the men died:

"... he suddenly screamed and the upper part of his body rose out of the water. He fell back and I saw that the water had become red with blood and that his foot had been bitten off. At this moment, I saw the grey form of a shark swimming excitedly around and I paddled away as fast as I could."

In the South Pacific, after a Japanese submarine torpedoed the troopship *Cape San Juan* in the South Pacific on November 11, 1943, no one knows how many went over the side before the ship sank. Of the more than 1,400 men aboard, most should have been able to leap into the sea after the torpedoes hit. When the merchantman *Edwin T. Meridith* arrived, crewmen saw countless sharks attacking men on life-rafts. "Time after time," a *Meredith* crewman later said, "I heard soldiers scream as the sharks swept them off the rafts. Sometimes the sharks attacked survivors who were being hauled to the *Meredith* with life ropes." A soldier who survived recalled, "I was sitting on the edge of a raft talking to my buddy in the darkness. I looked away for a moment, and when I turned back, he wasn't there anymore. A shark got him." Rescuers picked up 448 survivors. No one will ever know how many the sharks got.[6]

Leonard P. Schultz and Marilyn H. Malin, in their comprehensive worldwide list of shark attacks,[7] devote a section to air and sea disasters, which lists the *Nova Scotia* and other ships lost in action and stalked by sharks. Among the sources for the Schultz-Malin list were the files of the U.S. Coast Guard's Search and Rescue Agency, which compiled eyewitness reports of shark encounters. One tells of a Navy pilot who ditched his aircraft in the central Pacific. Soon after the pilot and his radioman hit the water, sharks appeared. As they floated in their lifejackets, a shark seized the radioman's right foot. From the pilot's report in the files:

"I told him to get on my back and keep his right foot out of the water, but, before he could, the shark struck again, and we were both jerked under water for a second. I knew that we were in for it as there were more than five sharks around us and blood all around us.

"He showed me his leg and not only did he have bites all over his right leg but his left thigh was badly mauled. He wasn't in any particular pain except every time they struck I knew it and felt the jerk. I finally grabbed my binoculars and started swinging them at the passing sharks.

"It was a matter of seconds when they struck again. We both went under and this time I found myself separated [from the radioman]. . . . I was also the recipient of a wallop across the cheek bone by one of the flaying tails of a shark. From that moment on I watched [the radioman] bob about from attacks. His head was under water and his body jerked as the sharks struck it. As I drifted away . . . sharks continually swam about and every now and then I could feel one with my foot. At midnight I sighted a [U.S. patrol] boat and was rescued after calling for help."

U.S. soldiers, sailors, and airmen went to war in the Pacific with little knowledge of shark perils. An advisory to naval airmen told them that sharks "constitute a negligible danger to Navy personnel." In 1994, the Navy issued *Shark Sense,* a pamphlet that said, "There is very little danger from sharks." Fear of the shark, said the pamphlet, "has originated because of wild and unfounded tales"—a hearkening back to the beliefs prior to the New Jersey attacks of 1916. The advice was incredibly wrong:

"Remember that the shark strikes with his mouth opened wide, and his vision blocked. If you can avoid his mouth by moving a foot or so out of his path, it is a miss for the shark . . . If you can attach yourself to him by grabbing a fin, when he turns for another attack, you aren't there; you are riding with him, behind his mouth and out of danger from his teeth. Hold tight and hang on as long as you can without drowning yourself. In the meantime, after missing his target, the shark may lose his viciousness and become his usual cowardly self."

George A. Llano, a U.S. Air Force research specialist who himself was a life-raft survivor, made a study of airmen who went down at sea during the war.[8] Of 2,500 reports, only thirty-eight mentioned contacts with sharks. But, as Llano remarked, "When sharks are successful, they leave no evidence, and the number of missing airmen who may have succumbed to them cannot be estimated. . . . Men have spent hours in the water among sharks without being touched, and in view of the evidence some of the escapes seem little short of miraculous. The one feature all accounts illustrate is the fact that, though clothing cannot be depended on to prevent attack, sharks are more apt to bite a bare than a clothed body."

Fear of sharks, whether the Navy believed in it or not, forced Navy officials to seek a shark repellent, a search that still goes on. And servicemen still occasionally find themselves amid sharks. In 1995, for instance, a Marine fell from the aircraft carrier *America* and spent thirty-six hours amid sharks of the Arabian Sea. He said that sharks bit at his fingers and toes but did not do any substantial damage. One wonders what kind of sharks he had met.

After World War II, as surfing, diving, and boating became increasingly popular, sharks kept doing what they had always done: feeding on prey. Now sharks were sensing—and sometimes coming into contact with—more members of a relatively rare prey species, human beings. For many human beings who were voluntarily in the water, as divers or surfers, swimming with sharks became, if not routine, then at least a sporadic thrill. Other human beings, safely in boats, did not expect such thrills. But the unexpected happened, and shark researchers are trying to find out why.

Shark attacks on boats have been going on for a long time. The 1963 Schultz-Malin list has a category on boat attacks, with entries going back to 1804. Some are intriguingly cryptic: "Canoe pushed 100 yards" or "6 sharks attacked" or "two boys; boat lifted a foot out of water" or "10-foot boat: attacked 20 times" or "Sailboat capsized, 3 persons drowned."

One of the incidents was reported in 1953 by John MacLeod, a lobsterman, who said that a shark had smashed his white dory off the southeastern coast of Canada's Cape Breton Island. MacLeod had been found clinging to the wreckage of the shattered dory. A fellow lobsterman, John Burns, had drowned. MacLeod said a white shark that had been following the dory suddenly pounced, smashing an eight-inch hole in the bottom of the hull and throwing both men into the sea. The shark swam on, leaving behind a tooth imbedded in a splintered board. William C. Schroeder, of the Museum of Comparative Zoology and the Woods Hole Oceanographic Institution, confirmed the story by identifying the tooth: It came from a white shark about twelve feet long and weighing 1,100 to 1,200 pounds.

An amazingly similar attack was reported from Florida in 1959. A boatman was sailing through water about eight to ten feet deep when a shark started circling him. "It was a flat, calm day and he could look up and see me clearly," the man reported. "Suddenly, he swam off about twenty or thirty feet and turned extremely fast back to the boat. He hit the boat right in the center and lifted the rear end clear out of the water. I have no doubt that he tried to knock me overboard." The boat owner said the rammer, which he identified as a tiger shark, ripped away a piece of fiberglass and wood about one foot in diameter.[9]

During a 1998 fishing trip off the Adriatic coast of Senigallia, Stefano Catalani caught a sand shark and strapped it to the side of the boat, a thirty-foot cabin cruiser. Then, he later recounted, "All at once, I saw this large greyish fin." A great white first gobbled down a metal bait container attached to the boat. Next, it ate the sand shark and began circling the boat as if it was the next target. Catalani sped for shore. Next day—after Catalani's video of the encounter appeared on Italian television—authorities shut down beaches along thirty miles of the coast. It was the first time in memory that a great white had been seen in the Adriatic. A year later, an Italian fisherman reported a similar attack in the Adriatic. He said he had just caught a tuna when a great white shark appeared, ate the tuna, and began to attack the boat. "It looked like an elephant," he said. "In thirty years as a fisherman, I've never seen anything like it. I shot at it with a spear gun. But the dart just bounced off its skin." The shark ceased the attack and swam off.

In South Africa, sharks have leaped into boats, charged boats, and stopped at least one boat with a suicidal bite on the whirring propeller. In February 1974, while a shark fisherman Danie Schoeman was looking for great whites in False Bay, sharks attacked his fifteen-foot boat five times. The first attacker jumped into the boat. Schoeman killed it with a lance. Two weeks later, a shark about the length of the boat charged and holed the boat above the waterline. Schoeman threw over a line baited with a small shark, and quickly hooked the big one. The infuriated shark dragged the boat for an hour and ten minutes, then turned and darted under the boat, rocking it violently in what turned out to be a death throe.

The third attack came in March 1974 when a shark banged the boat, putting another hole in it. In November 1976 a hooked sixteen footer dove, came up under the boat, and hit it so hard that the boat's stern rose nearly a foot above the sea. The shark chomped down on the transom, spitting out wood and fiberglass before Schoeman boated it. Schoeman also caught the fifth attacker, but only after it took another bite out of his scarred boat.[10]

In March 1982 a shark stopped a ninety-foot boat operated by the National Oceanic and Atmospheric Administration. While the boat was off Jacksonville, Florida, the shark started chasing it and finally slammed into the rudder, killing itself by tasting the port propeller. Another killed itself off the Isle of Wight when it hurled itself into a twenty-three-foot fishing boat. "It turned towards the boat and dived," a man who was in the boat told the *Times* of London. "Everything was quiet for a moment, and we thought it had swum away. Then there was a great rushing noise and suddenly the shark came surging out of the water about five yards away. It landed across the boat, which is only nine feet wide, so its head and tail were sticking over each side. The impact nearly sank the boat and it killed the shark outright."

Attack records include many incidents involving divers, particularly people who dive off boats. Sharks have been known to follow or seemingly stalk boats, perhaps because of the refuse that is tossed overboard. A sudden splash attracts stalking sharks—a good reason to be extremely vigilant when swimming off a boat. A Florida father who was diving with his children in Tampa Bay 1991 learned this lesson. Rick LeProvost and his three children were hanging onto a rope tied to the stern of a sailboat, playing a game he described as "jump off the boat and swim to Daddy." Suddenly, a shark grabbed his left thigh and tried to pull him under. His life vest probably kept him on the surface long enough to scream at his children to get into the boat and then get aboard himself.

"I got in the boat and lay on the deck. There was blood everywhere. I was lying there and I could just see over the side. I could see the shark just under the water, circling the boat," he told the *Petersburg Times*. He believed that the shark was waiting for the prey it had just tasted.

LeProvost and his sailing companion were both paramedics. So first aid was prompt and efficient. LeProvost only remembered two bites. But ashore, a surgeon found five bites—on his abdomen, left ankle, calf, and back thigh. He needed 120 stitches.

Researchers report numerous shark-boat encounters. From the field notes of S. D. Anderson and K. J. Goldman, shark researchers in the Farallon Islands:

First one shark, then another. Bit boat engine twice within 5–10 seconds. Then boat was bumped on port side and tail slap shot water (two times) into boat (really across it). Got soaked good. Shortly thereafter (10–15 seconds) shark on starboard side bumped boat, bit engine and tail slapped multiple times. Got completely soaked. It was incredible. Then another shark appeared. These sharks were 'hot' so we headed off.[11]

Great white attacks on boats are so numerous that some researchers believe a deep behavioral quirk is driving them. According to this theory, sharks, especially great whites, are at-tacking boats—and killing themselves on propellers—because they are investigating a strange entity in their ocean. The cu-riosity is perhaps comparable to the inquisitiveness that may trigger some of the "bump-and-bite" approaches to human beings. Because a 2,000- or 3,000-pound animal is doing the bumping, the impact can be disastrous to a boat or a person.

For centuries sailors told tales about sharks attacking sur-vivors of shipwrecks. Most scientists scoffed at the stories, which always lacked dates and exact locations. And the hu-man remains found in sharks could be explained away: They had drowned. But there often was a realistic, believ-able quality to those sea stories. Captain William Young, in-troduced in Chapter 2, recounted one that was told to him by a seafarer named Captain Ernie. Ernie had been working a ship out of Nassau, the *Una*, a small Bahamas steamer. She was bound for her homeport at Turks Island when she hit a coral reef.

"She had about seventy-five laborers aboard," Ernie recalled, "and when the little ship hit the reef, there wasn't much time for many of them to get into the lifeboats, or even on the life-rafts. Lots of them—God only knows how many—were dumped into the water and kept afloat by grabbing at whatever bobbed by. There wasn't much panic, though. That is, not until one of the passengers on a raft tumbled off and disappeared. Just one word was all he yelled: 'Shark!'

"All of a sudden, the sea was alive with those monsters from hell! They smashed into the rafts, overturning them and throwing screaming men into the sea. One of them even half-leaped out of the water and pulled a man right off a raft. Men tried to beat the sharks off with oars. The oars broke over their heads. Or a shark would grab an oar in his teeth and splinter it as if it was a toothpick. Some of the men went crazy and jumped right into the shark's jaws.

"How long the nightmare went on, Bill, I don't know. It ended as fast as it started. The sharks just disappeared. They didn't go away hungry, though. I'll vouch for that."

Since those days, shark researchers have documented many mass attacks on the dead and dying of air and sea disasters, tragedies that put human beings into the sea and sometimes add sharks to their torments. Each day in a world of desperate people, sharks stalk the makeshift craft that carry Cubans to Florida, Dominicans to Puerto Rico, illegal Asian immigrants to Australia. One such tragedy: A boat carrying about 160 Dominicans capsized on its way to Puerto Rico, a waystation on the voyage to a new life in America. Men, women, and children struggled in the sea. Forty or fifty sharks materialized. "It was an awful sight," a rescue worker said. The rescuers snatched about sixty people from the sharks.

A shrimp boat capsized in a storm off Australia's shark-prowled Queensland coast. Captain Ray Boundy, thirty-three years old, clung to the wreckage and watched sharks take his crew, Dennis Murphy, twenty-four, and Linda Horton, twenty-one.

The ferry *Doña Paz* collided with a tanker in the Philippines. More than 1,500 people died, said rescuers who, through the oily smoke and flames, saw sharks rising and eating. A ferry sinks in the Ganges-Brahmaputa delta, tipping 190 people into the water. Bull sharks take at least fifty of them. And those are only two of the crowded ferries that always seem to sink in the warm, turgid water that lures and hides the sharks.

When an airliner crashes into the sea, sharks may feast, but they do not kill. The tremendous impact may send out such a powerful vibration that the curious whitetips come from near and far. Those who have seen the autopsy photos say that airliner crash victims are already dead when the sharks arrive. But when a ship goes down, survivors live—to drown or to die in a shark's jaws.

Ships, little, unimportant ships, are always sinking in unimportant places. To name just one: A wooden cargo ship sailed from Aruba, off the coast of Venezuela, to deliver whiskey and frozen chickens to the Colombian port of Punta Gallinas, the northernmost point in South America. The ship had a captain and a crew of six. On May 29, 1998, somewhere in the Caribbean, a storm struck the little ship, breaking it up and hurling the crew and the chickens into the sea. And then the sharks came, drawn by the new, tantalizing scents. When the searchers found the wreck, there were three bodies ravaged by sharks. The others had mercifully drowned.

CHAPTER 10

Sharks to Fear

A surfer sits on his board, waiting for a wave off Gleneden Beach, Oregon, when he sees the water around him begin to boil. For a moment he thinks it's a seal. A shark grabs his right leg and pulls him into the water. The surfer kicks and pounds the shark, which releases him, and he heads for shore and medical aid with eight teeth marks on his thigh. They belong to a great white at least ten feet long.

Off a beach in South Africa, two teenage boys are fooling around as they swim out to anchored boats. One makes believe a shark has seized him and he begins flailing his arms, trying to look like the girl who was the victim in the movie *Jaws*. Then he and his pal tread water. Their pumping legs attract a shark. "I felt a hard thump on my side and I felt a vise clamp on my chest," the nineteen-year-old said later, describing the real shark attack he had mimicked only minutes before. Ashore, in the emergency room, a physician noted the spacing of the teeth marks in a wound from the shoulder blade to the lower edge of the rib case. The teeth belonged to a great white.

Two attacks, half a globe away, with different beginnings but the same ending: A shark took one bite, the victim survived, and the shark is positively identified as a great white about eight feet long.

There are some 400 shark species. Sharks in about 80 percent of these species grow to less than five feet and rarely encounter people. Of the other 20 percent, only thirty-odd species have been positively identified as attackers on people. But the reputation of some of those species varies—innocent in one part of the world, dangerous in another. Misidentification is frequent. After an attack, the species of shark that did the damage is the last thing on the minds of victims and witnesses as they recall blood-soaked moments of confusion and panic. The result is that the real attacker in many encounters is either not known or is identified incorrectly.

Beyond all others, three species are without doubt the most dangerous in the waters of the earth, and when they strike, there is rarely any mistaking their identity:

- The great white, star of *Jaws* and the shark responsible for attacks from California and Massachusetts to South Africa and Australia.
- The tiger shark, whose reputation for ferocity is worldwide.
- The bull shark, which attacks not only at sea and along shore but also in lakes and rivers.

These three species perpetrate most of the kinds of attacks classified by researchers as "bump and bite" and "sneak." A third kind of attack, labeled "hit and run," happens so quickly that surviving victims cannot identify the attacker. But the sharks that hit and run are inevitably large. They include the great hammerhead, shortfin mako, oceanic whitetip, the Galapagos shark, the sand tiger, and certain reef sharks, such as the Caribbean reef shark.[1]

In Australia, three sharks have been identified in fatal unprovoked shark attacks: the great white (called the white pointer in Australia), the tiger shark, and whaler sharks (the general name for several species of sharks that belong to the Carcharhinus genus). Other sharks considered potentially dangerous in Australia are the hammerhead, the Australian gray nurse shark, the blue shark, the mako, and, for waders especially, the wobbegong.

Here are the species that appear not only in blood-splattered seas but also in the lists of sharks that are dangerous to human beings.

Great White Shark
Also Known as White Pointer (Australia and South Africa), White Death (Australia).

Of the thirty or so fatal attacks reported in the world each year, great whites were most likely responsible for ten to twenty. But great whites are not always killers. Humans may survive white shark attacks because the great whites are more inquisitive than predatory—just a bite to see if a swimmer or a surfer is another kind of pinniped. That single bite, however, can kill if the bleeding victim does not get prompt medical aid.

Peter Klimley of the University of California at Davis, a leading authority on great whites, thinks that a great white can tell the relative fat content of an animal by first mouthing it gently. One researcher compared the action to the soft mouthing of bird dogs. Both animals get a great deal of information from their mouths.

If the shark senses the tensile resistance associated with blubber, the shark bites down hard. If not, the shark decides to save its energy for a meal that is more nutritious. "That's probably why most humans who are bitten are seldom killed," Klimley told a Discovery Channel interviewer. "We sometimes find sea otters floating dead with white teeth fragments stuck in their flesh. Unlike other marine mammals, sea otters rely on dense pelts rather than blubber to conserve warmth. From a white's perspective, the lack of fat makes them an undesirable meal. So after a shark mouths an otter, it tends to spit it out."

Not all shark experts agree with Klimley's hypothesis. George Burgess, director of the International Shark Attack File, points out that in a third of the attacks on humans, the white shark returns for a second bite. Burgess thinks more two-bite victims will die if medical aid is not swiftly available.

Seals and sea lions are the great whites' favorite prey, and both are usually attacked from below. When a great white strikes a seal, it usually kills it with a bite that causes fatal bleeding. Because sea lions are larger, the first upward strike—sometimes so powerful that the shark catapults itself out of the sea—usually is not lethal. The sea lion founders on the surface, bleeding, or makes its escape. To make a meal of either pinniped, the shark returns. If the prey was a seal, the shark dines on a carcass; if the prey was a sea lion, the shark has to kill it before dining.

Human beings, like sea lions, spend time on the surface. So humans are usually the target of the seal lion strategy: Strike from below, hard and swiftly. Take a bite. Let the prey bleed to death. With that minimum output of energy, the shark has produced a meal. There was no need to use up more energy struggling with an already doomed prey. Human beings, however, do not usually get a return visit. And if a rescuer appears, a great white almost always ignores the rescuer.

Other sharks may circle a prospective victim or signal aggression with body language. But the shark typically strikes quickly. Some victims have mentioned a thunderous sound just before impact. What they probably heard is the rush of water through the great white's gills as the colossal animal lunges forward at top speed.

As apex predators, great whites can essentially do what they want. But their behavior is controlled by what prey animals are available. Like other predators, great whites are opportunists. If there are no pinnipeds, they may seek meals in schools of fish. And people may be in or near those fish. This has led to the "mistaken identity" theory: Great whites mistake surfers on boards for seals. Whatever the reason, fully submerged people are far less vulnerable than those on the surface.

Apex predator or not, the great white can itself become prey. Observers in the Farallons have videotaped a rarely seen duel between a great white and an orca, or killer whale (*Orcas orca*), the largest member of the dolphin family and the world's largest predator of warm-blooded animals.[2] Witnesses saw a twenty-foot orca thrash a ten-foot great white to death and swim off with the shark in her jaws. She was well known to mammalogists as a member of the "LA Pod," a group of orcas that spend much of their time in waters off Los Angeles. She is the only orca known to prey on the sharks.

Research indicates that great whites refrain from arguing over prey—good news for humans, who only have to worry about one white instead of a pack. Although whites appear to be lone hunters, in fact the solitary behavior seems to stem from an innate tendency to leave each other alone.

Although the great white has become the most studied shark, little is known about it. One research says the great white is among the least understood of Earth's creatures. Studies have focused on their attack behavior, in the hope that the pattern of attacks on usual prey will provide clues to attacks on human beings. "The problem is that we only see sharks when they make active attacks on prey," says Klimley.

Great whites favor waters around seal colonies and do not usually enter estuaries and rivers with low salinities, as the bull shark does. When they are not preying on seal and sea lion colonies along the U.S. West Coast, they probably follow the whales migrating from the Gulf of Alaska to the Baja Peninsula, not to kill any but to feed on the carcasses of whales that die naturally.

For a long time, a shark caught in Australia in 1870 was cited as the world's biggest great white: thirty-six-and-a-half feet. But modern sleuthing showed the measurements had been wrong. The debate, which involves arcane questions about the way to measure a shark, now centers on claims of "biggest great white" by catchers in quest of recognition. British biologist Ian Fergusson, chairman of the Shark Trust, has studied the claims and asserts that no great white over nineteen and a half feet long has ever been validated. A typical shark sixteen feet long and weighing 4,500, he says, "is BIG, very BIG, and should need no further exaggeration to impress even the most discerning of viewers when seen up close."[3]

The teeth of young great whites seem to be designed for feeding on fish. As the sharks get older, their lower teeth change so that larger prey—such as seals and sea lions—can be grabbed and held. The bite of an adult great white, as described by research scientist John E. McCosker of the Steinhart Aquarium, consists of five steps spanning less than one second: (1) Lifts snout to enlarge gape; (2) drops lower jaw to make the gape even larger; (3) protrudes the upper jaw, "resulting in the startling—and terrifying—image of the white shark's upper jaw, teeth, gums, and connective tissue exposed and thrust forward from the roof of the mouth"; (4) lifts lower jaw; (5) retracts jaw and drops snout upon prey, using the leverage of the drop to snatch a large piece of flesh. The prey is pinned on the teeth of the lower jaw. The shark, having completed the bite, moves its head laterally to shear off the piece of flesh with the upper teeth.[4]

In 1998, the first modern sighting of a great white in the Adriatic was appropriated by experts on global warming. They said that changing oceanic temperatures were affecting the territorial spread of the shark. They predicted that great whites, following the shoals of its food fishes, would appear regularly in British waters within ten years.

The great white shark gets its name from its white belly, but its back and sides are a dark grayish black.

Tiger Shark

While Iona Asai was searching for pearls in the waters off an island in the Torres Strait, a tiger shark dove down upon him and took his head into its mouth. "When I felt his teeth go into my flesh, I put my hands around his head and squeeze his eyes until he let go me and I make for the boat," he said after recovering from the 1937 attack. His story sounds incredible, but there was the scar around his neck and the tooth that a surgeon removed. It was a tooth from the jaw of a tiger shark.

The skull of a horse was once found in a tiger shark not quite eleven feet long. The shark was able to swallow a horse's head whole for the same reason that it could try to swallow Iona Asai's head: Its upper and lower jaws have joints at each corner of the mouth. Strong, elastic muscles enable the shark to distend its mouth and manipulate the joints. Each jaw, upper and lower, is hinged in the center, so that the shark can form a large gaping opening. If that tiger shark's powerful jaws had closed fully around Iona Asai's head, he would have been beheaded.

191

From the Torres Strait and the shores of Australia, from India to Florida, tiger sharks are feared as the most dangerous of sharks. By some estimates, its all-time record for fatal attacks rivals that of the great white. In one study of 267 attacks with identifiable attackers, great whites were blamed for thirty-two and the tiger shark came in second with twenty-seven.[5] Unlike the great white, which may just take a bite and swim off, the tiger shark usually locks onto its prey. From the medical report of Dr. H. O. Spect, Sarasota, Florida, following a tiger shark's attack on an eight-year-old boy in 1958: "The patient was viciously attacked by a shark in shallow water off Longboat Key. In fact, he was pulled from the water with the shark still hanging onto his left leg and chewing the while. . . ." A surgeon "performed a high thigh amputation of the left leg and repaired multiple laceration of the left hand."

An inventory of tiger sharks' stomach contents conjures up a predator prowling near to shore, gobbling up whatever is there: dogs, boots, sacks of coal, a bag of potatoes, beer bottles, a pair of old trousers, a pair of shoes, the horns of a deer, twelve lobsters, turtles, squid, crabs, sea birds, poisonous sea snakes, other sharks, a black cat, the hind leg of a sheep, seagulls, unopened two-pound cans of green peas. Objects that cannot be digested remain intact in the stomach for some time and finally are regurgitated.

The omnivorous tiger bites with a rolling motion of its powerful jaws, enabling its big, saw-edged teeth to chop large prey into several pieces. So a twelve-foot tiger shark was able to devour another shark ten feet long. A thirteen-foot tiger shark caught in Australia had consumed thirty-two fish, averaging fifteen inches in length.

Tiger sharks seem to hunt mostly at night, coming closer to shore and eating almost anything that floats. A tiger shark swims slowly, then speeds up as it approaches prey.

Tiger sharks once were thought to take up permanent residence in an area. Hence, the hunts in Hawaii to eradicate the "killer shark" supposedly lurking off a beach following an attack. Recent research, however, showed that they traveled from island to island and sometimes swam long distances from one spot, not returning for weeks, if at all.

Tiger sharks are found in all tropical and subtropical seas and frequently appear in temperate seas. It is the most common large shark in the tropics, particularly the Caribbean and the Gulf of Mexico. Along the U.S. Atlantic coast in warm months, it often appears close to shore and sometimes enters river mouths and enclosed sounds.

Tiger sharks are known to grow to eighteen feet. They get their name from their stripes, which fade with age and finally disappear. They are sandy to dark gray on the upper body, off-white below. Some tiger sharks have dark smudges along their sides and black fin tips. A tiger's head is broad, its snout blunt.

Bull Shark
Also known as cub shark, ground shark, requiem shark. Local names: Ganges shark, Zambezi shark, Lake Nicaragua shark, river shark, freshwater whaler, estuary whaler, and Swan River whaler.

North of Perth, Australia, about thirteen miles from the sea, fifteen-year-old Graham Cartwright was swimming in the Swan River one day in 1969 when a shark rose through the seven feet of water and grabbed him by the left leg. The boy kicked at the shark with his other foot and screamed: "Help! Help! A shark's got me." To anyone familiar with what happened in Matawan Creek, New Jersey, in 1916, the scream was a terrifying echo. Like the boys swimming in Matawan Creek, the boy in Swan River would seem to be safe from sharks. He was not. Cartwright, with a deep, four-inch wound in his thigh, reached a hospital promptly and his leg was saved.

Bull sharks, which can prey in fresh, salty, or brackish waters, know few bounds. They often prey on fish in murky waters and probably mistake the splashing of a swimmer for a struggling fish. Dr. Leonard Compagno, one of the world's leading authorities on sharks, believes that the bull shark may be the most dangerous of all sharks and that its toll includes the boys of that New Jersey creek. By one count, bull sharks' record of fatal attacks ranks third behind great whites and tiger sharks.

Bull sharks are the dreaded sharks of Lake Nicaragua, the Ganges and Hooghly Rivers of India; Lake Jamoer in New Guinea and in numerous rivers and lakes in Asia, Mexico, Central and South America, and in St. Lucia Lake in South Africa. In Australia, bull sharks are found along the coasts and up rivers from Perth, around the northern coastline, and down the east coast to Sydney, New South Wales. They are found in tropical and warm-temperate waters throughout the world and have been known to challenge or attack divers, especially those carrying fish. Bull sharks can switch between salt and fresh water because their bodies can make the osmotic changes needed for passing from waters containing high amounts of salt to waters with little or no salt, or vice versa.

Bull sharks grow to about fourteen feet and weigh a maximum of 400 pounds. In the western Atlantic, they are found from southern Brazil to North Carolina, with some reported as far north as New York. They are abundant in the West Indies and the Gulf of Mexico, particularly off the Texas coast. The mouth of the Mississippi River is a favored birthing site for cub sharks, which gather there from May through July. Brackish waters are typical nursery sites for cub sharks. In such nurseries for sandbar sharks, bull sharks have been seen gorging on baby sandbar sharks.

Sand Tiger Shark
In Australia, gray nurse shark; in Africa, ragged tooth shark. Also known as sand shark, shovel-nose shark.

A shark of mixed reputation, the sand tiger has been accused in several abortive, non-fatal attacks. Divers, who encounter this shark frequently on coastal reefs, report that they are only dangerous if provoked. In aquariums, their fierce look and ceaseless swimming draw spectators who want to see "a real shark." Christopher W. Coates, director of the New York City Aquarium, once said of the sand tiger shark: "They can bite like hell and we don't trust them." They have been known to steal speared fishes from divers without attacking the divers.

Like great whites, sand tigers prey on pinnipeds. They can be fierce, initiated in predation as embryos, eating siblings *in utero* or feeding on unfertilized eggs. Scientific estimates put their maximum size to about six and a half feet, although divers have given estimates up to ten feet. They inhabit tropical and warm temperate waters throughout the world. Divers say they are usually not aggressive.

Most attacks in Australia prior to the 1970s were blamed on the sand tiger shark, (called the gray nurse shark by the Australians). Victims and witnesses said the shark was gray, the key identifier for the relatively innocent gray nurse shark. Branded a dangerous shark, it became a victim itself, and was nearly wiped out by aquatic vigilantes. The actual attackers were almost certainly white pointers, as the Australians call great whites, and "whalers," as bull sharks are known Down Under.

Great Hammerhead
The U.S. Navy once ranked the great hammerhead as the third most dangerous species, after the great white and

195

the tiger shark. (There are several hammerhead species; the Navy was considering only the largest species.) Records of attacks are relatively rare. But a report on a Florida victim, attacked off Palm Beach in 1931, vividly shows the damage a hammerhead can do:

"There were several jagged lacerations of right thigh and calf. The largest, ten inches long, was on the thigh. Here the muscles were torn from the bone but fortunately the large deep-seated blood vessels escaped injury. The cut on the right calf was about five inches long. In addition there were other smaller cuts on the right leg, and on the left were found abrasions and lacerations made presumably by the horny shagreen of the shark's skin as he threshed about the girl when she was striving to get away."[6]

Peter Klimley, a scientist who likes hammerheads, believes that a hammerhead attack is a defensive act. "Almost all sharks will show an aggressive display if cornered, as will most animals," he says. "If you corner a raccoon or a cat, it will attack." He also believes that because they are so easily identifiable, hammerheads get a full accounting for their acts.

The great hammerhead, the only hammerhead species considered a possible attacker, typically grows to fifteen feet; a twenty-footer has been reported. They are found in tropical and warm waters worldwide, inshore, sometimes in very shallow water, and at sea.

Mako

Three Australians, two men and a woman, were in a twenty-one-foot boat and fishing off New South Wales when a fifteen-foot mako shark took a bite out of the boat and sank it. One of the fishermen told a *Sunday Times* correspondent how it happened: "We had just started fishing about eight miles off shore when the shark hit us. I saw his body pass the boat, and then suddenly he ploughed straight into the bow. In three minutes the boat went down." Clinging to a small inflatable dinghy, the four watched the shark circling them for an hour and a half before it swam off. They were in the sea nine hours before rescuers found them.

Fishermen have been gasping out such stories for decades: You hook a mako and it turns on you, smashing into the boat, threatening you and everyone aboard, maybe even scratching you or biting you! From the viewpoint of the mako, a vigorous and powerful fish, these fish stories are hardly unprovoked attacks. But they go into the record and they make the mako, officially, a dangerous shark.

Pound for pound, it is one of the strongest of sharks. Clocked at twenty miles per hour, the mako has achieved the fastest speed ever recorded for a shark.

There are two types of mako, the most common is the short-fin mako; less common and less known is the long-fin mako (*Isurus paucus*). The short-fin is a powerful and weighty passenger for a sudden arrival in a fishing boat. A mako ten feet long may weigh more than 1,000 pounds. Makos may reach a length of thirteen feet or more.

In Polynesian legends, the mako is a reincarnated human being and must be treated with respect. This would be good advice for divers, for this shark can be aggressive. Divers who have encountered the mako say that it should especially be treated with caution when it swims in a figure-8 pattern and approaches with jaw agape—a possible prelude to an attack. The Maori of New Zealand apparently believed it was a "man-eater," for that is a rough translation of the Maori *mako-mako*.

The mako is a fierce, tireless fighter, leaping again and again to shake off the hook. Western writer Zane Grey, an enthusiastic shark fisherman, called the mako "the aristocrat of all sharks. His leaps are prodigious, inconceivably high. The ease and grace . . . is indescribable." Ernest Hemingway also fished for the mako. It is a marauding mako that consumes the marlin in Hemingway's *The Old Man and the Sea*.

It is found in tropical and warm temperate seas worldwide, and it follows warm waters toward the polar regions at the extreme northern and southern ends of its range.

Oceanic Whitetip

A Hawaiian diver was snorkeling between Oahu and Molokai, in the midst of a pod of forty or fifty pilot whales, when three oceanic whitetips materialized and began circling him, counterclockwise. One of the whitetips dropped its long pectoral fins and arched its back, like a hissing cat. The diver called out for his friends to bring their boat closer to him. The whitetip's snout was twitching from side to side. The diver prudently swam to the boat.

Whitetips often accompany pilot whales (*Globicephala sieboldii*) but do not prey on them. They may be finding prey stirred up by the whales or join in the whales' hunt for squid. Whitetips, which appear like apparitions at shipwrecks and air crashes at sea, are a worldwide species. They are usually found well offshore in deep waters, including depths near land, such as off Hawaii or along the edges of the continental shelf. By one authoritative estimate whitetips may be "the most abundant large animal, large being over one hundred pounds, on the face of the earth."[7]

Sandbar Shark
Also known as brown shark, ground shark. In Australia: Sandbar whaler or northern whaler.

A fast, sleek shark, the sandbar is considered dangerous in Australia, but without much evidence. They are found throughout the world, including some that found their way into the canals of Venice. They are also the most abundant sharks in Hawaiian waters.

The sandbar's common name comes from its habit of appearing as it crosses a sandbar, then disappearing again on the other side.

Blacktip Shark

In November 1990, a surfer in three feet of water off Boca Raton, Florida, fell off his board. He felt pain and instinctively swung at what had stabbed him. He pulled away a hand covered with blood. He had been bitten on the shoulder; his hand had grazed the shark's teeth. The surfer stumbled to shore and survived. The suspected attacker was a three- or four-foot blacktip shark.

Like dogs nipping at heels, blacktips are annoying and can inflict painful wounds. But they have never been blamed for a fatal attack.

The conspicuously black-tipped fins of this shark are often seen in tropical and sub-tropical seas. In Florida, they sometimes appear in large schools close to shore as they relentlessly follow and gorge on migrating menhaden. Farther offshore, fishermen have watched groups of blacktips soaring upward in the sea to hit a school of prey from below. Occasionally, a shark will leap into the air, somersault, and fall back into the sea. The antics seem to accompany feeding, which the swift, gregarious sharks turn into a frenzy.

They feed on smaller fishes, such as menhaden and sardines, and sting rays, whose stingers may end up imbedded in the sharks' jaws. Blacktips are often found in the stomachs of larger oceanic sharks, such as the tiger shark.

Lemon Shark

Long known as a shark of researchers, the lemon is mild. But it's a good idea to keep an eye on it. A lemon shark cruising around at the National Aquarium in Baltimore bit an underwater attendant for no apparent reason. The shark was later dispatched to the Atlantic Ocean. Lemon sharks are suspected of non-fatal attacks in Florida waters.

Blue Shark

These sharks, which may grow to sixteen feet, get on the "dangerous" list primarily because they have appeared at sea disasters, frightening rescuers with "feeding frenzies," a behavioral reflex that probably stems from the fact that blue sharks travel in groups. When a group tries to feed, the result inevitably is a "frenzy," a phenomenon that no longer is looked upon as a threat to people—unless they find themselves in the midst of it.

Other Sharks Labeled Dangerous
Silky Shark (Carcharhinus falciformis).

Another large, aggressive pelagic shark, it has been seen at disaster sites, competing with the whitetips, which dominate the scene of carnage. The silky's behavior, which somewhat parallels the whitetip's, has earned it a place on some lists of "dangerous sharks."

Galapagos Shark (Carcharhinus galapagensis).

Once thought to be an exclusively Pacific shark, one was identified in 1963 as the attacker of a swimmer in Magen's Bay on St. Thomas in the Virgin Islands. In the attack the swimmer lost a right hand and "enormous bites were taken from the left shoulder and the right thigh and hip." He was killed almost instantly. Next day, a large shark was caught. The swimmer's right hand, along with other remains, were found in the shark. Positive identification of the shark as the Galapagos shark was made by experts.[8]

Gray Reef Shark

A shark that grows to about six feet, it does occasionally bite human beings, especially divers carrying fish. But the reef shark's bite is painful, not fatal. Divers say that a reef shark gives a warning before snapping: It begins swimming in a circle. Then it lowers its pectoral fins and arches its back. "It has been known to become aggressive if it feels you are invading its territory," says a diver.

In 1973 Bill Curtsinger, an underwater photographer working for *National Geographic* magazine, was diving in a remote lagoon in Micronesia. A territorial gray reef shark came toward him. "It was twenty feet away and closing," he later wrote. "I saw it sweeping its head back and forth; its back arched like a cat's. The shark was speaking to me but at the time I didn't know the words. . . ." The shark raked his left hand and wounded his right shoulder.

"Harmless" Sharks

The quotes around the word harmless are, of course, ironic. These are sharks that mean no harm and do no harm—until someone harms or pesters them.

Nurse Shark

Sluggish, bottom-dwelling nurse sharks do get pestered. An incident reported by a diver: A companion straddled a large nurse shark and did what another rider had once told him: Hold on by grabbing the last of the gill slits (meaning those farthest from the mouth). He grabbed the other "last" slit—and the shark easily twisted its head and bit him. Nurse sharks will clamp a vise-like hold on unwary molesters—such as people who hope for an underwater ride. Documented attacks, nearly all provoked, have resulted in painful wounds. Nurses that have bitten divers ranged in size from *eighteeen inches* to nine feet. Nurse sharks are no kin to the gray nurse (*Carcharias arenarius*) of Australia, which has been indicted in many fatal attacks.

Angel Shark

Bottom-dwelling angel sharks, which are nearly as flat as a skate, belong to one genus (*Squatinidae*). The species are many, but the behavior of all is about the same. They burrow into the sand, wait until a small fish swims by, and then strike, grasping them with needle-like teeth. They also hunt crabs, lobsters, and skates, but it is their sudden strike from the sand that puts them on lists. Left alone, they certainly will not bother anyone. But if a diver picks up one of these five-foot creatures, he may learn why fishermen call them sand devils. Bothered, they can inflict a severe cut. "It is extremely fierce and dangerous to be approached," said an eighteenth-century British book on zoology. "We knew of an instance of a fisherman, whose leg was terribly torn by a large one of this species . . . which he went to lay hold of incautiously." A nineteenth-century Maryland fisheries report likened its behavior to "the unpleasant habits of the snapping turtle."

Zebra Shark (*Stegostoma fasciatum*)

Like angel sharks, zebra sharks (also called leopard sharks) are tempting objects for casual harassment. One of the few indictments against this little shark came from an anonymous reef diver who grabbed one by the tail. It turned on him and attached its jaws on the crotch of his wetsuit. He survived without injury.

Wobbegongs

Australian aborigines named these beautifully colored sharks, which are easily identified by three family features: A fringe of fleshy barbels or feelers around its mouth; deep grooves connecting each nostril with the mouth; a coloring pattern that blends in with the rocks and the weeds of the sea bottom. The spotted wobbegong grows to about ten and a half feet. They all have sharp teeth and powerful jaws. They will attack when disturbed or stepped on and can inflict a painful wound. The ornate wobbegong, which has fringes of flesh hanging like tassels from its mouth, grows to about nine feet and is a menace to unwary waders.

Cookie-Cutter Shark

When Hawaiian authorities found a body with two strange wounds on the back of it, they soon solved the mystery. This was the work of a cookie-cutter shark, a deep-water shark with razor-sharp teeth. It gets its name from its feeding technique: It places its mouth against the side of its prey, forming a suction with the aid of its tongue. It then sucks in a cylinder of flesh, rotating its body and tugging, scooping out a bite about the size of a golf ball. The cookie-cutter, which is only about twenty inches long, could not have killed the man. The autopsy report listed the wound as "probably post mortem" and gave the cause of death as "asphyxia by drowning." A cookie-cutter was also blamed in 1995 for an attack on a seven-year-old boy body-boarding off Haena, Kauai. The whirling little shark had removed a plug of flesh one inch deep and an inch and a half in diameter from the boy's left calf.

CHAPTER 11

Toward a Sharkproof Sea

Something was wrong with the propeller on a U.S. Navy boat anchored off Isla del Rey in the Gulf of Panama, about sixty miles southeast of the Pacific entrance to the Panama Canal. It was September 23, 1943, in the middle of World War II, and guarding the Panama Canal was a vital Navy mission. A twenty-year-old sailor put on swimming trunks and dived in to take a look at the propeller. As he surfaced, a shark grabbed his left leg. The sailor and the shark thrashed in the water for about one minute. Then the shark vanished, and shipmates pulled the sailor from the water, put a tourniquet on his thigh, treated him for shock, and sent him to a Navy hospital three hours away.

His left leg bore half a dozen deep wounds, arranged like arches. Some of the tooth marks were arrayed in two, three, and four rows. In the left knee, the most grievously wounded part of the leg, a surgeon extracted fragments of teeth. The surgeon stitched up an artery but could do little about a crushed bone and a nearly severed nerve. His patient was failing fast. Four hours after reaching the hospital he died of shock and loss of blood.

Capt. B. H. Kean of the U.S. Army Medical Corps saw the autopsy report and realized that the tragedy had produced proof that sharks could kill. He realized, too, that the tooth fragments could probably lead to an identification of the shark. The fragments went off to Dr. John Treadwell Nichols, curator of the Department of Fishes in the American Museum of Natural History—the scientist who had doubted the possibility of shark attacks back in 1919. Nichols identified the fragments as "tips of the teeth of a small so-called man-eater shark *Carcharodon carcharias,* and from a small individual of this species probably not more than 7 feet or so long."

Kean, meanwhile, found a 1929 report about a shark tearing off a Panamanian swimmer's leg in 1929 off Taboga Island, about thirty-five miles from where the sailor had been mauled. The 1929 shark had been caught two hours afterward; in it were the swimmer's leg and part of his bathing suit. Kean added that incident to his report.

"Controversy as to whether or not sharks will attack human beings has raged so violently in popular magazines and Sunday newspaper supplements," Kean wrote, "that the medical and military importance of the subject may have been obscured." Some people "have been inclined to ridicule or deny the danger of sharks. The present case is reported because scientific identification of a shark which attacked a human being is rare. . . . Conclusive evidence is at hand, therefore, that sharks will attack human beings. A discussion of frequency of such attacks in various parts of the world and of the use of shark repellents is beyond the scope of this report."[1]

Kean's report provides an insight into the state of shark science during World War II. To many like Kean, the debate over shark attacks still went on, even though E. W. Gudger, Associate Curator of Fishes at the American Museum of Natural History, had conceded in 1937 that attacks did occur.[2] Kean also did not know about work that was going on—because that work was, like the atomic bomb, a secret of war.

Dr. Harold J. Coolidge, on leave from the Harvard Museum of Comparative Zoology, was ostensibly involved in high-level public relations projects in Washington. That was his cover for assignment to the nation's wartime spy organization, the Office of Strategic Services (precursor to the Central Intelligence Agency). While on an OSS mission in the Caribbean, Coolidge met a plane crash survivor who told a horrifying story about the voracious sharks drawn to the crash. Coolidge, personally shocked by the story, learned that anxious mothers were writing their congressmen and President Roosevelt about the sharks. Coolidge took the shark problem directly to the White House and suggested that a scientific investigation be made into the feasibility of a chemical shark repellent. President Roosevelt, who had a special fondness for the Navy, reportedly ordered that the quest for a sharkproof sea be given top priority.

Some military leaders grumbled, arguing that the allotment of resources to a shark-repellent project would divert people and money from activities more directly concerned with fighting the war. Navy officials particularly resisted, maintaining that, since shark attacks were rare, it was psychologically unsound to overemphasize the menace. But, backed by the White House, proponents of the shark repellent won out with the argument that if a man in the water knew he had some kind of protection against sharks, he could devote more of his strength and wit to keeping himself alive.

The Office of Scientific Research and Development mobilized shark experts and survival specialists from the U.S. Navy's Committee on Medical Research, the Bureau of Aeronautics, and the U.S. Naval Research Laboratory.[3] W. Douglas Burden, president of the Marine Studios in Florida, managed the first experiments. Because the war had forced the closing of the Marine Studios, Burden set up repellent headquarters at the Woods Hole Oceanographic Institution in Woods Hole, Massachusetts.

Three smooth dogfish (*Mustelus canis*), each about three feet long, became the first experimental animals. They were killed with poisoned food in a dead-end search for slaying sharks. Research shifted to a search for something that would drive sharks away from a certain kind of potential food—U.S. servicemen. Successors to the first three dogfish were subjected to supersonics, ink clouds, stink bombs, and seventy-eight different substances, including several poison gases. Nothing worked.

Then Stewart Springer, a U.S. Fish and Wildlife scientist, remembered that a shark fisherman had once told him that if a shark died on an untended line, no more fishing was possible around that line. There was something about a dead shark that drove other sharks away. The Woods Hole dogfish turned tail when the scientists confronted them with an offering of very dead shark meat.

The principal chemical emitted by a rotting shark carcass was ammonium acetate, a type of acetic acid. Since the copper ion was found to exert a repellent chemical action, scientists decided to try the common chemical compound, copper acetate. Now they needed sharks for field tests. They could not find any along the Florida coast. According to lore about the frustrating search for sharks, Navy and U.S. Coast Guard vessels were assigned to the task in Cuban waters. Ernest Hemingway, a famed shark hunter, offered his services. On December 1, 1942, Secretary of State Cordell Hull cabled the American Embassy at Quito, Ecuador. After briefly describing the shark project, Hull ordered:

"You are requested to secure permission from the Ecuadorian government for the . . . necessary investigation of the territorial waters of Ecuador . . . You are also authorized to transmit reports from the investigators via diplomatic pouch. Please take up this matter on an urgent basis and report by telegraph."[4]

The researchers finally found a spot teeming with sharks in Ecuador's Gulf of Guayaquil, near the mouth of the Guayaquil River, and there the scientists tried out their "dead shark" repellent on small hammerheads, known as scalloped bonnetheads (*Sphyrna corona*), and two species of ground sharks that belonged to the same large family, Carcharhinidae, that contains the great white and other dangerous sharks.

Using mullet for bait, the researchers suspended lines eighteen to twenty-four feet deep. Some lines had a net bag containing the repellent. The tests showed that sharks struck again and again at the baited lines without the bags of repellent but stayed away from the repellent-bag lines. Convinced that the repellent worked on individual sharks, the experimenters next tried it on a pack of sharks in a feeding frenzy. Samples of the repellent were dispatched to a shrimp-trawling grounds near Mayport, Florida. The shrimp fishermen threw away the cleanings from the shrimp and "trash" fish that had been scooped up with the shrimp. As the shovelfuls of trash were dumped into the sea, fifty or seventy-five or more sharks followed the boat and excitedly feasted.

In a classified report on the use of the repellent against shark packs, one of the researchers said: "Sharks were attracted to the back of the shrimp boat with trash fish. The sharks appeared as a slashing, splashing shoal. We prepared a tub of fresh fish and another tub of fish mixed with repellent powder . . . I shoveled over the plain fish for 30 seconds while the sharks, with much splashing, ate them. Then I started on the repellent fish and shoveled for 30 seconds, after which I shoveled plain fish for 30 seconds, repeating the procedure three times.

"On the first trial the sharks were quite ferocious in feeding on the plain fish right at the stern of the boat. They cut fish for only about five minutes after the repellent mixture was thrown over. A few came back when the plain fish were put out immediately following the repellent. On a second trial 30 minutes later, a ferocious school fed for the 30 seconds that plain fish were supplied, but left as soon as the repellent was in the water. On the third trial we could not get the sharks nearer than 20 yards to the stern of the boat."

The repellent appeared to be an astounding success. The government ordered a high-priority program for manufacturing it in cakes to be attached to lifejackets. The repellent, which consisted of about 20 percent copper acetate and 80 percent nigrosine dye, diffused in the water as a blue-black cloud similar to the inky fluid ejected by squids when they become alarmed. The cloud was seen as a morale booster in itself because it provided anxious survivors with visible proof of protection. Servicemen were instructed to open the envelope and swish the cake around them when threatened by sharks.

"Shark Chaser," as the repellent was dubbed, became a military secret, and the purpose of its production was not disclosed to civilians who wondered what the awful smell was around the Borden Company's Shark Industries

Division plant in Salerno, Florida. Borden, which had been catching sharks to extract vitamin A from their livers, boiled down shark meat in great vats to extract the essence of the repellent. This dead-shark repellent manufacturing was soon supplemented by mass production of the chemical repellent.

The repellent was issued as a part of all Mae West (life-jacket) and life-raft equipment. How effective it was will never be known. Obviously, it did not work in the long-term mass exposure of men in disasters like the *Indianapolis* and *Juneau* sinkings. But thousands of men were set adrift in seas all over the world during the war, and undoubtedly the repellent provided many of them with at least an important psychological weapon against sharks. "Beyond question, the greatest value of the Shark Chaser was the mental relief and sense of security it afforded the men who had it on hand," observed George A. Llano, the Air Force research specialist who made a study of wartime survival at sea.[5]

Evaluation of Shark Chaser after the war showed mixed results at best. Dr. Albert Tester, a University of Hawaii zoologist, summed up the reports: "I do not think at the present time that we have a sure-fire repellent of any kind. There are sharks and sharks. One repellent may work with the tiger shark, but not with the gray sharks we have here in Hawaii. Another may work with the gray and not with the Tiger." The British Shallow Water Diving Unit at Nassau tested shark repellent under conditions that would be more pertinent to recreational divers. "The use by us of shark repellent [copper acetate] did not prove anything," the British reported. "It does not seem reasonable to suppose that a shark in the fury of an attack would pause or retreat from its headlong rush for food because it did not care for the smell of the repellent. Again, if the repellent were effective, it would be only so down tide."

When the repellent was tried on a pack of sharks consuming dead whales in Australia, some sharks were repelled while others in their frenzy ate the packets of Shark Chaser. Some skeptical researchers wondered if the blue-black dye, rather than the copper acetate, was actually discouraging the sharks.

Continuing research included a bizarre experiment by U.S. Navy Commander H. David Baldridge, Jr. He decided to see how sharks reacted to mammals in distress. Since he could not put people in that kind of distress, he chose another mammal: the standard laboratory white rat: *Rattus norwegicus.* He attached a light fishing line to the rats' tails or, by a clip, to the fur at the napes of their necks and dropped them into tanks containing lemon, dusky, tiger, or nurse sharks. Confronted with a live rat, they all had essentially the same response, as described by Baldridge: "The initial reaction was curiosity as evidenced by close approaches and occasional direct bumps by the noses of the sharks. After a few minutes and in the absence of stimuli other than the even swimming motions of the live rat, the sharks appeared to ignore the mammal."[6]

When the tethered rats squirmed and made irregular swimming motions, the sharks still ignored them, even though those motions in prey animals (including people) supposedly inspired an attack. Blood is also a proven attractant, but, Baldridge learned, not from a bleeding rat, dead or alive. The only exception was a small tiger shark that "mouthed a bleeding dead rat." Sharks finally were aroused by rats whose fur was coated with the bodily juices of bonito or "mullet blend" (recipe: Place a mullet and some water in a blender and switch on high). Sharks also reacted to dead rats whose intestines were exposed. And sharks did show interest when a rat was dropped into a pen, leading Baldridge to conclude that an attack "could be provoked by increasing the level of splashing by repeatedly lifting and dropping the rat into the water."

Baldridge believed that his experiments gave credence to the quest for a chemical repellent. The rats doused with fish fluids demonstrated that an unattractive animal could become attractive "by changing only the degree of olfactory and/or chemical stimulation." This, he said, pointed out the need for "determination of the chemical substances which pass into the sea from the body of a human swimmer under various conditions of stress, exercise, and diet." He also cautioned spear fishermen to not emulate the fish-tainted rats by carrying strings of bleeding dead fish.

Shark Chaser found its way into the survival kits that early astronauts carried into space and that U-2 pilots carried on their perilous flights over the Soviet Union. NASA put Shark Chaser into the marker dye released from Apollo space capsules when they hit the sea. After at least one landing, the splashdown attracted sharks. "Nothing happened," a NASA spokesman said, "except maybe the frogmen who helped in the recovery worked faster than usual. The sharks only circled and watched."[7]

When Shark Chaser entered the burgeoning world of civilian sea adventurers, it gave comfort but did not convince skeptics of its usefulness. The effort to develop Shark Chaser, however, had inspired new interest in shark matters, and this in turn led those early researchers to form what became the International Shark Research Panel. This is undoubtedly the most important legacy of Shark Chaser. It may not have worked that well in repelling sharks but it did attract researchers.

A promising chemical repellent came with the discovery, by shark researcher Eugenie Clark, that a small flatfish, the Moses sole (*Pardachirus marmoratus*) prevented sharks from biting down on it by secreting a chemical. When Dr.

Clark presented live or dead soles to sharks in an experiment at sea, the fish repelled at least four species of shark in the open sea, usually for more than ten hours.

To protect large numbers of people, another kind of repellent was needed. The idea goes back to South Africa in 1904, when the Durban City Council erected a large semicircular enclosure around their shark-prowled beach. Battered by the surf, the net became so badly damaged that it was torn down in 1928. After a 1945–1951 string of twenty-one attacks—seven fatal—Durban tried again, this time adopting a technique, developed in Australia in 1937. Large-meshed nets had been anchored seaward of the breaker zone at many Sydney beaches. The mesh nets, designed to trap sharks by snaring their gills, killed many sharks and stopped attacks at the beaches.

In 1952, Durban erected seven gill nets, each about 140 yards long, along the Durban beachfront. In the first year 552 sharks were caught in the nets and Durban began a long era free of shark attacks.

Elsewhere on the sharky South African coast, however, the sharks continued to strike. After five fatal attacks in 107 days—between Black December 1957 and Easter 1958—resorts in towns along the KwaZulu-Natal coast, trying to lure back panicky vacationers, desperately erected flimsy nets in the surf zone and proclaimed shark-free swimming. This did not work. So in 1964 Durban-style shark nets were installed at some of the larger holiday resorts north and south of Durban and the Natal Provincial Administration created the Natal Anti-Shark Measures Board (now called the Natal Sharks Board), which was "charged with the duty of approving, controlling, and initiating measures for safeguarding bathers against shark attacks."

By March 1966 fifteen beaches had protective nets, which the Sharks Board eventually took over. Just as the development of Shark Chaser inspired sustaining U.S. research on sharks, the creation of the Natal Sharks Board (NSB) ushered in a new era of shark research in South Africa. The removal of "Anti-Shark" from the board's name signaled a change in mission, from killing sharks to preserving them. The nets came under new scrutiny.

The nets had been steadily reducing shark populations. While fewer and fewer sharks were trapped in the nets, more and more dolphins, sea turtles, and other marine creatures died in them. The NSB has started studying the use of baited lines as an alternative to shark nets. These lines, which are used to protect beaches in Queensland, Australia, target sharks. And the nets are cleared daily. Sharks that are still alive are tagged and released; selected dead sharks are brought in for study.

For years, the NSB had been experimenting with electrical force fields in hopes that these could somehow lead to electrically protected beaches. But unwieldy cables designed to produce the field were too difficult to handle and were no match for the coast's heavy seas. Besides, there was the fear that electrical charges powerful enough to hold sharks off at sea might endanger swimmers. The research, however, did pay off by leading to the Protective Oceanic Device—the Shark POD. It generates electromagnetic fields near a diver, driving off sharks, which are extremely sensitive to electrical fields. The theory behind the POD is that, startled by a sudden increase in an electrical field, a shark will dart away.

In 1992 the NSB commissioned two famed shark enthusiasts, Ron and Valerie Taylor of Australia, to test a prototype of the POD, first in a shark tank and then against great whites at sea. Valerie Taylor had already tried another shark

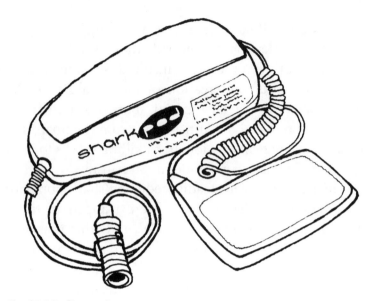

The SharkPOD diver unit.

protective measure: a chain-mail suit. While she was diving in it in Australian waters, a gray reef shark snapped at her, biting her face and ripping away her air hose. She reached the surface with four teeth punctures at a vulnerable spot, the gap between the hood and the suit. A tiny tooth fragment remained in her jaw.

Valerie and Rod dove with the POD off South Africa's Dyer Island, site of an immense seal colony preyed upon by great whites. The Taylors made a film showing the POD driving off the sharks. "We felt invincible after that first dive," she later wrote. "There were a dozen or more sharks around, of which five appear on film, and they all kept their distance." On another dive, in the Coral Sea off South Australia, they noticed the sharks' eyes twitching at the same rate as the electric pulse emitted by the POD. "Once the sharks were feeding, they showed a serious reluctance to stop, even though obviously affected by the pulse (eyes blinking, mouth twitching, gills cramping). The POD would stop them approaching the baits, but when turned off to let them get their teeth into the fish, then reactivated, they would not release the food."

In another experiment with tiger sharks, they found that while the POD would keep tiger sharks away from bait, once they started eating, the POD did not work. If the tigers released the bait, even for a few seconds, the activated POD stopped them from continuing to feed. "They would circle, obviously wanting to return," Valerie Taylor wrote, "but the radiating electric field would keep them away." During these tests, lemon sharks, a great hammerhead, a reef shark, and a tawny shark also came to the baits and reacted the way the tiger sharks did. "These experiments reinforced our feeling that once a shark starts eating, the desire to feed overrides the instinct of self-preservation. No matter how unpleasant the irritation of a POD, it will not release its meal."[8]

In its latest form, the POD, powered by a 90-volt battery, generates a pulsing electric field between two electrodes, one on the diver's tank and the other on the diver's fin. The theory is that the pulsing, radiating fields around the POD irritate the sharks' electro-receptors and drive them away. The POD's electrical field forms an elliptical "shield" up to about twenty feet around a swimmer. It is rated to last seventy-five minutes before needing a recharge.

Divers wore PODs when they searched for the wreckage of Swissair Flight 111 off Halifax in 1998. The divers wanted to ward off any sharks that might be drawn to the bodies of the 229 people killed in the crash.

Perhaps electricity will work. So much has been tried: The bubbling "water barrier" on a New Jersey beach, the Shark Survival Sack for air and ship disaster victims to climb into, the gun that fired a projectile that injected gas into the body of a shark at high pressure, the toxin syringe

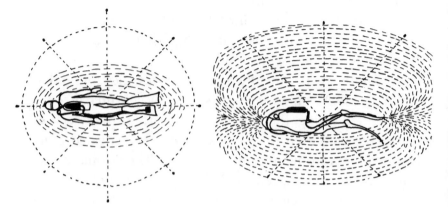

Protective electrical field generated by the SharkPOD.

weapon that took several minutes to work and put the shark in a very bad pre-death mood.

Then there was Simo, the bottle-nosed dolphin (*Tursiops truncates*), trained to attack sharks by bumping into them. The idea was that dolphins like Simo would patrol beaches and keep them clear of sharks. At the Mote Marine Laboratory, Simo learned to bump a sandbar shark and a nurse shark. Next came a bull shark, which looks very much like a sandbar shark. Simo knew better. He became visibly disturbed and instead of attacking "raced around the pool squeaking and clicking, clearly under severe psychological stress."[9] Simo could tell when he was facing a shark that could easily kill him. How, no one knows. But Simo showed more sense than some people who chose to swim with sharks without knowing much about them.

CHAPTER 12

Looking for Trouble

The signs posted on the beach warned of sharks. But Claudio Roberto Florencio de Freitas was an indestructible twenty-two-year-old surfer. So he plunged into the surf off Praia da Boa Viagem Beach, four miles from Recife, northern Brazil's major port and capital of Pernambuco state.

The shark, most likely a great white, cruised amid several surfers and chose Claudio, clamping down on his left arm. Claudio screamed and saw the shark swim off with his forearm in its mouth. Brave friends gathered around him and got him to shore and then to a hospital. But it was too late. He had bled to death, another victim of a beach notorious for shark attacks. The November 1998 attack produced the ninth fatality in six years. All the victims were surfers.

On May 1, 1999—Brazil's Labor Day holiday—twenty-one-year-old Charles Barbosa Pires was surfing with two friends off Recife's Boa Viagem Beach when a shark grabbed his right leg, inflicting a deep wound. He struck at the shark, driving it off. As he struggled shoreward, either that same shark or another one slashed the surfer's hands. By then, three lifeguards were swimming toward him. They towed him ashore and got him to a hospital, where physicians well experienced in shark bites saved his life. On the day after Christmas 1999 came another Pernambuco attack, this one on a boy who survived but lost a leg.

Surfers have a saying about places like Praia da Boa Viagem Beach: "Once you go into the water, you're part of the food chain." There is much truth to that. Worldwide, surfers are the targets of sharks more often than victims in any other recreational group. Their kicking and splashing on the surface resemble the movement of shark prey. And there is more to it than that. Surfers and sharks, psychologically, are like moths and a flame. In the year of the attack on Claudio Roberto Florencio, surfers accounted for 69 percent of all 1998 attacks recorded by the International Shark Attack File.

Windsurfers, the fast moving newcomers to surfing, thought that they were immune until 1982. That was the year that a shark struck at a windsurfer, Scott Shoemaker, who was speeding along the sea off Hookipa Beach, Hawaii. In an instant a shark—probably a small reef shark—smashed into his board and bit down on his thigh, sending him dangling from his boom. Shoemaker pushed the shark off and crawled onto the board. Expecting another attack, he rearranged his rig and sailed to shore. Friends took him to a hospital, where his leg was saved.

The water was murky off a remote beach on Wailuaiki Bay, a surfing spot on Hawaii's Maui Island. On that day in 1993, windsurfer Roddy Lewis says he was thinking, *This is perfect water for sharks.* A few seconds after that thought flashed into his mind, a shark ten to twelve feet long clutched his leg. Lewis beat the shark on the head, driving it off. Lewis caught a wave and surfed to shore, where physicians managed to save Lewis's leg.

Attacks on windsurfers may introduce a new type of shark behavior—a territorial defense toward an oncoming intruder whose speed startles the shark. The theory comes from Elise MacGregor of *Windsurfing* magazine, who suggests that "sharks view the speeding, sharp-nosed, sharp-finned windsurfing boards that slam into them as a threat." She recounted a story from a windsurfer who witnessed a shark pursuing a windsurfer all the way to the beach.

Winds can whip these swift surfers far from shore, lessening the chance of quick rescue. In May 1999, twenty-two-year-old Tony Donoghue was windsurfing in Hardwicke Bay in South Australia, where great whites are regularly seen. When he had not returned by day's end, friends reported him missing. Next day, searchers picked up a shredded wetsuit, then, a couple of miles away, a scratched sailboard, and a torn harness. "There's no doubt he was taken by a shark," a police spokesman said, adding that police doubted his body would ever be found.

Some traditional surfers believe that the sharp increase in attacks on their brethren has to do with a change in equipment. Small paddleboards (bellyboards), which have been popular in recent years, may give less protection from shark attack than the more traditional large surfboards. And the smaller board, with four limbs hanging off it, may be mistaken for a seal, particularly by a great white.

Surfer Magazine in March 1993 reported a sharp increase in shark attacks on surfers off popular beaches in California, Florida, Australia, and Oregon. Between 1982 and 1987 there had been twenty shark attacks in California and Hawaii. Between 1987 and 1993 there were thirty-three—and the overwhelming number of victims were surfers. In Oregon there were ten non-fatal attacks on surfers between 1976 and 1991. The reason for the increase in attacks was an increase in surfers.

In the early 1950s, when surfing was beginning to become popular around Santa Cruz, California's "Surf City," there were probably no more than 1,500 surfers. Now, along the entire U.S. West Coast, there are more than 500,000, and their numbers are growing. Also contributing to the good times for the shark and bad times for the surfer was the Marine Mammal Protection Act, passed in 1972. It saved the pinnipeds and at the same time imperiled more surfers. No longer hunted, the sea lions prospered. The bigger population attracted pelagic great whites to hunting areas closer to shore, where the surfers were.

Surfers are so committed to surfing that they do not seem to notice the sharks or care about how habits of surfers happen to coincide with the habits of sharks: Both favor dusk and dawn, the surfers for surfing, the sharks for eating. And surfers often hunt for the perfect wave in areas where sharks hunt for food. Sharks are invisible to surfers, but surfers are not only visible but also very tempting to sharks.

John E. McCosker, a renowned shark researcher, first tested the surfer-as-seal theory off Dangerous Reef in Australia in 1985. He placed a mannequin in a wetsuit on a surfboard and put it in water chummed by animal blood. A great white attacked the board, although there was neither blood nor meat on the board or the mannequin. In another experiment, McCosker put a dummy in a scuba suit sixty feet below the surface. The dummy was not attacked until McCosker attached a fish to it (imitating the spear fishermen who tie a speared fish to a line about the waist). That *did* attract a shark. "I think you're much better off underwater than at the surface," McCosker told an interviewer. "In fact, I'm convinced you're better off, and I think the experiment proves it."

Sharks find surfboards so attractive that scientists take advantage of this behavior by using boards to lure sharks. When biologists Peter Pyle and Scot Anderson wanted to film close-up images of feeding sharks in the Farallon Islands, they made old surfboards their camera platforms, knowing that sharks were drawn to surfboards. Tethered to a boat or to shore, the surfboards float out to feeding areas as a visual stimulus to attract sharks. When the sharks attack the surfboard, their images are caught on videotape by a camera mounted on the board. If a shark could show disappointment, it would show on those videotapes.

A surfer in a shiny black wetsuit probably looks like an elephant seal or sea lion to a shark hunting its favorite prey. Or surfers also may look like a school of mullet, says George Burgess, director of the International Shark Attack File. "Here in Florida," he observes, "the soles of the feet and palms of the hands tend to be much lighter than the rest of the surfer's tanned skin. Black-tip sharks, who are very good at distinguishing contrast, naturally perceive the flashing white as fish bellies." (In a classic example of foot-as-mullet, a California surfer was straddling a surfboard waiting for a wave when a shark sank its teeth into his left leg. He suffered severe cuts around the knee.)

Like white sharks along the California coast, sharks in Oregon eat seals and sea lions, preying on large colonies in Winchester Bay and the Rogue, Blanco, and Orford reefs, and in other smaller colonies. And, as in California, surfers place themselves in the same waters with sharks and pinnipeds. Surfers call a certain area off the California coast the Red Triangle. Another biological red triangle forms when shark, seal, and surfer occupy the same water.

John Forse, fifty years old and thirty-six years a surfer, was straddling his surfboard about 150 yards off Gleneden Beach on an April day in 1998 when he saw swirling water and assumed that a seal was nearby. It was a fifteen-foot shark. "The next thing I knew I felt this pressure on my thigh. No pain, it was more like a vise grip," he told an *Oregonian* interviewer. "He pulled me under maybe ten to twelve feet. We were thrashing around down there and he came back up."

The teeth on the great white's lower jaw dug into Forse's new board; his upper teeth sank into Forse's right thigh, etching a curving, foot-long wound with twelve tooth marks.

The shark came back to the surface and then started down again. Forse was still attached to his board by a quick-release cord. "I knew that sharks had a sensitive spot on their nose, but that was about six feet away, so I couldn't reach it. His dorsal fin was about a foot away. So I started beating on the back of it. He started down a second time and the cord snapped. He must've bitten it in half. The whole thing took, oh, twenty seconds." Forse climbed back up on the board, which had a crescent bite out of it, and paddled into shore.

Forse was the twelfth surfer attacked by a shark off the Oregon and Washington coasts between 1976 and 1998. In the twelve recorded Oregon incidents, five of the surfers were injured. The seven others escaped with bitten surfboards. One of the California surfers bitten during that high tide of attacks was John Regan, who was quite sure that the shark that slightly injured him—"took one bite and took off"— mistook him, in his all-black wetsuit, for a seal. That was the second time a shark bit Regan. Two years before, while spear-fishing, he was bitten on the other leg by a shark.

Elsewhere in the surfer world, the story was the same. For about a week, surfers off Ponta do Uuro, Mozambique, had noticed large shoals of fishes feeding close to shore. Most of them knew that those fishes brought sharks. One of the surfers was lying on his board with his legs in the water. The shark came and bit him, inflicting a wound on his right leg about eight inches across, not deep enough to cause damage.

In South Africa, the sea was "warm, dirty, and choppy" at the mouth of the Buffalo River near East London. A surfer about 200 yards offshore felt something grab him. A shark bit his left calf with a bite big enough to encompass his foot. "I turned around and clouted it," the surfer said later, "and it let go and swam away."

A thirty-one-year-old Japanese surfer was sitting on his surfboard waiting for a wave when, witnesses said, he suddenly disappeared. Tooth marks on the surfboard indicated that the shark was a great white. It had bitten off both of the surfer's legs, along with his right arm and shoulder. The attack occurred off Sunayama Beach in Miyako Island, a small island in the Ryukyu Island chain that is south of the major Japanese islands.

Speaking on the hundreds of attacks on seals and sea lions by great whites, researcher Peter Klimley says, "They clearly make a decision on what they are going to swallow. Most surfers they just spit out."

There were twenty-six divers on the boat that sailed to St. Crispin's Reef, about forty miles off Port Douglas, a gateway to Australia's Great Barrier Reef, on January 25, 1998. Twenty-four divers came back. Eileen Lonergan, twenty-nine, and Thomas Lonergan, thirty-three, were accidentally left behind.

They were never seen again. But over the following months fishermen found a diving fin with *Eileen L* printed on the bottom, a wetsuit hood, and a wetsuit torn at the rear. Searchers also found a diver's slate. On one side were jotted details of dives and the names of fish they had seen. On the other was written: "Please help us. Find us soon before we die." Under this message they signed their names, address, and phone number.

Ben Cropp, a veteran diver who served as search adviser during the hunt for the Lonergans, is an authority on Australian sharks. He believed that a tiger shark probably attacked them within forty-eight hours after the dive boat sailed off without them. "You'd appear a helpless animal to them," he told an interviewer. "By night the tide would have ebbed and they would be swept back to the outer reef." Tiger sharks, he said, often spend the days in deep water and venture to shallow reefs at night looking for food. St. Crispin's is one such outer reef.

Shark-diver interaction at a glance:

Body Parts Injured in 234 Shark Attacks on Divers	
Body Parts	**Attack percentage**
Leg	79.4
Calf/knee	31.6
Thigh	23.5
Foot	20.5
Toe	3.8
Arm	64.9
Arm	28.6
Hand	16.2
Shoulder	10.3
Finger	9.8
Torso	44.0
Chest	9.8
Abdomen/stomach	9.4
Buttocks	8.5
Back	6.4
Waist	5.6
Genitals	4.3
Head	10.3
Head/neck	10.3
SOURCE: INTERNATIONAL SHARK ATTACK FILE	

Rodney Orr, spearfishing on a surfboard at the edge of California's Red Triangle, had taken his limit of abalone and was going back for black snapper and ling. As he kicked away from his board, he felt as if a boat had run over him. "The lights went out," Orr recalled. For a moment, darkness tinged with blood enclosed him. Then, "Just at the edge of vision I saw something, but I didn't realize what it was, and then the little light dawned, and what I could see [were] the gills on this white shark." Continuing his recollection of that day in 1990, he told a *Nova* interviewer, "And the shark was like ten, eleven feet long, and it closed on me, but when I looked back at it, it had closed the distance by half, and then it started coming in fast. And I knew it was after me.

"But I tried to get behind this rock. And when I tried to get behind it, the shark came in on my left side, his mouth just opened up, and his jaw actually just came out of his mouth. And I had a row of teeth marks up in my scalp where he bit down. And the worst damage was probably to my nose and to my lower eye, because I had a hole through the upper eyelid and the bottom eyelid. All I could see was, really, was the teeth out of my, you know, from my left eye. And I could see about ten or twelve teeth.

"I think he realized that I wasn't a seal at that time. But why he didn't finish biting the head off me, why he didn't thrash, I don't know. It's just luck of the draw."

With one hand Orr lashed out at the great white with his spear gun; with the other hand he struck at the teeth that had just holed his eyelids. Then, perhaps ten seconds after the attack began, the shark let him go and he was delivered from the shark's mouth. He paddled to shore and was taken to a hospital and saved with eighty stitches.

On a compilation of California shark attacks, Orr is listed as a victim with "minor wounds." He appears twice on the list because he had also been attacked by a great white in 1961. That time, his wetsuit suffered the damage.

Like surfers, divers often find themselves in waters inhabited by sharks. Most divers follow rules designed to keep them away from sharks. If they see—or *sense*—a shark, they try to slip away. Teddy Tucker, the legendary Bermuda treasure diver, says that diving in crystal-clear, 85-degree water can make you forget about the rules. He has seen countless sharks in seas from Bermuda to New Zealand. Now the director of the Bermuda Underwater Exploration Institute, Tucker has translated his respect for sharks into a save-the-sharks video, produced by the institute in cooperation with the New England Aquarium.

"It's a good idea to quit diving late in the day, when the sharks become more active," he advises. "I counted eight of them around us late one afternoon while working on the Old Spaniard [his name for a sixteenth-century wreck]. And they circled ever closer until we decided to reboard the boat.

"Diving on the outer reef required your constant attention. At five P.M., you did not require a watch. First arrivals were small dusky sharks from four to four and a half feet long. They would arrive in a group until the number of sharks could not be counted. It was necessary to keep a constant lookout. As long as one did not move quickly, you were safe. However, when the sharks' pace started to speed up it was time to get back to the boat."

Teddy's dusky sharks belong to one of at least twelve species in Bermuda waters. Sharks, especially tiger sharks, are not well publicized in balmy Bermuda. When an 800-pound tiger shark was caught near Bermuda's shore in 1999, John Barnes, the director of Agriculture and Fisheries, quickly issued an assurance that shark attacks were rare. But he did add a warning about the sharks' nocturnal habits:

"Skinny dipping in the middle of the night might not be a good idea, or swimming while there's a full moon."

Bermuda has had few shark attacks. One in the 1980s was hushed up, according to the *Bermuda Sun,* "for fear the screaming headlines would scare away the tourists." But the sharks certainly are there. In contrast to Tucker's prudent advice to get out when you see them, a Bermuda spear fisherman pursued a shark, was attacked, but survived a brazen attempt to make a shark a fish of prey. "I was out with a group of people three or four miles off shore to the west of the north channel trying to catch two or three fish for dinner," he told the *Sun.* At the edge of the reef, a five-foot shark suddenly appeared "and it came straight at me." The shark swam close, then swam away—and the diver decided to "have a go at it."

He got close enough to the shark to spear it. After thrashing around, it swam off. By then, another man had joined the spear fisherman in the water. The shark made a large circle and "came straight back at me like he knew I was the one that did him in." In the short scuffle that followed, the shark bit the spear fisher on the arm and swam away.

Spear fishermen are in constant danger if sharks are nearby. The underwater fisherman's catches bleed, putting the catcher in the midst of a chum trail. Inexperienced spear fishermen carry their catch on a stringer or tether. Experience teaches them to put the catch in a bag that can be dropped when a shark appears. The shark wants the bag, not the person holding it. But, if he insists. . . . Smart fishermen also watch the tides, spear fishing on the incoming tide, when fewer sharks are likely to be inshore from the fisher. On an outgoing tide, sharks from offshore may be attracted to the fishing site.

When challenged, spear fishers are supposed to give up their catch. An example of what happens otherwise came in the Bahamas when a diver, fishing the inside-reef zone, speared a fish at about the same time that a bull shark appeared. The spear fisherman clutched the fish close to his chest. The shark darted for the fish, biting not only the fish but also part of the man's neck and face.

"I blew it. Please don't blame the shark," Kevin King told Gary Adkison, a doctor who was trying to repair King's chewed right elbow. A shark bit King in August 1999 while he was spear fishing off Grand Cay, Bahamas. King had seen the shark, warned his friends to leave, but decided to spear one last fish. He did—and then the shark hit him, mauling his elbow. "The shark shook him very violently and hard to get Kevin to let go of the grouper," Adkison told the Florida *Sun-Sentinel.* "The shark knew in which arm Kevin held the grouper."

Spear fishermen, Adkison said, "must understand that you are competing with the shark and that his job is to eat sick, wounded animals. The key is to be alert that the predators can show up at any time and always have a boat nearby to get the bleeding fish out of the water."

Instinct usually impels people *away* from sharks. Even surfers, windsurfers, and divers who enter shark-prowled waters do not want to get close to a shark. But there are sports divers who seek out sites known to attract sharks. The wrecks of the *Papoose* and the *Tarpon,* in waters up to 140 feet deep off North Carolina, are popular spots for swimming with sharks without the protection of a cage. In California, divers tell each other about places with sharks because, for these divers, sharks are the major attraction.

Diving enthusiasts say that some of the most famous dive sites—off Australia's Great Barrier Reef, on Palau's Blue Corner, off Costa Rica's Cocos Island, in the Galapagos Islands—do not disturb the sharks or the environment. But some observers fear that the parade of divers may have effects on the sharks' behavior, particularly their ageless repertoire for reproduction, territoriality, and aggression.

Tourist divers, an ever-increasing new breed, will pay high fees to get what they want: guaranteed close encounters of the selachian kind. Sharks have become objects for observation, rather than man-eaters to avoid. The very word *shark* attracts these divers. Advertisements for dive trips lure tourist divers to such places as Shark Junction in Grand Bahama Island, Shark Reef in Cat Cays, Bimini; Shark Buoy and Bull Shark Wall on New Providence Island in the Bahamas.

Travel brochures urge tourists to *Reach out and touch a shark!* Put on Scuba gear and then even feed a shark! Or ride a great white by grabbing a sixteen-footer's tail—a stunt that made the cover of a diving magazine. All this happens in the new realm where paying customers can snuggle up to sharks. (Divers have a name for it: Addictive Shark Diving Disorder, "the uncontrollable urge to leap out of a perfectly good boat into a sea filled with toothed elasmobranches.")

"Play with more than 30 Nurse sharks," urges one advertisement. Another, for a shark-feed operation, says, "You can also do a training course and hand-feed the sharks yourself. You wear a chain mail suit and a video is taken of you." That is the promise from one of the many shark-feeding operations in the Bahamas, a choice site for divers (and moviemakers) in search of sharky, crystal-clear waters. And another: "Get up and swim with the sharks during the feed. Touch them if you like. They will not harm you. They see you only as another big predator there for a meal. If you stay bonded to the sand you might as well have stayed at home and watched it all on video."

There may be more shark-feeding spots in the Bahamas than anywhere else in the world. The industry is served by fishermen who catch the shark bait and companies that specialize in producing fish blood for chumming. The most common shark to perform for Bahaman divers is the Caribbean reef shark, which grows to about eight feet. Other species include the relatively harmless nurse sharks and the silky—a large, aggressive shark whose unusually smooth skin gives it its popular name.

At one of the Bahaman sites, the host of the shark feast "hypnotizes" reef sharks by stroking them, a phenomenon also observed in great whites. A diver who witnessed this later recounted how the feeder lifted the shark off the sandy seafloor by its dorsal fin and presented it to tourist divers, who then stroked its tail. He next pulled a dead fish from a container and waved it in front of the shark's jaws. The shark instantly devoured the fish.

At Walker's Cay, divers ("bait-mates") pay to attend a shark feed that is called a Shark Rodeo. As many as seventy sharks, most of them Caribbean reef sharks, are drawn to a "chumsicle," a rebar tree festooned with the fish heads and tails discarded by sports fishermen. Divers swim around or over the chumsicle and watch the sharks feed on the bait. When the sharks finish their meal and swim off, divers scramble to pick up the teeth broken off on the rebars. In a variation at Stuart Cove's, divers drop to the bottom (about thirty-five feet down) and form a circle. A shark feeder then brings down a crate of "chum chunks" and puts it in the middle of the circle, attracting the reef sharks, which swarm toward the shark feeder, who wears chain-mail sleeves and gloves. He pulls out chunks with a spear and holds up the morsels for passing sharks to grab while the bait-mates photograph their encounters.

Shark diving without the protection of a cage is a natural step for thrill seekers in wetsuits. South Africa introduced shark-cage diving in the early 1990s at Dyer Island, Gansbaai, near Africa's southernmost tip. The commercial cage industry spread through southern Africa, where thousands of divers now pay to drop into shark-filled seas—including a treat that sounds like a nightmare: a nighttime dive in the midst of great whites.

At first the cage operators clashed with concerned users of the same seas. Commercial fishermen and abalone divers called the cage divers "cowboys" and claimed that they would drive away fish or bring in more sharks, or both. "The sharks can see the people in the cages and on the boats," said one veteran diver, "and they learn to associate people and their scent with both the food and the excitement generated in the operation." Cage operations were blamed for a flurry of six attacks on South African surfers and divers in the space of five weeks. Although only one of the attacks was near a cage, anti-cage groups charged that cage diving had either habituated or excited sharks into attacking swimmers and surfers.

Eventually, the Department of Sea Fisheries developed a code of conduct that set up standards for equipment and the training of cage operators. Chumming was banned in the Dyer Island Channel—nicknamed "Shark Alley," because it runs between Dyer, an island full of birds, and Gyser Rock, the island home to some 60,000 fur seals. The two islands form a protected nature reserve.

Regulations are also appearing elsewhere in the realm of tourist-luring sharks, a realm that includes—besides the Bahamas and South Africa—Cocos Island in the Indian Ocean, Bora Bora and Rangiroa Atoll in French Polynesia, Bikini in the Marshall Islands, the Galapagos, the Revillagigedo Islands and the Sea of Cortez in Mexico, Cuba, and Papua New Guinea. One of Australia's great white expeditions is led by thoroughly scarred Rodney Fox, probably the world's best known survivor of a great white.

The National Marine Fisheries Service has banned shark-baiting along the 360-mile central California coast, but cage diving goes on elsewhere on the U.S. West Coast. Surfers helped to get the ban after protesting about a cage-diving enterprise that lured sharks by dumping slaughterhouse offal into the sea. Hawaii prohibits feeding to lure sharks in sixteen areas, primarily to protect surfers.

Environmentalists, along with spear fishers, have been campaigning against underwater shark feedings by divers, maintaining that such feedings train sharks to associate humans with food. Spear fishermen in Florida reported encounters with aggressive sharks that harass and snap at them. Several fishermen were injured by sharks exhibiting what the fishermen saw as dangerous new behavior. Florida's Fish and Wildlife Conservation Commission took the first step toward banning or closely regulating the practice by voting unanimously to make it illegal for divers, instructors, and anyone else in the water to feed fish. One of the commissioners, Edwin Roberts, could speak firsthand about the issue. He told of a dive trip with his children to Sombrero Light off Marathon, a shark-feeding site. "The nurse sharks ran me and my kids out of the water," Roberts said. "I was having to beat [the sharks] to keep them off my kids."

George Burgess, adding the weight of the International Shark Attack File to the controversy, said that the inevitable accident provoked by dive-tour encounters will ruin the work of scientists who, ever since *Jaws*, have fought to tame the public image of the shark as a man-eating predator. "Almost certainly when a dive-tour attack happens, it will be videotaped and that tape will appear on one of the tabloid TV shows," said Burgess, director of the ISAF. "The shark will be blamed for the attack." Attacks that have occurred have been relatively mild. A dive master in the Bahamas was severely bitten on the arm and leg by a Caribbean reef shark;

a tourist was bitten on the head by a shark at an underwater feeding site in the Bahamas on a non-feeding day. Critics of shark-feeding say there have been other, unpublicized incidents.

Some shark-feeding operations employ shark cages, which look simple enough to operate. Customers are lowered into cages while operators chum the area. Things can go wrong: A shark can get caught in the cage ropes; a shark can pull the cage free of the boat and take the passengers for a ride. Several places in California and Australia clothe the customers in chain-mail suits. But many feeders, including popular attractions in the Bahamas and Florida, do not provide diving tourists with any protective gear. Some of the latter supposedly "train" their customers to feed sharks by hand.

Burgess, to see for himself, joined in an unprotected feeding dive in the Bahamas. "The experience," he reported, "was exhilarating. . . . I did not feel threatened by the sharks swimming above, in front, and behind me as we knelt on the sand bottom of a natural amphitheater. I did note one blacktip, apparently low in a dominance order that was confined to the perimeter of the circling mass of sharks and fishes and was reluctant to approach the chum ball in the center. It exhibited apparent displacement or frustration behavior involving periodic mouth gaping, increasing over time, and occasional erratic swimming movements, including hunching of the back and dropping of the pectoral fins. This type of behavior has been observed immediately prior to attacks on divers during shark feeding dives at other sites in the Bahamas. . . ."[1]

Shark-cage diving, he believes, is generally safe, although some operators and customers have been bitten when they stuck out their hands. Some divers in chain mail have been wounded, as have those wearing no protection.

Although chain-mail suits offer some protection from small to medium-size sharks, Burgess noted that the tooth tips of even small sharks can penetrate the mesh and wound the wearer (as happened to a pioneer chain-mail wearer, Valerie Taylor). Such large sharks as whites, tigers, bull, and dusky can cut through the mesh, and even if their teeth do not penetrate, their powerful jaws can produce crushing injuries.

"The metal mail," Burgess says, "may even be electro-magnetically attractive to some species of sharks; whites, in particular, are well-documented biters of metal objects, such as ship hulls and propellers." Another report of a shark drawn to an electrical field came from a shark-feed site off the village of Ponta do Ouro in Mozambique. Divers there view tiger sharks, hammerheads, silvertips, and bull sharks (known locally as Zambezi sharks). During one dive, a bull shark, more than eight feet long, smashed into a digital be-tacam, ignoring the betacam operator and two companions.

In the Bahamas, where shark-feed divers are usually un-protected, Burgess has collected reports of more than a dozen injuries in the last several years. "Most of these," he says, "have not been publicized in the media because of effi-cient damage control by local operators. Perhaps fortu-nately for the event promoters, most of the victims were host dive masters who presumably knew well what they were getting into, but a serious injury to a diving tourist is inevitable."

Are bait-attracted sharks more likely to attack people than other sharks? Burgess' answer: "Based solely on obser-vations of baited carcharhinids in the Bahamas, which seem to largely ignore divers, one may be tempted to suggest 'no more' or even 'less' of a threat." But put a concentration of both sharks and humans in the same place at the same time and you get what Burgess calls "an increased opportunity for an attack." He also worries about placing one source of food like the chum ball in the midst of an uncontrolled number of sharks. Some may become so conditioned to getting free food that when they find none, they may attack. Burgess wonders if that is what happened when a shark attacked the diver swimming at a Bahamas feeding site on a non-feeding day.

No shark is more dangerous than the great white, which normally eats large prey. Unlike the reef sharks or even the blue sharks lured to feeding sites, great whites frequently kill on first strike. Burgess points out that even a theoretically safe cage dive with great whites challenges basic axioms for avoiding attack: avoid diving in an area known to be frequented by sharks; avoid diving in waters known to contain animal carcasses and blood; do not touch sharks; avoid wearing shiny objects—such as the cage itself—and contrasting colors while diving. Failure to obey those axioms led to more than twenty-four reported attacks. Although none of those attacks occurred during shark feeds, they could have, and, Burgess, in a chilling prophecy, says, "I can predict unequivocally that it will."

Burgess and other scientists are concerned about the way shark feeding is disrupting the ecosystem. "Concentrations of sharks (and bony fishes) I witnessed at the Bahamas feeding site are unnatural," he says. ". . . The sharks and some bony fishes at these sites are now trained show animals that reside in the area and have become at least partially dependent on free food. Similar entrainment has been reported from feeding sites in Australia. We do not know if local populations are increasing such that they can concentrate at these sites while still maintaining their natural levels of density and distribution over adjacent areas.

"That the Bahamas sharks are indeed entrained is demonstrated by their response to the sound of a boat's motor.

Dive operators routinely rev their engines as they approach the feeding site in order to attract the sharks ('calling in our babies' is the expression used by operators at one site). Sharks rapidly come to the site, surrounding the boat long before the first free food or diver hits the water (sound Pavlovian?). Similar behavior has been noted in Australia. . . . If sharks appear whenever a motorboat visits a region, anglers are likely to lose their hooked catches to opportunistic sharks or have the sharks frighten away potential catches. Skin/scuba divers seeking sharkless diving will encounter unwelcomed escorts. . . . We have heard of a diver who had a shark follow his outboard motor-driven boat from dive stop to dive stop, eventually ending in a bite."

Shark feeding at U.S. and Caribbean sites evolved from the practice of "riding" whale sharks and manta rays at Indo-Pacific tourist spots. U.S. laws prohibit the harassment of marine mammals, but sharks do not have such federal protection. Nor do sharks get included in the kind of prohibition that is enforced at Biscayne National Park in Florida, where visitors are forbidden to feed or interact with any fish. For Biscayne, this is just a natural extension of a National Parks policy: Don't feed wild animals.

For professionals, there is no alternative. They must dive, driven not by hobby or obsession but by a need to make a living. Even professionals who know the shark do not really know the shark.

In the Caribbean off the Yucatán peninsula lies the Mexican island of Mujeres. There in May 1992, Greg Marshall, a marine biologist who is also a filmmaker for *National Geographic Television,* was planning to attach his Crittercam to a shark. The Crittercam is a video camcorder and data-logging system, both controlled by a miniature computer. The system, housed in a small titanium cylinder, is attached to a shark or other underwater creature by a small barb or suction cup. A fail-safe mechanism on the barb or suction cup releases the device, and a radio-tracking device leads searchers to the floating Crittercam with its roll of creature-in-action film.

Mexican fishermen, who knew that the waters around Mujeres often teemed with sharks, were hired to catch a shark that would carry a Crittercam. They succeeded. But when Marshall stuck the barb into the shark's skin, it escaped. "Nobody felt they were in any immediate danger," John Bredar, *National Geographic Television* producer, later reported. Underwater cameraman Nick Caloyianis dived in, unaware that a fisherman was trying to recapture the shark. Then, as Bredar told the story on the *Geographic* Web site, "One of the fishermen popped up out of the water screaming, 'He bit him! He bit him!' And then Nick popped out of the water moaning, 'Oh my God! Oh God! Oh God!' and fell into the boat clutching his arm, bleeding profusely."

As the boat sped back to shore, someone called ahead to a small military installation and asked for an ambulance. "Nick was in shock and had lost a lot of blood. First we cut Nick out of his wet suit. He had major lacerations all over his right arm up to his elbow and deep lacerations down to the bone around his hand and fingers. Then a similar kind of classic shark bite on his leg.

"One of these medical guys was trying to put a tourniquet on Nick's arm. If somebody's life is in danger, you put a tourniquet on. Otherwise, you're at risk of losing the limb, because you cut off the blood supply to the entire limb. I was shocked that this guy was doing this and said, 'NO! NO! NO!' We realized we had to get out of this place. Nick was going to get worse, not better.

"The ambulance was waiting. They pushed Nick into the back of the ambulance and one of the attendants shut the door on Nick's leg. This poor guy has been attacked by a shark. He's been abused in one medical facility. We're going to another one and they close the door on his leg!

"Finally, we get to the hospital. The only reassuring medical thing in the entire day is that we're greeted by a doctor. I know he's a doctor because he's wearing golf clothes. It's a national holiday in Mexico and clearly any doctor worth his salt would be playing golf. Finally we felt, OKAY. Things are going to be okay.

"They start working on Nick's wounds. It was the most gruesome thing I've ever seen. The margin between serious accident and tragedy was paper thin because the shark was so close to ripping into Nick's major arteries—literally centimeters away."

The fishermen eventually recaptured the shark and the *National Geographic* team got the Crittercam attached. According to Bredar, the shark that attacked Caloyianis was the first animal to carry a Crittercam successfully in the ocean. There was poetic justice to that, for it had been a shark that had inspired Marshall six years before. During a close, but uneventful, encounter, Marshall noticed a large remora stuck onto the shark's belly. "I realized," he later said, "that by substituting a video camcorder for the sucker-fish we could record images from the shark's perspective."

Although Bredar and Marshall wanted to release the shark that would star in their *National Geographic* film, the fishermen insisted on killing it, saying, "The shark has tasted human blood, it's been in our water. We live in these waters. We're going to kill it." The fishermen cut out the jaws, which were presented to Caloyianis in the hospital.

Caloyianis made a complete recovery. Four months after the attack—which he classified as provoked—he was back in the sea, filming blue sharks off Block Island.

★ ★ ★

"There has been a general trend, over the last decade or so, for divers to grow increasingly over-confident when encountering sharks," writes Jeremy Stafford-Deitsch, a world-renowned underwater photographer.[2] "Indeed, as more and more divers feed various species of reef shark on tropical reefs, with only the rarest of mishaps, a cavalier tendency has slowly, but imperceptibly gained ground: Because some species of shark can, under certain conditions, be relatively safely encountered, there is a growing assumption that many, if not all, sharks can be approached/fed/photographed underwater without risk. However the only way to learn what can and cannot be done is trial and error—and error, when dealing with sharks, can lead to disastrous results."

He singled out the silky shark as an example. Easy to identify underwater (sharp-pointed head, thin-bodied), the silky is not usually thought of as a dangerous shark. But, during a dive at the Sha'ab Rumi Reef in the Sudanese Red Sea, four silky sharks appeared, and schools of fishes, clearly unnerved, disappeared, "as if expecting trouble." At that point, several bottle-nosed dolphin also appeared.

Stafford-Deitsch suddenly realized he was breaking several of his own safety rules: "I was swimming with sharks when there were dolphins present. (The sharks can mistake you for an injured dolphin.) I was swimming with large, open-water sharks on my own. I was swimming with sharks as dusk approached—and many species of shark are crepuscular in their feeding habits. . . .

"I looked below into the gloom and gulped. The two largest sharks were powering up from below towards me at the same alarmingly rapid pace. My instincts shrieked danger. At the last moment they stopped right in front of me. I nervously took a blurred shot as I tried to convince myself that they would calm down, circle, return to the gloom, and circle again. But they didn't retreat an inch. Instead their heads were sweeping from side to side as they worried their way ever closer. I decided I needed to gain some respect and kicked the bigger one in the head with my fin. It shuddered, spun in an angry circle and immediately returned to its original position hovering inches from my fins, twitching and trembling in a mass of nervous energy. I kicked it. . . ."

He could hear the engine of the inflatable dive boat. He headed for the top of a reef, from which he could yell to be picked up. But the sharks were following him. He sensed that if he stopped they might charge him. "Then the larger shark surged past my left fin and was effortlessly alongside, fearlessly watching me with its yellow eye. I clunked the shark on the snout with the butt of my Nikonos. It ignored this puny blow and continued to glide parallel, watching. . . .

"Then I heard the roar of the inflatable as it sped up to the side of the reef. The sharks, distracted, retreated a little. It was the first moment of doubt, of distraction, of hesitation that had registered in the silkies since I had re-entered the water. That moment's hesitation saved me: The noisy arrival of the inflatable had broken the pitiless, prehistoric spell that bonds hunter to hunted. The sharks backed off enough to allow me to turn and swim for the boat.

"What lessons did I learn? What lessons should others learn from this? Our ignorance about sharks and their behaviour in the wild is all but total. I had glimpsed how rapidly the rules can change, how irrelevant everything I thought I knew could instantly become. Most sharks are not dangerous most of the time. But dusk is a special time. And I only just got away with it on this occasion—more sober, more respectful, more daunted than before. And with more grey hairs."

Some tips for divers:

- If you see a shark's behavior change—especially arched back, pectoral fins held stiffly down and a rigid side-to-side head movement—you are being told to back off immediately or you will be attacked. (Researchers say that virtually all serious attacks on a reef are by territorial sharks defending their space.)
- If you see any large shark cruising near you—particularly hammerheads, tiger, bull, or lemon sharks—leave the area. These four species are responsible for more serious or fatal attacks upon divers fully underwater than any other, including the great white.
- Your dive boat itself may attract sharks. Boat motors and metallic hulls seem to be attractants for some sharks. Anchored boats also seem to draw inquisitive sharks, as do buoys, and other inanimate objects. In a study of such behavior by great whites, scientists concluded that the sharks "often strike unfamiliar objects to determine potential food value," even when they did not resemble familiar prey. "It would seem," the scientists wrote, "that grasping an unfamiliar object would be the only reliable method of determining palatability."[3]

CHAPTER 13

If It Happens . . .

In the Gulf of Aqaba, between the Sinai Peninsula and the desolate coast of Saudi Arabia, Martin Richardson had dived out of a boat and was swimming with a pod of five bottle-nose dolphins. After a few minutes, he screamed. The men in the boat saw his body fly through the air and realized sharks were attacking him. But they knew that anyone surrounded by dolphins was safe from shark attack. The men jumped into an inflatable boat and headed for Richardson. Three dolphins were circling around Richardson, who had been bitten on the back, shoulder, and chest. Swift medical treatment saved him.

A diver was in a friend's boat, hunting lobsters in the Florida Keys in August 1999, when he spotted a pod of dolphins and decided to jump in. As he attempted to join the dolphins, a seven-foot bull shark swam up to him. When he tried to kick it away, another shark bit his other leg, inflicting five small wounds. He, like many before him, had thought that dolphins protected swimmers from sharks. (Incidentally, he also violated the Federal Marine Mammal Protection Act, which prohibits the harassing of dolphins, including trying to swim with them.)

You *can* be attacked by sharks while you are swimming with dolphins. And perhaps dolphins will protect you if an attack comes. But the point, lost to most admirers of dolphins, is that both those beloved mammals and the shark often pursue the same prey. They happen to be in the water at the same time. And if another mammal in the form of a human being appears, anything can happen.

Sharks often are called unpredictable, but that statement reflects our scant but growing knowledge of sharks, rather than the behavior of the sharks themselves. A person who is attacked has a survival edge if he or she has learned some fundamental facts about shark behavior.

Can I avoid a shark attack?

No question has an easy answer. But questions can be answered in the dolphin way: Yes and no. Anything can happen.

Where are sharks likely to be?

Many shark attacks occur in nearshore waters, typically inshore of a sandbar where sharks may be confined at low tide. Sharks may also congregate along steep drop-offs, near channels or at river mouths, where they usually find food. More than 85 percent of attacks are in water no deeper than *five feet.*

Why do sharks attack?

Some attacks may be purely out of curiosity, such as a shark investigating prospective new prey. Or the attack may be a territorial response; researchers know little about territoriality in sharks. But since most predator activity on land involves staking out a territory, that same behavior

246

may also occur among sharks, especially large sharks. A great white feeding on a sea lion off the Farallon Islands in California, for example, seems to warn off other sharks by slapping its tail, producing a visual and audible signal. A human being straying into this kind of a situation may be in trouble.

Similarly, some attacks may be triggered when the victim unintentionally trespasses into some ritualistic behavior, interrupting or annoying a shark engaged in a courtship ritual. Some scientists speculate that shark attacks on humans often are cases of mistaken identity.

What are the shark's moves in a typical attack?

Researchers believe that there are three kinds of unprovoked attacks: hit-and-run, bump-and-bite, and sneak.

Hit-and-Run

In September 1994 a woman swimming in chest-deep water near Hilton Head Island, South Carolina, was bitten by a shark, which left an eighteen-inch wound that ran diagonally from her thigh to chest. She survived. It was the first attack in the area since 1988, when a man was bitten on the arm by a shark about three miles away.

Both encounters are classified as hit-and-run attacks. In such an attack—typically in the surf zone—a swimmer or surfer is the target. The victim seldom sees the attacker, and the shark does not return after inflicting a bite. Most hit-and-run attacks are probably due to mistaken identity. Often water visibility is poor and the waves are high. Currents may be running. And there may be many swimmers or surfers in the water.

Some of these attacks could also involve social behaviors unrelated to feeding, such as dominance behaviors similar to those observed in land animals.

Injuries are usually relatively small wounds, often on the leg below the knee, and are seldom life-threatening.

Bump-and-Bite

A diver who entered the water at a Caribbean reef at night had to know that he was taking a chance. But he wanted to retrieve a piece of equipment he had left on the sea floor. He jumped out of his boat and walked through the shallow water. Suddenly, he felt something brush his legs. He does not remember how he got back into the boat. A shark researcher, he knew he was the lucky victim of a bump-and-bite attack: A lemon or nurse shark had been checking out its territory. The shark meant no harm, the researcher said.

Sometimes the victims do not get off as easily. In many cases, the bump precedes an attack, which involves a bite and then, usually, flight from the scene by the shark.

Sneak

A woman swimming off Monastery Beach in Carmel Bay, California, felt two "bangs" to her leg. For a moment she thought she had been hit by a playful swimmer. Then she felt pressure on her leg and yelled, "I'm stuck." She thought she was in some kind of trap. Leaning down in the water and grabbing her leg, she realized "it was a shark and was about a foot away from my face. . . . I think the shark still had my foot in its mouth, and I think it either bit deeper or was releasing my leg because I felt more pain and not just pressure." (Many shark victims report no immediate pain, probably due to intense shock.) Other swimmers got the woman to shore, where prompt medical aid saved her and her leg. The attacker was a great white twelve- to thirteen-feet long.

This sneak attack ended with a living victim. Many, especially those launched by a great white, do not, one reason being that great whites often make repeated strikes.

In sneak attacks, particularly by great whites, the attack follows a pattern that researchers have named "bite-and-release" or "bite-and-spit" behavior. The shark grabs the victim, usually pulls him or her under the water, then suddenly lets go and swims away, leaving a badly wounded victim behind. Why? Researchers offer two theories:

- The shark may be following observed energy-saving behavior with pinniped prey: Mortally wound the prey, let it bleed to death, then come back and eat it.
- After tasting the prey, the shark finds it unpalatable and goes off in search of something better.

Whatever the shark's reason for bite-and-release, that bite is not usually powerful enough to be fatal. The victim has a chance of survival if help and a hospital are nearby.

No shark has been more extensively studied than the great white. Whole books have been written about great whites.[1] But there is no way to predict how a great white will react if you meet one. An analysis of 484 shark attacks in Australian waters—within 200 nautical miles of Australia, the Torres Strait Islands, and the Cocos Islands—showed that 180 were fatal. In the thirty-four attacks that great whites are known to have made, twenty-one were fatal.

That same Australian study shows that great whites, at least in Australia, do not consistently practice "bite-and-spit" behavior.[2] In 26 percent of the cases, the body was consumed or taken away. The Australian researcher, John West, analyzed the sequence of events in a great white attack and discerned four "orders":

First order: Circled or swam toward victim

Second order: Grabbed victim or bit surfboard; grabbed victim and surfboard

Third order: Swam away (sometimes with victim in mouth); circled victim again; made second attempt to bite; grabbed victim again

Fourth order: Swam away (again sometimes with victim in mouth); circled victim; grabbed the victim again; followed victim to shore

What does a potential victim make of that? One answer: great whites have a repertoire of behavior, and "bite-and-spit" seems to be in that repertoire. But the great white's choice of moves is unpredictable. There is one thing to take comfort in: In most cases West analyzed, the victim was grabbed and quickly released.

The best way to avoid a shark attack is to use common sense, the basis for the following rules. If you are swimming, diving, or surfing in a new area, ask local people about the area's shark history. In Florida and Hawaii, tourists who don't know the water are frequently the victims.

At times, along many shores, sharks congregate close to shore to feed. This is particularly true in Florida. Great numbers of nurse, blacktip, and sand sharks are often reported as they follow their food source close to the shoreline or are cruising the waters because of the abundance of fish. A group of sharks off Tyndall Air Force Base, near Panama City, Florida, for example, was so closely packed that a biologist said they looked like bodysurfers riding small waves and bumping into each other. Most of them ranged in size from three to eight feet. The beaches were closed on that particular day. But beach closings are bad for business. So sometimes when sharks congregate inshore, tourists don't know about it and get nipped among the fishes that the sharks are hunting.

General Advice for Swimmers and Surfers[3]

- *Never swim alone.* Swim, dive, or surf with other people. Sharks are more likely to attack a solitary individual.
- Don't swim where sharks congregate, such as between sandbars, near steep drop-offs, or near channels.
- Don't enter the water if sharks are known to be present and evacuate the water if sharks are seen.
- Don't swim in dirty or turbid water. (Note how many attacks described in this book took place in murky water.)
- Don't wander too far from shore, especially if you insist on swimming alone. This isolates you and places you far away from help.
- Avoid being in the water during darkness or twilight hours. Sharks are most active during these times and have a competitive sensory advantage.
- Don't enter the water if you are bleeding from an open wound. Women when menstruating should avoid waters known to have sharks. Don't urinate. Remember that a shark's olfactory sense is extremely acute.
- Don't wear shiny jewelry because the reflected light resembles the sheen of fish scales.
- If you see garbage or the effluents of sewers, get out. (Who wants to swim there anyway, sharks or no?) Also, avoid swimming around the mouths of rivers or streams. Sometimes these waterways deliver fish to waiting sharks, or they may contain items that attract sharks, such as drowned animals or offal.
- Avoid waters being fished by sport or commercial fishermen, especially if there are signs of feeding activity or

bait fishes are being thrown into the water. Diving seabirds are good indicators of such activities.

- Sightings of dolphins do not indicate the absence of sharks. Both dolphins and sharks often eat the same food items.
- Avoid uneven tanning and bright-colored clothing: Sharks see contrast particularly well. Bright yellow—color used for life rafts!—has been dubbed "yum-yum yellow" by experimenters who have tested shark vision. Some researchers believe that if divers' wetsuits were yellow instead of black, there might be more attacks on divers.
- Refrain from excessive splashing.
- Don't allow dogs in the water with you; their erratic movements could attract sharks.
- Never harass a so-called "harmless" shark. Some divers decide to tweak the tail of a nurse shark—or even try to ride it.
- If you see a shark swimming in a jerky, rigid pattern, assume it is in a threat display and is about to make an aggressive move. Get away!
- If schooling fish start to behave erratically or congregate in large numbers, leave the area.
- Don't swim near people who are fishing or spear fishing, or near sewage outfalls. If a shark is sighted in the area, leave the water as quickly as possible and stay calm. A shark may interpret panicky movements as a fish in distress.

Studies of attacks show that the victims' activities—swimming, scuba diving, snorkeling, surfing—somewhat determine the strategy of a shark's attack. The activities also determine the strategy of the victim's defense. But some defenses apply in all situations. So familiarize yourself with all of them so that you will be aware of the full spectrum of defenses against shark attack.

You are swimming about fifty yards from shore when you feel something brush against your right leg. . . .

Advice to Victims

- Try to remain calm. Amazingly, most survivors have remained calm. Perhaps the shock of the attack takes over and the victim's psyche reverts to a primordial defensive reaction.
- You cannot know what will inspire a particular shark to attack. If you make a threatening move, the shark may react by attacking or by swimming off. You must depend upon intuition or some knowledge of shark behavior.

Photographer Bill Curtsinger says that before a gray reef shark attacked him underwater, "I saw it sweeping its head back and forth; its back was arched like a cat's. *The shark was speaking to me, but at the time I didn't know the words.*"

- As an absolute last move—when you see the shark's jaws gape or feel its teeth sink into your leg—strike out with your hands and feet, aiming at the shark's snout, if possible. This is a desperate, life-at-stake act. You risk wounds whose blood may intensify your attraction as prey. Your defensive acts cannot hurt the shark. What you are trying to do is ward it off, drive it away, make it decide that you are not worth the effort. There is no way of knowing whether striking out will save your life, but many fighting survivors have survived.

Shouting underwater or blowing bubbles has often produced a "startle response, " which can buy time or even send the shark swimming away. Watch out, though, for another try. Some sharks have been observed going off and then circling around the intended victim. By then, rescue may be near. By never swimming alone, you always have help nearby. Rescuers usually have their courage rewarded by not becoming a target themselves. H. David Baldridge (whose advice is the foundation of this chapter) notes "numerous examples of rescuers not being injured even though they went immediately to the aid of the victim. They at times actually fought with the shark, and even on occasion placed themselves as barriers between the attackers and their victim."

- If you have a spear gun or a club, says Baldridge, "Keep fully in mind the limitations of such devices . . . and do not expect them to accomplish the impossible. Such weapons, if used improperly, may serve only to further agitate the shark. Use available spears and knives first to fend off the shark and attempt to wound the fish only as a last resort. Sharks often seem to react with increased vigor to efforts at sticking it with pointed objects."

Powerheads and other weapons designed to kill sharks may so enrage a shark that it will attack wildly and draw the attention of other sharks. If you do have such a weapon and think you are able to fire it accurately, aim for the top of the head between the eyes, or the side of the head right through an eye. You may have only two or three seconds to aim and fire.

- Some sharks—even big, aggressive sharks—have darted away in response to a desperate poke in the eye or on the snout. One victim drove away a shark by grabbing a gill slit. Others have used underwater cameras as weapons. We will never know what the last moves were of victims who did not survive. But we do know that in case after case last-hope defensive acts bought time for the victim and led to at-sea rescues.

Hitting or stabbing a shark is suicidal unless it is the last, desperate act of someone fighting to live at a moment close to death. Captain Jonathan Brown, commander of an Air Force C-124 Globemaster that crashed in the Pacific in 1958, did fight a shark. His experience is a cautionary tale.

Brown and two other members of the crew of nine survived the crash. The three men fashioned a raft out of a piece of wood and buoyed it up with mail sacks. They clung to this during the night. At dawn, the sharks appeared. For a while, shark repellent seemed to keep them away.

Then they came closer. "We'd do a lot of yelling and the sharks would back off and look the situation over," Brown said later. "We don't know how many there were. I don't know how big they were. They seemed to be attracted to anything of light color. We were wearing black socks and our flight suits, which was a help."

One of the sharks seemed to single Brown out. It charged him. "The shark had me by the shoulder and was shaking me," Brown recalled. "We yelled, thrashed, and kicked about in the water trying to get rid of it.

"Finally, I beat on its head with my fist, and it let go."

Brown's last act of defense worked. The shark swam off, though it remained nearby in the water, along with others, until, after twelve hours amid the circling sharks (most likely oceanic whitetips), the three survivors were rescued.

The desperate yet purposeful defense Captain Brown and his companions put up shows the only kind of thinking that gives anyone a chance in the water against an attacking shark. No defense guarantees survival, for the odds are against anyone who is facing an onrushing shark.

Advice to Divers

- *Never dive alone.* The presence of your diving buddy might deter an attack. And, if anything happens to you (including shark attack), help is nearby.
- Don't wander off from a group. You become a tempting solitary target.
- Don't provoke a shark, including small, so-called "harmless" sharks.
- Don't keep caught fish, dead or alive, on your person or tethered to you on a stringer. Get all speared or otherwise wounded fish out of the water immediately.
- Don't spearfish in an area for a long time. Sharks may be drawn there by your prolonged quick movements or by the accumulation of body juices from wounded fish.
- Avoid wearing contrasting colors or elaborately decorated wetsuits.

    Consider the attack on a diver with elaborate tattoos of animals on his legs. The shark that attacked him zeroed in on the legs, removing tissue that included the tattoos. Coincidence? No one knows for sure.
- Leave the water as soon as possible after sighting a large shark. This advice is given in vain to those divers who *want* to see sharks. Just remember: You are in its territory and it makes the rules. See Bill Curtsinger's remarks above about the need to interpret shark body language.
- Carry a shark billy or plan to use the butt of a speargun as a defensive weapon. They have been known to hold an aggressive shark at bay. A typical billy: a three-foot-long wooden, glass-fiber, or metal club with one end roughened to give purchase against the skin of a shark.

    Pacific islanders for centuries have used clubs against sharks, smacking them on the snout to drive them off. Jacques Cousteau recommended that divers carry a shark billy. "After seeing sharks swim on unshaken with harpoons through their heads, deep spear gashes on their bodies, and even after sharp explosions near their brains, we place no reliance in knives as defensive arms," Cousteau wrote.

Photographer Jeff Rotman has used a club against sharks. As he reported in *Sharks, Challengers of the Deep*, "often a shark approaches a diver by making several passes in smaller and smaller circles. Sometimes it breaks out of the circle to charge right at you and veers off just a few feet in front of you. . . . If it comes too close, a smack on the snout, which is very sensitive, sends the clear signal, 'I am not wounded and not easy prey.' While a few species are in fact very dangerous to be in the water with, most are not."

- Take advantage of your fully submerged status by always being aware of movements and presences below, above, and around you.
- Don't maneuver a shark into a position between yourself and any obstacle, such as a reef, sandbar, or boat.
- Avoid diving at dusk and at night.
- Don't surface until you reach your dive boat. Fully submerged divers have a better chance than divers who are partially submerged—especially divers who splash and swim in panic, inadvertently producing a pattern that resembles a prime quarry: prey in distress.

First Aid

Back in 1947, in St. Augustine, Florida, when shark attacks were still being called attacks by barracuda, a male swimmer was rescued soon after the attack and taken to a local hospital. One leg was badly mangled and he suffered other injuries as well. The leg was amputated, and he was given blood transfusions. But he died from what physicians called shock and hemorrhage.

That rarely happens today in places where sharks attack often enough to keep medical emergency room doctors and nurses savvy about what to do when an ambulance delivers a patient bleeding from wounds inflicted by a large animal. Ultimately, that medical skill skews all the statistics on attacks, for it is what happens to the victim, on the beach and in the hospital, that usually means the difference between life and death.

Many people whose lives were saved on the beaches of Australia can thank a doctor who has gone down in South African shark-attack history as "Dr. S. Feinberg of Port Shepstone." He was called to administer to so many shark victims that he made up a medical kit, ever ready for him to snatch up on his way to a victim. The kit has come to be known as the Feinberg Pack. On December 1957, the pack was used to treat a young girl whose arm had been bitten off at the shoulder. Taken to shore bleeding to death, she was given intravenous fluids—the first such treatment given to a shark victim on the beach.

The Feinberg Pack was eventually distributed to lifesaving clubs at more than thirty beaches in South Africa. It contains a synthetic blood plasma substitute and equipment for administering fluids intravenously. There are also plastic cannulae, fine flexible plastic tubes that are preferred over needles because they do not damage veins when a victim is moved. There are also a medical tourniquet, wound dressings to be used as pressure pads, artery forceps to arrest bleeding from major blood vessels, a butterfly needle in case of vascular collapse, and a "space blanket" of aluminized plastic to place around or shade the victim.[4] In a study that ran from 1962 to 1988, every victim treated with a Feinberg Pack survived.

South African shark-attack specialists have classified shark-inflicted wounds into three grades:

Grade I: Major arteries severed. Blood loss is so great that the victim can only live for minutes without aid.

Grade II: One artery severed; abdominal wounds with breaching of abdominal wall; minor arteries severed. Victim can survive if prompt and correct treatment is given on the beach.

Grade III: One minor artery severed; superficial limb wounds; superficial abdominal wounds with no breaching of abdominal wall. Victim will always survive if treated correctly on the beach.

Medical researchers in South Africa say that one important factor in the recovery of victims is the fact that they are usually in good health when they are attacked.

Australia has had more than 180 recorded fatal attacks. Seashore emergency rooms there know about treating victims of shark attacks. From experts who manage Australia's Shark Attack File come these suggestions for first aid, once the victim is removed from the water:

- Treat the patient immediately on-site.
- Stop the bleeding immediately by applying direct pressure above or on the wound. A tourniquet may be used if a pressure bandage cannot control bleeding.
- Reassure the patient. It is important for the victim to know that he or she is in caring hands. A South African surfer who had his right leg torn away told of a young woman who held his hand as he awaited aid on the beach: "She was holding my hand all the time. I was very cold and could feel the warmth from her body flow into me. It was then I thought I would live . . ." He survived after a five-hour operation requiring more than 2,000 stitches.

- Send for an ambulance and medical personnel. Do not move the patient if badly injured.
- Cover the patient lightly with clothing or a towel.
- Give nothing by mouth.

Hawaii's shark-wise lifeguards provided these first-aid instructions:

For skin scrapes and minor bites: Scrub directly in the wound with clean gauze or a cloth soaked in clean, fresh water. Press on the area to stop bleeding. If bleeding persists, or the edges of a wound are jagged or gaping, the victim likely needs stitches. Taping a small bite shut is often an effective alternative, but may leave a more visible scar than suturing. For numbness or inability to move a finger or toe normally, see a doctor immediately. Victims who appear pale, sweaty, and nauseated are in danger of fainting. Lower the victim to the ground.

Wounds where a major artery or vein is severed: A victim can die rapidly from blood loss. Often, a rescuer can stop bleeding from large, severed blood vessels by firmly pressing anything handy (swimsuit, towel, hand) directly on the wound. Such pressure usually causes the vessel to clamp down in spasm, and clots begin to form. In the water, however, this procedure can be nearly impossible, especially while helping a victim to shore or to a boat. In these cases, when bleeding may be fatal, a tourniquet is appropriate. Trying a surfboard leash or dive mask strap around a massively bleeding limb could save a life.

Help a bleeding victim get out of the water as quickly as possible. At the beach, or in the boat, control bleeding by pressing directly on the wound, then remove any tourniquets. Leaving a tourniquet on can cause permanent injury. Maintaining pressure on the wound, take the victim to an emergency room as quickly as possible.

★ ★ ★

Peter Klimley, who has seen numerous attacks on pinnipeds, agrees with other researchers who say that attacking sharks are motivated by either defense or hunger. "The majority of sharks, small and large, will bite divers when they unknowingly approach too closely, violating the species' individual space," Klimley says. When this happens, the sharks usually display a threatening behavior. The gray reef shark, for example, "will swim rapidly in tight loops in front of the diver and lower its pectoral fins, arch its back, lower its tail, and point its snout upward. The mouth may be opened and closed repeatedly to reveal the shark's teeth. If approached too closely, the shark may bite the diver, but will usually remove no flesh. This behavior is analogous to a cat's arching its back, bristling its hair, and baring its teeth and hissing. The best way to avoid a defensive attack is to recognize the threat behavior and slowly move away from the shark in the opposite direction."

Great whites, tiger sharks, and bull sharks, all big enough to consume a human being, may see a human swimmer, surfer, or diver as a potential meal. So Klimley advises people to avoid swimming and diving near places where there are concentrations of animals that these shark species prey on. For great whites, that means near colonies of seals and sea lions. Tiger sharks prowl near islands with large populations of sea birds. Bull sharks swim near shore in pursuit of shoals of fish. Or they feed at river mouths or up the rivers.[5]

But why don't these big sharks finish off their human meals after an attack?

Klimley's theory: People might not be fat enough. "Fat," he points out, "has twice the energy value that muscle does. Seals and sea lions have a layer of fat, unlike birds, humans, and sea otters." By selectively hunting fatty animals, the shark makes its best energy investment. Bony mammals are not worth the effort.

If you have information about a shark attack, historic or new, make a copy of the questionnaire on pages 267–275 and send it by regular mail or E-mail to the International Shark Attack File. If several people witnessed an incident, the ISAF would appreciate it if you would ask each one to fill out a copy of the questionnaire independently so that ISAF analysts can get each person's unbiased perspective on the incident. The addresses are:

gburgess@flmnh.ufl.edu.

International Shark Attack File
American Elasmobranch Society
Florida Museum of Natural History
University of Florida
Gainesville, Florida 32611

APPENDIX A

Popular and Scientific Species Names

Australian gray nurse shark (*Odontaspis taurus*)
basking shark (*Cetorhinus maximus*)
blacktip shark (*Carcharhinus limbatus*)
blacktip reef shark (*Carcharhinus melanopterus*)
blue shark (*Prionace glauca*)
bramble shark (*Echinorhinus brucus*)
brown shark (*Carcharhinus plumbeus*)
bull shark (*Carcharhinus leucas*)[1]
blacktip shark (*Carcharhinus limbatus*)
Caribbean reef shark (*Carcharhinus perezi*)
cookie-cutter shark (*Isistius brasiliensis*)
dusky shark (*Carcharhinus obscurus*)
dwarf dogshark (*Etmopterus perryi*)
gray nurse shark (*Odontaspis arenarius*)
gray reef shark (*Carcharhinus amblyrhynchos*)
great white shark (*Carcharodon carcharias*)[2]
Galapagos shark (*Carcharhinus galapagensis*)
Greenland shark (*Somniosus microcephalus*)

great hammerhead shark (*Sphyrna mokarran*)
lemon shark (*Negaprion brevirostris*)
mako [short-fin] (*Isurus oxyrynchus*)
mako [long-fin] (*Isurus paucus*)
nurse shark (*Ginglymostoma cirratum*)
oceanic whitetip shark (*Carcharhinus longimanus*)
ornate wobbegong (*Orectolobus ornatus*)
sand tiger (*Odontaspis taurus*)[3]
sandbar shark (*Carcharhinus plumbeus*)
scalloped bonnethead (*Sphyrna corona*)
scalloped hammerhead (*Sphyrna lewini*)
silky shark (*Carcharhinus falciformis*)
sixgill shark (*Hexanchus griseus*)
silky shark (*Carcharhinus falciformis*)
silvertip shark (*Carcharhinus albimarginatus*)
smooth dogfish (*Mustelus canis*)
spinner shark (*Carcharhinus brevipinna*)
spiny dogfish (*Squalus acanthias*)
spotted wobbegong (*Orectolobus maculatus*)
tawny nurse shark (*Nebrius ferrugineus*)
tiger shark (*Galeocerdo cuvier*)
whale shark (*Rhincodon typus*)
whitetip reef shark (*Triaenodon obesus*)

APPENDIX B

Instructions for Reporting a Shark Attack to the International Shark Attack File

If information is uncovered about a potential shark attack, historic or new, please ask the victim and/or any witnesses to fill out a questionnaire, or if more appropriate fill it out yourself based on information you've developed, and forward it (them) to the International Shark Attack File by traditional mail or electronically through e-mail.

If multiple parties witnessed an incident, we would appreciate it if you would ask them to fill out a copy of the questionnaire independently so that we can get their unbiased perspectives on the incident. Inclusion of any corroborative documentation (such as newspaper articles; police, medical, or autopsy reports; photographs of the victim, gear worn by the victim, and the attack site; etc.) is also most appreciated, as is environmental information (e.g. water temperature, water salinity, tidal state, habitat, etc.). The goal is to gather as much information as possible relevant to the attack.

In addition to investigating the environmental factors and activities of the victim and the shark involved in an incident, we are very interested in documenting the medical aspects of an attack. If possible, we would welcome photographs of the wounds and the permission to request copies of relevant medical records. These data are used in on-going medical studies examining the effectiveness of various modes of medical action, especially as related to infection by Vibrio (aquatic microorganisms that can cause serious diseases). Any supplied information, including the questionnaire and any such medical records, are considered confidential and will be used only by screened professional biological and medical researchers. The press is explicitly barred from ISAF cases files.

The questionnaires can be downloaded in English, French, and Portuguese (in Word 6.0 format) from on the ISAF web site: www.flmnh.ufl.edu/fish/sharks/ISAF/ISAF.htm The filled-out questionnaire can then be e-mailed as an attachment to gburgess@flmnh.ufl.edu. Or it can be mailed to the museum address on the questionnaire.

International Shark Attack File
American Elasmobranch Society
Florida Museum of Natural History
University of Florida
Gainesville, Florida 32611
U.S.A.
George H. Burgess, Director
(352) 392-1721
FAX 352-846-0287
E-mail: gburgess@flmnh.ufl.edu

ABBREVIATED SHARK ATTACK QUESTIONNAIRE

This questionnaire submitted by:

Name:

Address:

Phone number:

(1) VICTIM

Name:

Address:

Phone number:

(2) TREATING PHYSICIAN/HOSPITAL

Name:

Address:

Phone number:

Photos taken of victim's wounds?

(3) DATE OF ATTACK

month/day/year:

(4) TIME OF ATTACK

(   ) (A.M.) *or* (P.M.)

(5) LOCATION OF ATTACK

Ocean:

Country:

State/province:

County:

Specific locality:

Longitude-latitude (if available):

(   ) Salt water (   ) Fresh water (   ) Brackish water

(6) GENERAL OUTCOME OF ATTACK

(   ) Fatal

(   ) Non-fatal

(7) NATURE OF INJURIES

Please describe details of injuries:

(8) ACTIVITY OF VICTIM

Wading/sitting activity in shallow water:

(   ) Victim in shallow water, no specific activity information

(   ) Wading

(   ) Erratic splashing, horseplay, etc.

(   ) Standing still on bottom

(   ) Sitting on bottom

(   ) Other shallow water activity than above

OR

Surface activity:

(   ) Aboard a boat

(   ) Swimming

(   ) Floating, little or no motion (includes use of flotation gear)

(   ) Treading water (includes use of flotation gear)

(   ) Snorkeling (includes use of mask and fins with or without snorkel)

(   ) Riding surfboard/boogie board

(   ) Aboard float, raft, innertube, etc.

(   ) Other surface activity than above

(   ) Bodysurfing, planing on waves

OR

Subsurface activity:

( ) Subsurface or diving activity, no details

( ) Scuba diving

( ) Free diving (no gear) or subsurface swimming

( ) Free diving with mask and/or fins, with or without snorkel

( ) Pearl diving

( ) Hard hat diving

( ) Other diving/subsurface activity than above

OR

Water entry or exit other than wading:

( ) Entering water (jumping, diving, falling, etc.)

( ) Leaving water (ladder, side of boat, etc.)

( ) Entry or exit other than above

(9) RACE AND SEX OF VICTIM

( ) Caucasian/white male

( ) Negroid/black male

( ) Mongolian/Oriental male

( ) Malayan/Polynesian male

( ) Male, race unknown or other than above

( ) Caucasian/white female

( ) Negroid/black female

( ) Mongolian/Oriental female

( ) Malayan/Polynesian female

( ) Female, race unknown or other than above

(10) AGE OF VICTIM

( ) years old

(11) WATER CLARITY AT TIME OF ATTACK

( ) Attack did not occur in the water

( ) Clear

( ) Turbid/murky

( ) Muddy

(12) DEPTH AT WHICH ATTACK OCCURRED

( ) Attack did not occur in the water

( ) Attack occurred at surface

( ) Attack occurred in ( ) of water

(13) TOTAL DEPTH OF WATER AT ATTACK SITE

( ) The total depth of the water at the attack site was
( ) deep.

(14) FISHING ACTIVITY BY VICTIM

( ) Victim was not fishing

( ) Fish being hooked

( ) Fish being netted

( ) Spearfishing

( ) Carrying/holding fish

( ) Other fishing activity as specified: _____

---

(15) FISHING ACTIVITY BY OTHERS NEAR VICTIM

( ) Other persons were not fishing nearby

( ) Fish being hooked

( ) Fish being netted

( ) Spearfishing

( ) Carrying/holding fish

( ) Other fishing activity as specified: _____

---

(16) GENERAL ACTIVITY OF OTHERS NEAR VICTIM

( ) Other person(s) were not nearby

( ) Normal bathing/swimming

( ) Splashing/horseplay, etc.

( ) Thrashing/flailing, etc.

( ) Diving/underwater activities

( ) Wading

(   ) Unusually loud voices/noises

(   ) Surfing, with or without board

(   ) Other activity as specified: _____

_____

(17) NUMBER OF PERSONS IN WATER WITHIN 10 FEET OF VICTIM

(   ) No other persons were within 10 feet of victim

(   ) The number of people within 10 feet of victim was
(   )

(18) NUMBER OF PERSONS IN WATER WITHIN 10–50 FEET OF VICTIM

(   ) No other persons were within 10–50 feet of victim

(   ) The number of people within 10–50 feet of victim was
(   )

(19) WERE THERE OTHER PERSONS IN GENERAL AREA (MORE THAN 50 FEET AWAY)?

(   ) Yes

(   ) No

(20) SHARK BEHAVIOR

(   ) The shark was not seen

(   ) The shark was seen and its behavior was as follows:

Shark attack behavior at time of initial strike:

( ) Attack did not occur in water or shark did not contact victim

( ) Minimum of turmoil, victim initially unaware of situation

( ) Sudden violent interaction between shark and victim

AND

Shark behavior during subsequent strikes:

( ) Attack did not occur in water or shark made only one strike

( ) Shark made multiple/repeated deliberate strikes

( ) Frenzied behavior

( ) Released initial hold, quickly bit victim again

AND

Shark behavior after final strike:

( ) Attack did not occur in water

( ) Shark remained attached to victim and had to be forcibly removed

( ) Shark remained in immediate area of attack

( ) Shark followed victim/rescuers toward shore

( ) Shark seen to leave area of attack

( ) Shark not seen after final strike

( ) Shark remained attached to victim after final strike, released hold without use of force by victim/rescuer(s)

(21) TYPE OF SHARK INVOLVED

( ) The shark was not seen well enough to describe its appearance

( ) At least part of the shark was seen. *Please describe with as much detail as possible what the shark looked like (color, shape of body and fins, shape of teeth, etc). Use back of page if necessary:*

(22) SIZE OF ATTACKING SHARK

( ) The shark was not seen well enough to estimate its size

( ) The estimated total length of the shark was (   )

(23) CLOTHING/GEAR WORN BY VICTIM:

Please describe the color and type of clothing and/or diving gear worn by the victim, including jewelry:

(24) NARRATIVE

Please describe the circumstances surrounding the attack (use additional pages as necessary). Audio or video tape is acceptable but must be understandable.

NOTES

Prelude

[1]Scientific names are used on the first reference to a species. For a list of popular and scientific names of sharks mentioned, see page 263.

[2]The 100 million toll, in commercial fisheries, was an 1989 estimate by Dr. Samuel Gruber, chairman of the Shark Specialist Group of the International Union for the Conservation of Nature and Natural Resources (IUCN) Species Survival Commission.

[3]Information on the California law's history comes primarily from "More Rare Than Dangerous: A Case Study of White Shark Conservation in California," Chapter 45, *Great White Sharks*. (For full information on cited books, see Select Bibliography.)

[4]See *Journal of Clinical Oncology*, November 1998.

Chapter 2

[1]Murphy, R.C., and Nichols, J.T. "The Shark Situation in the Waters About New York." *Brooklyn Instit. Arts Sciences, Brooklyn Mus. Quarterly*, 3 (4). 1916.

[2]*Shark! Shark! The Thirty-Year Odyssey of a Pioneer Shark Hunter*. Gotham House, 1934.

[3]T.S. Wallett in *Shark Attack in Southern African Waters and Treatment of Victims*. Struik, Cape Town, South Africa.

[4]Bigelow, H. B., and Schroeder, W. C. *Fishes of the Western Northern Atlantic*, Memoir No. 1; Part One, Lancelets,

Cyclostomes, Sharks; Part Two, Sawfishes, Guitarfishes, Skates, Rays and Chimaeroids. Sears Foundation of Marine Research, Yale University, 1948.

[5]*Sharks and Survival.*

[6]"Shark Attack Against Man: A Program of Data Reduction and Analysis." Baldridge later published his research in *Shark Attack.*

[7]All temperatures in the book are given in Fahrenheit.

[8]"Shape Discrimination and Visual Predatory Tactics in White Sharks," Chapter 21, *Great White Sharks.*

[9]http://www.flmnh.ufl.edu/fish/Sharks/ISAF/ISAF.htm

[10]Patricia Garfield, president of the Association for the Study of Dreams.

Chapter 4

[1]Linbaugh, C. (1963). "Field notes on sharks" in *Sharks and Survival* (P.W. Gilbert, ed.).

[2]Peter Pyle and Scot D. Anderson; see "The Behavior of White Sharks and Their Pinniped Prey during Predatory Attacks," Chapter 16, *Great White Sharks.*

[3]The four pinniped species are the northern elephant seal (*Mirounga angustirostris*), the California sea lion (*Zalophus californianus*), the Steller sea lion (*Eumetopias jubatus*), and the harbor seal (*Phoca vitulina*).

[4]John E. McCosker and Robert N. Lea, "White Shark Attacks in the Eastern Pacific Ocean: An Update and Analysis," Chapter 39, *Great White Sharks.*

[5]Ibid.

Chapter 5

[1]*Shark Bites,* by Greg Ambrose, 1996. The Bess Press, P.O. Box 22388, Honolulu, HI 96823.

Chapter 6

[1]Most of the descriptions of the attacks and wounds in this chapter come from *Shark Attack in Southern African Waters and Treatment of Victims* by T. S. Wallett. Struik, Cape Town, South Africa, 1983.

[2]Ibid.

[3]Davies, D.H. *About Sharks and Shark Attack.*

[4]"Shark attack off the east coast of South Africa, 22nd January, 1961." *Oceanographic Research Institute Investigational Report 4.*

[5]Marie Levine, "Unprovoked Attacks by White Sharks Off the South African Coast," Chapter 40, *Great White Sharks.*

[6]The board's statement was based on an article by one of its scientists, Geremy Cliff, in *Africa Environment and Wildlife* 6(5): 86–87.

Chapter 7

[1]Australian whaler sharks belong to the genus *Carcharhinus,* but there is no agreement on a single species name. Several species have been put forth as "whalers," including *C. brachyurus,* also known as the narrowtooth, the New Zealan whaler, or the copper shark. *Carcharhinus ahenea,* which once had the common name "bronze whaler," has been retired by taxonomists. That Latin name once had been the species name for the gray nurse, now known as *Odontaspis taurus* (also known as the sand tiger shark).

[2]John West, "White Shark Attacks in Australian Waters," Chapter 41, *Great White Sharks.*

[3]Coppleson's record keeping evolved into *Shark Attack,* published in 1958 by Angus & Robertson, Sydney.

[4]The catch is described by Capt. William Young, a shark fisherman of the time. See *Shark! Shark!* by W.E. Young and H.S. Mazet. New York: Gotham House, 1933.

[5]Brown recounts the attack in his book, *Sharks The Silent Savages.*

[6]See Note 2.

[7]"Worldwide Patterns of White Shark Attacks on Humans," by George H. Burgess and Matthew Callahan (International Shark Attack File); Chapter 42 in *Great White Sharks.*

[8]See Fox's account in *Great White Shark.*

[9]Wadrop gave his account in an e-mail to an Internet shark page, http:// www.ozemail.com.au.

[10]Sources: Australian Bureau of Statistics, Canberra; John West, Shark Attack File, Taronga Zoo, Sydney; Dr. Graham Webb, Darwin; Dr. Doug Walker, Operation Sticky Beak, Sydney.

Chapter 8

[1]Steel, R. *Sharks of the World.* New York: Blandford Press, 1985.

[2]The shark was found by the Shark Specialist Group of the World Conservation Union, with assistance from the World Wildlife Fund.

[3]See *The Sharks of Lake Nicaragua* by Randy Wayne White (The Lyons Press, 1999) and *Savage Shore: Life and Death with Nicaragua's Last Shark Hunters* by Edward Marriott (Metropolitan Book, 2000).

[4]The historical background on the Lake Nicaragua shark comes from *The Natural History of Sharks.*

[5]The story is told in *Sharks Are Caught at Night* by François Poli (translated by Naomi Walford). Regnery Co., Chicago, 1959.

Chapter 9

[1]Capt. Charles B. McVay, III, commanding officer of the *Indianapolis*, was found guilty by court martial of hazarding his ship's safety by failing to zigzag. But he was restored to active duty without punishment. McVay was the first U.S. Navy officer to be court martialed for losing his ship to an enemy in at least a century. In 1968 McVay committed suicide.

[2]James and Finneran, the former executive director of the *Indianapolis* Survivors Memorial Organization, posted their recollections on the organization's Internet site.

[3]Information about the *Indianapolis* tragedy comes from the survivors cited and accounts in *Final Voyage: The Sinking of the USS* Indianapolis by Dan Kurzman (Pocket Books, 1992) and *All The Drowned Sailors: The Cover-Up of America's Wartime Disaster at Sea* by Raymond B. Lech (Stein & Day, 1982).

[4]*The Natural History of Sharks* by Thomas H. Lineaweaver III and Richard H. Backus (Lyons & Burford, 1970).

[5]Information on the battle from *World War II: The Encyclopedia of the War Years 1941–1945* by Norman Polmar and Thomas B. Allen (Random House, 1996).

[6]Information about the *Nova Scotia* and the *Cape San Juan* from *About Sharks and Shark Attack*.

[7]"A List of Shark Attacks for the World," Schultz and Malin, *Sharks and Survival*.

[8]G. A. Llano, *Airmen Against the Sea*.

[9]"The Florida Shark Story," by Robert F. Hutton, Educational Series Pamphlet No. 13, Florida State Board of Conservation.

[10]David H. Davies (see Note 6) gathered the information about the attacks on Schoeman's boat.

[11]A. Peter Klimley, Peter Pyle, Scot D. Anderson, "Tail Slap and Breach. Agonistic Displays among White Sharks?" Chapter 22, *Great White Sharks*.

Chapter 10

[1]For scientific names, see "Popular and Scientific Names," page 263.

[2]But "in relative terms it is no more of a 'killer' than an insectivorous frog or a beef-eating human," notes Ronald M. Nowak, in the definitive *Walker's Mammals of the World*.

[3]From a Fergusson e-mail also quoted in the *National Geographic Magazine*, April 2000.

[4]John McCosker, "The Massively Destructive First Bite," *Great White Shark*.

[5]"Shark Attack: A Program of Data Reduction and Analysis," by H. David Baldridge. Contributions from the Mote Marine Laboratory. Vol. 1, No. 2 (1974).

[6]"The Florida Shark Story," by Robert F. Hutton, Florida State Board of Conservation, Pamphlet No. 13, issued March 30, 1959.

[7]*The Natural History of Sharks*.

[8]The story of the identification of the shark is told on page 144 of *The Book of Sharks*.

Chapter 11

[1]"Death Following Attack by Shark Carcharodon Carcharias," Capt. B. H. Kean, *Journal of American Medicine* July 22, 1944.

[2]E. W. Gudger, "Will Sharks Attack Human Beings?" *Natural History*. Vol. XL, No. 1 (1937).

[3]Zahuranec, B. J. 1983. *Shark Repellents From The Sea—New Perspectives*. H. David Baldridge, "Shark Research and the U.S. Navy."

[4]Information on the search for the repellent came originally from the research of Harold W. McCormick, co-author, with Thomas B. Allen and Captain William E. Young, of *Shadows in the Sea*, Chilton Books, 1963. A revised edition, by Allen, was published by Lyons & Burford in 1997. Technical information comes from "Development of the U.DS. Navy 'Shark Chaser' Chemical Shark Repellent" by Richard L. Tuve, Chapter 17 in *Sharks and Survival*.

[5]Llano, G. A. *Airmen Against the Sea*.

[6]H. David Baldridge, Jr., "Reaction of Sharks to a Mammal in Distress," *Journal of Military Medicine*, May 1966.

[7]The incident is revealed in "Sharks: Wolves of the Sea," by Nathaniel T. Kenney in the February 1968 issue of *National Geographic Magazine*.

[8]The Taylors made an hour-long documentary, "Shark POD," based on the experiments. Her remarks are taken from an Internet digest of the documentary.

[9]*Shark Attack in Southern African Waters and Treatment of Victims* by T. S. Wallett. Struik, Cape Town, South Africa, 1983.

Chapter 12

[1]Burgess, George H. 1998. Diving with elasmobranchs: a call for restraint. *Shark News* 11:1–4. This entire issue of *Shark News*, as well as others, appeared on the IUCN Shark Specialist Group pages hosted at http://www.flmnh.ufl.edu/fish.

[2]Published on the Internet.

[3]Ralph S. Collier, Mark Marks, Ronald W. Warner, "White Sharks Attacks on Inanimate Objects along the Pacific Coast of North America," Chapter 19, *Great White Sharks*.

Chapter 13

[1]To name two excellent ones: *Great White Sharks* and *Great White Shark*.

[2]"White Shark Attacks in Australian Waters," by John West, Chapter 42, *Great White Sharks* (cited above).

[3]Derived from International Shark Attack File advice; advice from the Australian Shark Attack File; and "Shark Attack: A Program of Data Reduction and Analysis" by H. David Baldridge. Contributions from the Mote Marine Laboratory. Vol. 1, No.2, 1974. Baldridge is also the basic source for the "Advice to Divers" and "Advice to Victims."

[4]The Feinberg Pack is described in from *Shark Attack in Southern African Waters and Treatment of Victims* by T. S. Wallett. Struik, Cape Town, South Africa, 1983.

[5]Klimley suggests that anyone wanting advice on avoiding shark attacks should read the book edited by him and Ainley (cited above), especially Chapter 44 by H. David Baldridge, Jr.: "Comments on Means for Avoidance or Deterrence of White Shark Attacks on Humans." See also Klimley's 1974 article, "An inquiry into the causes of shark attacks," in *Sea Frontiers*, 20(2):66–76.

Appendix A

[1]Also known as the Zambezi shark and Lake Nicaragua shark.

[2]"White shark" is the scientifically preferred popular name, but most popular accounts still, quite understandably, give the shark the additional adjective "great."

[3]Other scientific names for both the sand tiger and the Australian gray nurse shark include *Carcharias taurus, C. arenarius,* and *Eugomphodus taurus.* Not all authorities believe that "sand tiger" and "gray nurse" are common names for the same species.

SELECTED BIBLIOGRAPHY

Besides drawing from my own books (*The Shark Almanac,* 1999, and *Shadows in the Sea,* 1996, both published by the Lyons Press, New York), I obtained valuable insights from the following publications. Many of the initial descriptions of the attacks came from newspapers that are cited in the text. I also made extensive use of the publicly available data collected by the International Shark Attack File, the Australian Shark Attack File, and the Shark Research Institute.

Baldridge, H. D. *Shark Attack.* Berkley Publishing Corp., New York. 1974.

Bigelow, H. B., and Schroeder, W. C. *Fishes of the Western Northern Atlantic, Memoir No. 1; Part One, Lancelets, Cyclostomes, Sharks; Part Two, Sawfishes, Guitarfishes, Skates, Rays and Chimaeroids.* Sears Foundation of Marine Research, Yale University, New Haven. 1948.

Brown, Theo W. *Sharks: The Silent Savages.* Sports Illustrated Book, Little, Brown, Boston. 1973.

Coppleson, V. M. *Shark Attack.* Angus & Robertson, London. 1959.

———. A Review of Shark Attacks in Australian Waters Since 1919. *Medical Jour. Australia,* 2(19):680–687. November 4, 1950.

———. Shark Attacks in Australian Waters. *Medical Jour. Australia,* 1 (15):449–467. 1933.

Davies, David H. *About Sharks and Shark Attack.* Shuter and Shooter, Pietermaritzburg. 1964.

Discovering Sharks. A volume, containing 24 papers, honoring the work of Stewart Springer. American Littoral Society, Highlands, New Jersey. 1990.

Ellis, Richard and John E. McCosker. *Great White Shark.* HarperCollins, New York. 1991.

Ellis, Richard. *The Book of Sharks.* Grosset & Dunlap, New York. 1976.

Gilbert, P. W. (ed.). *Sharks and Survival.* D. C. Heath and Company, Boston. 1963.

Klimley, A. P. and D. G. Ainley (eds.). *Great White Sharks: The Biology of* Carcharodon carcharias. Academic Press, San Diego. 1996.

Lineaweaver, Thomas H., III, and Richard H. Backus. *The Natural History of Sharks.* Lippincott, Philadelphia. 1969.

Llano, G. A. *Airmen Against the Sea, An Analysis of Sea Survival Experiences.* Maxwell Air Force Base, Alabama; Arctic, Desert, Tropic Information Center, Research Studies Institute, Publication G-104. (See also "Sharks vs. Men," by G. A. Llano, *Scientific American,* Vol. 196, No. 6, June 1957).

McCosker, J. E. "White Shark Attack Behavior: Observations of and Speculations about Predator and Prey Strategies." 1985. *Memoirs of the Southern California Academy of Science* 9: 123–35.

National Geographic magazine articles: "Sharks at 2,000 Feet," Dr. Eugenie Clark, and Emory Kristof, pages 681–691,

November 1986; "Sharks: Magnificent and Misunderstood," Dr. Eugenie Clark, pages 138–187, August 1981; "A Jawbreaker for Sharks,"; Valerie Taylor, pages 664–665, May 1981; "Into the Lairs of Sleeping Sharks," Dr. Eugenie Clark, pages 570–584, April 1975; "Close Encounters With the Gray Reef Shark," Bill Curtsinger, pages 45–67, January 1995; "Great White Sharks," Peter Benchley, pages 1–29, April 2000.

Reader's Digest. *Sharks: Silent Hunters of the Deep*. Reader's Digest. Sydney, Australia.

Springer, Victor G. and Joy P. Gold. *Sharks in Question: The Smithsonian Answer Book*. Smithsonian Institute Press. Washington, D.C. 1989.

Stafford-Deitsch, Jeremy. *Shark: A Photographer's Story*. Sierra Club Books, San Francisco. 1988.

Stevens, J. D. (ed.). *Sharks*. Facts on File Publications. New York. 1987.

Zahuranec, B. J. *Shark Repellents From The Sea—New Perspectives*. American Association for the Advancement of Science, Washington, DC, AAAS Selected Symposium 83. 1983.

INDEX

Note: Italicized page numbers refer to charts and illustrations.

289